ANGLO-SAXON GRAMMAR
AND EXERCISE BOOK

C. Alphonso Smith,

Editor

COMPLETE UNABRIDGED

Anglo-Saxon Grammar and Exercise Book, by

C. Alphonso Smith This eBook is for the use of anyone anywhere at no cost and with almost no restrictions whatsoever. You may copy it, give it away or re-use it under the terms of the Project Gutenberg License included with this eBook or online at www.gutenberg.net

Title: Anglo-Saxon Grammar and Exercise Book with Inflections, Syntax, Selections for Reading, and Glossary

Author: C. Alphonso Smith

Release Date: February 15, 2010 [EBook #31277]

Language: English

Character set encoding: ISO-8859-1

*** START OF THIS PROJECT GUTENBERG EBOOK ANGLO-SAXON GRAMMAR ***

Produced by Louise Hope, Barbara Tozier, Bill Tozier and the Online Distributed Proofreading Team at http://www.pgdp.net

---

[Transcriber's Note:

This text is intended for users whose text readers cannot use the "real" (Unicode/UTF-8) version of the file. Characters that could not be fully displayed are shown in alternative forms:

Ââ Êê Îî Ôô Ûû (circumflex in place of macron or "long" mark; the circumflex in its own right does not occur) y: Æ: æ: (long y and æ; the sequence "y:" does not occur in the Old English material, and "æ:" does not occur at all)

Characters with more than one diacritic (rare), and some less common combinations such as accented æ, are shown "top to bottom" in brackets: [´â] [´æ] (long a with accent, æ with accent). Greek words (also rare) have been transliterated and shown between +marks+; there should be no confusion between this and the + as printed.

The short vowels e and o are sometimes shown with ogonek (reversed cedilla). In the introductory section on vowel sounds, and in the overall Glossary, these are shown as [E,] [e,] [O,] [o,]. Elsewhere the ogonek was simply omitted; there are no minimal pairs (different words distinguished only by this sign).

See the Poetry section (between V and VI in Part III, Readings) for display of characters specific to that section.

Italics are shown with *lines*. Boldface is shown with #hash marks#. In the printed book, boldface was used for all Anglo-Saxon other than exercises and reading passages; it has been omitted from the e-text except when necessary for clarity.

In references to numbered Sections, "Note" may mean either an inset Note or a footnote.

In the prose reading selections (pages 99-121), page numbers and line breaks have been retained for use with the linenotes and Glossary.

Page numbers are shown in [[double brackets]]. In the verse selections, line numbers in the notes have been replaced with line numbers from the original texts, printed in brackets as shown. The distinction between linenotes and numbered footnotes is in the original.

Single brackets [] and asterisks * are in the original, as are the symbols + = < >. Text in [[double brackets]] was added by the transcriber.]

ANGLO-SAXON GRAMMAR

AND EXERCISE BOOK

With Inflections, Syntax, Selections for Reading, and Glossary

By

C. ALPHONSO SMITH, Ph.D., LL.D.

Late Professor of English in the United States Naval Academy

ALLYN and BACON Boston New York Chicago Atlanta San Francisco

---

IAI

Norwood Press J. S. Cushing & Co.--Berwick & Smith Norwood Mass. U.S.A.

PREFACE.

The scope of this book is indicated in § 5. It is intended for beginners, and in writing it, these words of Sir Thomas Elyot have not been forgotten: "Grammer, beinge but an introduction to the understandinge of autors, if it be made to longe or exquisite to the lerner, it in a maner mortifieth his corage: And by that time he cometh to the most swete and pleasant redinge of olde autors, the sparkes of fervent desire of lernynge are extincte with the burdone of grammer, lyke as a lyttell fyre is sone quenched with a great heape of small stickes." --*The*

Governour, Cap. X.

Only the essentials, therefore, are treated in this work, which is planned more as a foundation for the study of Modern English grammar, of historical English grammar, and of the principles of English etymology, than as a general introduction to Germanic philology.

The Exercises in translation will, it is believed, furnish all the drill necessary to enable the student to retain the forms and constructions given in the various chapters.

The Selections for Reading relate to the history and literature of King Alfred's day, and are sufficient to give the student a first-hand, though brief, acquaintance with the native style and idiom of Early West Saxon prose in its golden age. Most of the words and constructions contained in them will be already familiar to the student through their intentional employment in the Exercises.

For the inflectional portion of this grammar, recourse has been had chiefly to Sievers' *Abriss der angelsächsischen Grammatik* (1895). Constant reference has been made also to the same author's earlier and larger *Angelsächsishe Grammatik*, translated by Cook. A more sparing use has been made of Cosijn's *Altwestsächsische Grammatik*.

For syntax and illustrative sentences, Dr. J. E. Wülfing's *Syntax in den Werken Alfreds des Grossen, Part I.* (Bonn, 1894) has proved indispensable. Advance sheets of the second part of this great work lead one to believe that when completed the three parts will constitute the most important contribution to the study of English syntax that has yet been made. Old English sentences have also been cited from Sweet's *Anglo-Saxon Reader*, Bright's *Anglo-Saxon Reader*, and Cook's *First Book in Old English*.

The short chapter on the Order of Words has been condensed from my *Order of Words in Anglo-Saxon Prose* (Publications of the Modern Language Association of America, New Series, Vol. I, No. 2).

Though assuming sole responsibility for everything contained in this book, I take pleasure in acknowledging the kind and efficient assistance that has been so generously given me in its preparation. To none do I owe more than to Dr. J. E. Wülfing, of the University of Bonn; Prof. James A. Harrison, of the University of Virginia; Prof. W. S. Currell, of Washington and Lee University; Prof. J. Douglas Bruce, of Bryn Mawr College; and Prof. L. M. Harris, of the University of Indiana. They have each rendered material aid, not only in the tedious task of detecting typographical errors in the proof-sheets, but by the valuable criticisms and suggestions which they have made as this work was passing through the press.

C. ALPHONSO SMITH.

Louisiana State University, Baton Rouge, September, 1896.

PREFACE TO THE SECOND EDITION.

In preparing this enlarged edition, a few minor errors in the first edition have been corrected and a few sentences added. The chief difference between the two editions, however, consists in the introduction of more reading matter and the consequent exposition of Old English meter. Both changes have been made at the persistent request of teachers and students of Old English.

Uniformity of treatment has been studiously preserved in the new material and the old, the emphasis in both being placed on syntax and upon the affinities that Old English shares with Modern English.

Many obligations have been incurred in preparing this augmented edition. I have again to thank Dr. J. E. Wülfing, Prof. James A. Harrison, Prof. W. S. Currell, and Prof. J. Douglas Bruce. To the scholarly criticisms also of Prof. J. M. Hart, of Cornell; Prof. Frank Jewett Mather, Jr., of Williams College; and Prof. Frederick Tupper, Jr., of the University of Vermont, I am indebted for aid as generously given as it is genuinely appreciated.

C. ALPHONSO SMITH.

August, 1898.

PREFACE TO THE FOURTH EDITION.

Among those who have kindly aided in making this edition free from error, I wish to thank especially my friend Dr. John M. McBryde, Jr., of Hollins Institute, Virginia.

C. ALPHONSO SMITH.

University of North Carolina, Chapel Hill, February, 1903.

TABLE OF CONTENTS.

PART I.--INTRODUCTION.

Chapters

* * * * * * * *

OLD ENGLISH

GRAMMAR AND EXERCISES

* * * * * * * * *

OLD ENGLISH GRAMMAR AND EXERCISE BOOK.

PART I.

INTRODUCTION.

CHAPTER I.

HISTORY.

1. The history of the English language falls naturally into three periods; but these periods blend into one another so gradually that too much significance must not be attached to the exact dates which scholars, chiefly for convenience of treatment, have assigned as their limits. Our language, it is true, has undergone many and great changes; but its continuity has never been broken, and its individuality has never been lost.

2. The first of these periods is that of OLD ENGLISH, or ANGLO-SAXON,[1] commonly known as the period of *full inflections*. *E.g.* #stân-as#, *stones*; #car-u#, *care*; #will-a#, *will*; #bind-an#, *to bind*; #help-að# (= #ath#), *they help*.

It extends from the arrival of the English in Great Britain to about one hundred years after the Norman Conquest,--from A.D. 449 to 1150; but there are no literary remains of the earlier centuries of this period. There were four[2] distinct dialects spoken at this time. These were the Northumbrian, spoken north of the river Humber; the Mercian, spoken in the midland region between the Humber and the Thames; the West Saxon, spoken south and west of the Thames; and the Kentish, spoken in the neighborhood of Canterbury. Of these dialects, Modern English is most nearly akin to the Mercian; but the best known of them is the West Saxon. It was in the West Saxon dialect that King Alfred (849-901) wrote and spoke. His writings belong to the period of Early West Saxon as distinguished from the period of Late West Saxon, the latter being best represented in the writings of Abbot Ælfric (955?-1025?).

[Footnote 1: This unfortunate nomenclature is due to the term *Angli Saxones*, which Latin writers used as a designation for the English Saxons as distinguished from the continental or Old Saxons. But Alfred and Ælfric both use the term *Englisc*, not Anglo-Saxon. The Angles spread over Northumbria and Mercia, far outnumbering the other tribes. Thus *Englisc* (= *Angel* + *isc*) became the general name for the language spoken.]

[Footnote 2: As small as England is, there are six distinct dialects spoken in her borders to-day. Of these the Yorkshire dialect is, perhaps, the most peculiar. It preserves many Northumbrian survivals. See Tennyson's *Northern Farmer*.]

3. The second period is that of MIDDLE ENGLISH, or the period of *leveled inflections*, the dominant vowel of the inflections being e. *E.g.* #ston-es#, #car-e#, #will-e#, #bind-en# (or #bind-e#), #help-eth#, each being, as in the earlier period, a dissyllable.

The Middle English period extends from A.D. 1150 to 1500. Its greatest representatives are Chaucer (1340-1400) in poetry and Wiclif (1324-1384) in prose. There were three prominent dialects during this period: the Northern, corresponding to the older Northumbrian; the Midland (divided into East Midland and West Midland), corresponding to the Mercian; and the Southern, corresponding to the West Saxon and Kentish. London, situated in East Midland territory, had become the dominant speech center; and it was this East Midland dialect that both Chaucer and Wiclif employed.

NOTE.--It is a great mistake to think that Chaucer shaped our language from crude materials. His influence was conservative, not plastic. The popularity of his works tended to crystalize and thus to perpetuate the forms of the East Midland dialect, but that dialect was ready to his hand before he began to write. The speech of London was, in Chaucer's time, a mixture of Southern and Midland forms, but the Southern forms (survivals of the West Saxon dialect) had already begun to fall away; and this they continued to do, so that "Chaucer's language," as Dr. Murray says, "is more Southern than standard English eventually became." See also Morsbach, *Ueber den Ursprung der neuenglischen Schriftsprache* (1888).

4. The last period is that of MODERN ENGLISH, or the period of *lost inflections*. *E.g. stones, care, will, bind, help*, each being a monosyllable. Modern English extends from A.D. 1500 to the present time. It has witnessed comparatively few grammatical changes, but the vocabulary of our language has been vastly increased by additions from the classical languages. Vowels, too, have shifted their values.

5. It is the object of this book to give an elementary knowledge of Early West Saxon, that is, the language of King Alfred. With this knowledge, it will not be difficult for the student to read Late West Saxon, or any other dialect of the Old English period. Such knowledge will also serve as the best introduction to the structure both of Middle English and of Modern English, besides laying a secure foundation for the scientific study of any other Germanic tongue.

NOTE.--The Germanic, or Teutonic, languages constitute a branch of the great Aryan, or Indo-Germanic (known also as the Indo-European) group. They are subdivided as follows:

{ North Germanic: Scandinavian, or Norse. { { { Old High German, Germanic { East Germanic: Gothic. { (to A.D. 1100,) { { { High German { Middle High German, { { { (A.D. 1100-1500,) { { { West Germanic { { New High German. { { (A.D. 1500-.) { { Low German { Dutch, { Old Saxon, { Frisian, { English.

CHAPTER II.

SOUNDS.

#Vowels and Diphthongs.#

6. The long vowels and diphthongs will in this book be designated by the macron (̄). Vowel length should in every case be associated by the student with each word learned: quantity alone sometimes distinguishes words meaning wholly different things: #fôr#, *he went*, #for#, *for*; #gôd#, *good*, #God#, *God*; #mân#, *crime*, #man#, *man*.

Long vowels and diphthongs:

â as in father: #stân#, *a stone*. æ: as in man (prolonged): #slæ:pan#, *to sleep*. ê as in they: #hêr#, *here*. î as in machine: #mîn#, *mine*. ô as in note (pure, not diphthongal): #bôc#, *book*. û as in rule: #tûn#, *town*. y: as in German grün, or English green (with lips rounded):[1] #bry:d#, *bride*.

The diphthongs, long and short, have the stress upon the first vowel. The second vowel is obscured, and represents approximately the sound of *er* in *sooner, faster* (= *soon-uh, fast-uh*). The long diphthongs (æ: is not a diphthong proper) are êo, îe, and êa. The sound of êo is approximately reproduced in *mayor* (= *mâ-uh*); that of îe in the dissyllabic pronunciation of *fear* (= *fê-uh*). But êa = æ:-uh. This diphthong is hardly to be distinguished from *ea* in *pear, bear*, etc., as pronounced in the southern section of the United States (= *bæ-uh, pæ-uh*).

7. The short sounds are nothing more than the long vowels and diphthongs shortened; but the student must at once rid himself of the idea that Modern English *red*, for example, is the shortened form of *reed*, or that *mat* is the shortened form of *mate*. Pronounce these long sounds with increasing rapidity, and *reed* will approach *rid*, while *mate* will approach *met*. The Old English short vowel sounds are:

a as in artistic: #habban#, *to have*. æ as in mankind: #dæg#, *day*. e, [e,] as in let: #stelan#, *to steal*, #s[e,]ttan#, *to set*. i as in sit: #hit#, *it*. o

as in br*oa*d (but shorter): #God#, *God*. [o,] as in n*o*t: #l[o,]mb#, *lamb*. u
as in f*u*ll: #sunu#, *son*. y as in m*i*ller (with lips rounded)[1]: #gylden#,
golden.

NOTE.--The symbol [e,] is known as *umlaut*-e (§ 58). It stands for
Germanic *a*, while e (without the cedilla) represents Germanic *e*. The
symbol [o,] is employed only before m and n. It, too, represents
Germanic *a*. But Alfred writes #manig# or #monig#, *many*; #lamb# or
#lomb#, *lamb*; #hand# or #hond#, *hand*, etc. The cedilla is an
etymological sign added by modern grammarians.

[Transcriber's Note: The diacritic is not a cedilla (open to the left) but
an ogonek (open to the right).]

[Footnote 1: Vowels are said to be round, or rounded, when the
lip-opening is rounded; that is, when the lips are thrust out and
puckered as if preparing to pronounce *w*. Thus *o* and *u* are round
vowels: add *-ing* to each, and phonetically you have added *-wing*. *E.g.*
go^{w}ing, su^{w}ing.]

#Consonants.#

8. There is little difference between the values of Old English
consonants and those of Modern English. The following distinctions,
however, require notice:

The digraph #th# is represented in Old English texts by ð and þ, no
consistent distinction being made between them. In the works of
Alfred, ð (capital, Ð) is the more common: #ðâs#, *those*; #ðæt#, *that*;
#bindeð#, *he binds*.

The consonant #c# had the hard sound of *k*, the latter symbol being
rare in West Saxon: #cyning#, *king*; #cwên#, *queen*; #cûð#, *known*.
When followed by a palatal vowel sound,--e, i, æ, ea, eo, long or
short,--a vanishing *y* sound was doubtless interposed (*cf.* dialectic
k^{y}ind for *kind*). In Modern English the combination has passed into
ch: #cealc#, *chalk*; #cîdan#, *to chide*; #læ:ce#, *leech*; #cild#, *child*;
#cêowan#, *to chew*. This change (*c* > *ch*) is known as Palatalization.
The letter g, pronounced as in Modern English *gun*, has also a palatal

value before the palatal vowels (*cf.* dialectic *g^{y}irl* for *girl*).

The combination #cg#, which frequently stands for #gg#, had probably the sound of *dge* in Modern English *edge*: #ecg#, *edge*; #secgan#, *to say*; #brycg#, *bridge*. Initial #h# is sounded as in Modern English: #habban#, *to have*; #hâlga#, *saint*. When closing a syllable it has the sound of German *ch*: #slôh#, *he slew*; #hêah#, *high*; #ðurh#, *through*.

9. An important distinction is that between voiced (or sonant) and voiceless (or surd) consonants.[2] In Old English they are as follows:

VOICED. VOICELESS.

g h, c d t ð, þ (as in *th*ough) ð, þ (as in *th*in) b p f (= v) f s (= z) s

It is evident, therefore, that ð (þ), f, and s have double values in Old English. If voiced, they are equivalent to *th* (in *th*ough), *v*, and *z*. Otherwise, they are pronounced as *th* (in *th*in), *f* (in *fi*n), and *s* (in *s*in). The syllabic environment will usually compel the student to give these letters their proper values. When occurring between vowels, they are always voiced: #ôðer#, *other*; #ofer#, *over*; #rîsan#, *to rise*.

NOTE.--The general rule in Old English, as in Modern English, is, that voiced consonants have a special affinity for other voiced consonants, and voiceless for voiceless. This is the law of Assimilation. Thus when *de* is added to form the preterit of a verb whose stem ends in a voiceless consonant, the d is unvoiced, or assimilated, to t: #settan#, *to set*, #sette# (but #treddan#, *to tread*, has #tredde#); #slæ:pan#, *to sleep*, #slæ:pte#; #drencan#, *to drench*, #drencte#; #cyssan#, *to kiss*, #cyste#. See § 126, Note 1.

[Footnote 2: A little practice will enable the student to see the appropriateness of calling these consonants voiced and voiceless. Try to pronounce a voiced consonant,--*d* in *den*, for example, but without the assistance of *en*,--and there will be heard a gurgle, or *vocal murmur*. But in *t*, of *ten*, there is no sound at all, but only a feeling of tension in the organs.]

#Syllables.#

10. A syllable is usually a vowel, either alone or in combination with consonants, uttered with a single impulse of stress; but certain consonants may form syllables: *oven* (= *ov-n*), *battle* (= *bæt-l*); (*cf.* also the vulgar pronunciation of *elm*).

A syllable may be (1) weak or strong, (2) open or closed, (3) long or short.

(1) A weak syllable receives a light stress. Its vowel sound is often different from that of the corresponding strong, or stressed, syllable. *Cf.* weak and strong *my* in "I want my lárge hat" and "I want m[´y] hat."

(2) An open syllable ends in a vowel or diphthong: #dê-man#, *to deem*; #ðû#, *thou*; #sca-can#, *to shake*; #dæ-ges#, *by day*. A closed syllable ends in one or more consonants: #ðing#, *thing*; #gôd#, *good*; #glæd#, *glad.*

(3) A syllable is long (*a*) if it contains a long vowel or a long diphthong: #drî-fan#, *to drive*; #lû-can#, *to lock*; #slæ:-pan#, *to sleep*; #cêo-san#, *to choose*; (*b*) if its vowel or diphthong is followed by more than one consonant:[3] #cræft#, *strength*; #heard#, *hard*; #lib-ban#, *to live*; #feal-lan#, *to fall*. Otherwise, the syllable is short: #ðe#, *which*; #be-ran#, *to bear*; #ðæt#, *that*; #gie-fan#, *to give.*

NOTE 1.--A single consonant belongs to the following syllable: #hâ-lig#, *holy* (not #hâl-ig#); #wrî-tan#, *to write*; #fæ-der#, *father.*

NOTE 2.--The student will notice that the syllable may be long and the vowel short; but the vowel cannot be long and the syllable short.

NOTE 3.--Old English short vowels, occurring in open syllables, have regularly become long in Modern English: #we-fan#, *to weave*; #e-tan#, *to eat*; #ma-cian#, *to make*; #na-cod#, *naked*; #a-can#, *to ache*; #o-fer#, *over*. And Old English long vowels, preceding two or more consonants, have generally been shortened: #brêost#, *breast*; #hæ:lð#, *health*; #slæ:pte#, *slept*; #læ:dde#, *led.*

[Footnote 3: Taken separately, every syllable ending in a single consonant is long. It may be said, therefore, that all closed syllables are long; but in the natural flow of language, the single final consonant of a syllable so often blends with a following initial vowel, the syllable thus becoming open and short, that such syllables are not recognized as prevailingly long. *Cf.* Modern English *at all* (= *a-tall*).]

#Accentuation.#

11. The accent in Old English falls usually on the radical syllable, never on the inflectional ending: #bríngan#, *to bring*; #st[´â]nas#, *stones*; #bérende#, *bearing*; #[´î]delnes#, *idleness*; #fr[´ê]ondscipe#, *friendship*.

But in the case of compound nouns, adjectives, and adverbs the first member of the compound (unless it be ge- or be-) receives the stronger stress: #héofon-rîce#, *heaven-kingdom*; #ónd-giet#, *intelligence*; #sôð-fæst#, *truthful*; #gód-cund#, *divine*; #éall-unga#, *entirely*; #bl[´î]ðe-lîce#, *blithely*. But #be-h[´â]t#, *promise*; #ge-béd#, *prayer*; #ge-f[´ê]alîc#, *joyous*; #be-sóne#, *immediately*.

Compound verbs, however, have the stress on the radical syllable: #for-gíefan#, *to forgive*; #of-línnan#, *to cease*; #â-cn[´â]wan#, *to know*; #wið-stóndan#, *to withstand*; #on-sácan#, *to resist*.

NOTE.--The tendency of nouns to take the stress on the prefix, while verbs retain it on the root, is exemplified in many Modern English words: *préference, prefér; cóntract* (noun), *contráct* (verb); *ábstinence, abstaín; pérfume* (noun), *perfúme* (verb).

CHAPTER III.

INFLECTIONS.

#Cases.#

12. There are five cases in Old English: the nominative, the genitive, the dative, the accusative, and the instrumental.[1] Each of them, except the nominative, may be governed by prepositions. When used without prepositions, they have, in general, the following functions:

(*a*) The nominative, as in Modern English, is the case of the subject of a finite verb.

(*b*) The genitive (the possessive case of Modern English) is the case of the possessor or source. It may be called the *of* case.

(*c*) The dative is the case of the indirect object. It may be called the *to* or *for* case.

(*d*) The accusative (the objective case of Modern English) is the case of the direct object.

(*e*) The instrumental, which rarely differs from the dative in form, is the case of the means or the method. It may be called the *with* or *by* case.

The following paradigm of #mûð#, *the mouth*, illustrates the several cases (the article being, for the present, gratuitously added in the Modern English equivalents):

Singular. Plural.

N. mûð = *the mouth.* mûð-as = *the mouths.*

G. mûð-es[2] = *of the mouth* mûð-a = *of the mouths* (= *the mouth's*). (= *the mouths'*).

D. mûð-e = *to* or *for the* mûð-um = *to* or *for the mouths. mouth.*

A. mûð = *the mouth.* mûð-as = *the mouths.*

I. mûðe = *with* or *by means* mûð-um = with *or* by means of the mouth.
of the mouths.

[Footnote 1: Most grammars add a sixth case, the vocative. But it seems best to consider the vocative as only a *function* of the nominative *form.*]

[Footnote 2: Of course our "apostrophe and *s*" (= *'s*) comes from the Old English genitive ending -es. The *e* is preserved in *Wednesday* (= Old English #Wôdnes dæg#). But at a very early period it was thought that *John's book*, for example, was a shortened form of *John his book.* Thus Addison (*Spectator*, No. 135) declares *'s* a survival of *his.* How, then, would he explain the *s* of *his*? And how would he dispose of *Mary's book*?]

#Gender.#

13. The gender of Old English nouns, unlike that of Modern English, depends partly on meaning and partly on form, or ending. Thus #mûð#, *mouth*, is masculine; #tunge#, *tongue*, feminine; #êage#, *eye*, neuter.

No very comprehensive rules, therefore, can be given; but the gender of every noun should be learned with its meaning. Gender will be indicated in the vocabularies by the different gender forms of the definite article, #sê# for the masculine, #sêo# for the feminine, and #ðæt# for the neuter: #sê mûð#, #sêo tunge#, #ðæt êage# = *the mouth, the tongue, the eye.*

All nouns ending in #-dôm#, #-hâd#, #-scipe#, or #-ere# are masculine (*cf.* Modern English wis*dom*, child*hood*, friend*ship*, work*er*). Masculine, also, are nouns ending in -a.

Those ending in #-nes# or #-ung# are feminine (*cf.* Modern English good*ness*, and gerundial forms in -*ing*: see*ing* is believ*ing*).

Thus #sê wîsdôm#, *wisdom*; #sê cildhâd#, *childhood*; #sê frêondscipe#, *friendship*; #sê fiscere#, *fisher(man)*; #sê hunta#, *hunter*; #sêo gelîcnes#, *likeness*; #sêo leornung#, *learning*.

#Declensions.#

14. There are two great systems of declension in Old English, the Vowel Declension and the Consonant Declension. A noun is said to belong to the Vowel Declension when the final letter of its stem is a vowel, this vowel being then known as the *stem-characteristic*; but if the stem-characteristic is a consonant, the noun belongs to the Consonant Declension. There might have been, therefore, as many subdivisions of the Vowel Declension in Old English as there were vowels, and as many subdivisions of the Consonant Declension as there were consonants. All Old English nouns, however, belonging to the Vowel Declension, ended their stems originally in a, ô, i, or u. Hence there are but four subdivisions of the Vowel Declension: a-stems, ô-stems, i-stems, and u-stems.

The Vowel Declension is commonly called the Strong Declension, and its nouns Strong Nouns.

NOTE.--The terms Strong and Weak were first used by Jacob Grimm (1785-1863) in the terminology of verbs, and thence transferred to nouns and adjectives. By a Strong Verb, Grimm meant one that could form its preterit out of its own resources; that is, without calling in the aid of an additional syllable: Modern English *run*, *ran*; *find*, *found*; but verbs of the Weak Conjugation had to borrow, as it were, an inflectional syllable: *gain*, *gained*; *help*, *helped*.

15. The stems of nouns belonging to the Consonant Declension ended, with but few exceptions, in the letter n (*cf.* Latin *homin-em*, *ration-em*, Greek +poimen-a+). They are called, therefore, n-stems, the Declension itself being known as the n-Declension, or the Weak Declension. The nouns, also, are called Weak Nouns.

16. If every Old English noun had preserved the original Germanic stem-characteristic (or final letter of the stem), there would be no difficulty in deciding at once whether any given noun is an a-stem,

ô-stem, i-stem, u-stem, or n-stem; but these final letters had, for the most part, either been dropped, or fused with the case-endings, long before the period of historic Old English. It is only, therefore, by a rigid comparison of the Germanic languages with one another, and with the other Aryan languages, that scholars are able to reconstruct a single Germanic language, in which the original stem-characteristics may be seen far better than in any one historic branch of the Germanic group (§ 5, Note).

This hypothetical language, which bears the same ancestral relation to the historic Germanic dialects that Latin bears to the Romance tongues, is known simply as *Germanic* (Gmc.), or as *Primitive Germanic*. Ability to reconstruct Germanic forms is not expected of the students of this book, but the following table should be examined as illustrating the basis of distinction among the several Old English declensions (O.E. = Old English, Mn.E. = Modern English):

{ {Gmc. *staina-z*, {(1) a-stems {O.E. #stân#, { {Mn.E. *stone*. { { {Gmc. *hallô*, {(2) ô-stems {O.E. #heall#, I. Strong or Vowel { {Mn.E. *hall*. Declensions { { {Gmc. *bôni-z*, {(3) i-stems {O.E. #bên#, { {Mn.E. *boon*. { { {Gmc. *sunu-z*, {(4) u-stems {O.E. #sunu#, { {Mn.E. *son*.

{(1) n-stems {Gmc. *tungôn-iz*, { (Weak {O.E. #tung-an#, { Declension) {Mn.E. *tongue-s*. { { { {Gmc. *fôt-iz*, { {(*a*) {O.E. #fêt#, II. Consonant {(2) Remnants { {Mn.E. *feet*. Declensions { of other { { Consonant { {Gmc. *frijônd-iz*, { Declensions {(*b*) {O.E. #frîend#, { { {Mn.E. *friend-s*. { { { { {Gmc. *brôðr-iz*, { {(*c*) {O.E. #brôðor#, { { {Mn.E. *brother-s*.

NOTE.--"It will be seen that if Old English #êage#, *eye*, is said to be an n-stem, what is meant is this, that at some former period the kernel of the word ended in -n, while, as far as the Old English language proper is concerned, all that is implied is that the word is inflected in a certain manner." (Jespersen, *Progress in Language*, § 109).

This is true of all Old English stems, whether Vowel or Consonant. The division, therefore, into a-stems, ô-stems, etc., is made in the interests of grammar as well as of philology.

#Conjugations.#

17. There are, likewise, two systems of conjugation in Old English: the Strong or Old Conjugation, and the Weak or New Conjugation.

The verbs of the Strong Conjugation (the so-called Irregular Verbs of Modern English) number about three hundred, of which not one hundred remain in Modern English (§ 101, Note). They form their preterit and frequently their past participle by changing the radical vowel of the present stem. This vowel change or modification is called *ablaut* (pronounced *áhp-lowt*): Modern English *sing, sang, sung*; *rise, rose, risen*. As the radical vowel of the preterit plural is often different from that of the preterit singular, there are four *principal parts* or *tense stems* in an Old English strong verb, instead of the three of Modern English. The four principal parts in the conjugation of a strong verb are (1) the present indicative, (2) the preterit indicative singular, (3) the preterit indicative plural, and (4) the past participle.

Strong verbs fall into seven groups, illustrated in the following table:

PRESENT. PRET. SING. PRET. PLUR. PAST PARTICIPLE.

I. Bîtan, *to bite*:

Ic bît-e, *I bite* or *shall bite*.[3] Ic bât, *I bit*. Wê bit-on, *we bit*. Ic hæbbe ge[4]-biten, *I have bitten*.

II. Bêodan, *to bid*:

Ic bêod-e, *I bid* or *shall bid*. Ic bêad, *I bade*. Wê bud-on, *we bade*. Ic hæbbe ge-boden, *I have bidden*.

III. Bindan, *to bind*:

Ic bind-e, *I bind* or *shall bind*. Ic bond, *I bound*. Wê bund-on, *we bound*. Ic hæbbe ge-bund-en, *I have bound*.

IV. Beran, *to bear*:

Ic ber-e, *I bear* or *shall bear*. Ic bær, *I bore*. Wê bæ:r-on, *we bore*. Ic hæbbe ge-bor-en, *I have borne*.

V. Metan, *to measure*:

Ic met-e, *I measure* or *shall measure*. Ic mæt, *I measured*. Wê mæ:t-on, *we measured*. Ic hæbbe ge-met-en, *I have measured*.

VI. Faran, *to go*:

Ic far-e, *I go* or *shall go*. Ic fôr, *I went*. Wê fôr-on, *we went*. Ic eom[5] ge-far-en, *I have (am) gone*.

VII. Feallan, *to fall*:

Ic feall-e, *I fall* or *shall fall*. Ic fêoll, *I fell*. Wê fêoll-on, *we fell*. Ic eom[5] ge-feall-en, *I have (am) fallen*.

[Footnote 3: Early West Saxon had no distinctive form for the future. The present was used both as present proper and as future. *Cf.* Modern English "I go home tomorrow," or "I am going home tomorrow" for "I shall go home tomorrow."]

[Footnote 4: The prefix ge- (Middle English *y-*), cognate with Latin *co* (*con*) and implying completeness of action, was not always used. It never occurs in the past participles of compound verbs: #oþ-feallan#, *to fall off*, past participle #oþ-feallen# (not #oþ-gefeallen#). Milton errs in prefixing it to a present participle:

"What needs my Shakespeare, for his honour'd bones, The labour of an age in piled stones? Or that his hallow'd reliques should be hid Under a star-*ypointing* pyramid." --*Epitaph on William Shakespeare*.

And Shakespeare misuses it in "Y-ravished," a preterit (*Pericles* III, *Prologue* I. 35).

It survives in the archaic *y-clept* (Old English #ge-clypod#, called). It appears as *a* in *aware* (Old English #ge-wær#), as *e* in *enough* (Old English #ge-nôh#), and as *i* in *handiwork* (Old English #hand-ge-weorc#).]

[Footnote 5: With intransitive verbs denoting *change of condition*, the Old English auxiliary is usually some form of *to be* rather than *to have*. See § 139.]

18. The verbs of the Weak Conjugation (the so-called Regular Verbs of Modern English) form their preterit and past participle by adding to the present stem a suffix[6] with *d* or *t*: Modern English *love, loved*; *sleep, slept*.

The stem of the preterit plural is never different from the stem of the preterit singular; hence these verbs have only three distinctive tense-stems, or principal parts: *viz.*, (1) the present indicative, (2) the preterit indicative, and (3) the past participle.

Weak verbs fall into three groups, illustrated in the following table:

PRESENT. PRETERIT. PAST PARTICIPLE.

I. Fremman, *to perform*:

Ic fremm-e, *I perform* or *shall perform*. Ic frem-ede, *I performed*. Ic hæbbe ge-frem-ed, *I have performed*.

II. Bodian, *to proclaim*:

Ic bodi-e, *I proclaim* or *shall proclaim*. Ic bod-ode, *I proclaimed*. Ic hæbbe ge-bod-od, *I have proclaimed*.

III. Habban, *to have*:

Ic hæbbe, *I have* or *shall have*. Ic hæf-de, *I had*. Ic hæbbe ge-hæf-d, *I have had*.

[Footnote 6: The theory that *loved*, for example, is a fused form of *love-did* has been generally given up. The dental ending was doubtless an Indo-Germanic suffix, which became completely specialized only in the Teutonic languages.]

19. There remain a few verbs (chiefly the Auxiliary Verbs of Modern English) that do not belong entirely to either of the two conjugations mentioned. The most important of them are, #Ic mæg# *I may*, #Ic mihte# *I might*; #Ic con# *I can*, #Ic cûðe# *I could*; #Ic môt# *I must*, #Ic môste# *I must*; #Ic sceal# *I shall*, #Ic sceolde# *I should*; #Ic eom# *I am*, #Ic wæs# *I was*; #Ic wille# *I will*, #Ic wolde# *I would*; #Ic dô# *I do*, #Ic dyde# *I did*; #Ic gâ# *I go*, #Ic êode# *I went*.

All but the last four of these are known as Preterit-Present Verbs. The present tense of each of them is *in origin* a preterit, *in function* a present. *Cf.* Modern English *ought* (= *owed*).

CHAPTER IV.

ORDER OF WORDS.

20. The order of words in Old English is more like that of Modern German than of Modern English. Yet it is only the Transposed order that the student will feel to be at all un-English; and the Transposed order, even before the period of the Norman Conquest, was fast yielding place to the Normal order.

The three divisions of order are (1) Normal, (2) Inverted, and (3) Transposed.

(1) Normal order = subject + predicate. In Old English, the Normal order is found chiefly in independent clauses. The predicate is followed by its modifiers: #Sê hwæl bið micle læ:ssa þonne ôðre hwalas#, *That whale is much smaller than other whales*; #Ond hê geseah twâ scipu#, *And he saw two ships*.

(2) Inverted order = predicate + subject. This order occurs also in independent clauses, and is employed (*a*) when some modifier of the predicate precedes the predicate, the subject being thrown behind. The words most frequently causing Inversion in Old English prose are #þâ# *then*, #þonne# *then*, and #þæ:r# *there*: #Ðâ fôr hê#, *Then went he*; #Ðonne ærnað hy: ealle tôweard þæ:m fêo#, *Then gallop they all toward the property*; #ac þæ:r bið medo genôh#, *but there is mead enough*.

Inversion is employed (*b*) in interrogative sentences: #Lufast ðû mê?# *Lovest thou me?* and (*c*) in imperative sentences: #Cume ðîn rîce#, *Thy kingdom come*.

(3) Transposed order = subject ... predicate. That is, the predicate comes last in the sentence, being preceded by its modifiers. This is the order observed in dependent clauses:[1] #Ðonne cymeð sê man sê þæt swiftoste hors hafað#, *Then comes the man that has the swiftest horse* (literally, *that the swiftest horse has*); #Ne mêtte hê æ:r nân gebûn land, siþþan hê from his âgnum hâm fôr#, *Nor did he before find any cultivated land, after he went from his own home* (literally, *after he*

from his own home went).

[Footnote 1: But in the *Voyages of Ohthere and Wulfstan*, in which the style is apparently more that of oral than of written discourse, the Normal is more frequent than the Transposed order in dependent clauses. In his other writings Alfred manifests a partiality for the Transposed order in dependent clauses, except in the case of substantival clauses introduced by #þæt#. Such clauses show a marked tendency to revert to their Normal *oratio recta* order. The norm thus set by the indirect affirmative clause seems to have proved an important factor in the ultimate disappearance of Transposition from dependent clauses. The influence of Norman French helped only to consummate forces that were already busily at work.]

21. Two other peculiarities in the order of words require a brief notice.

(1) Pronominal datives and accusatives usually precede the predicate: #Hê hine oferwann#, *He overcame him* (literally, *He him overcame*); #Dryhten him andwyrde#, *The Lord answered him*. But substantival datives and accusatives, as in Modern English, follow the predicate. The following sentence illustrates both orders: #Hy: genâmon Ioseph, ond hine gesealdon cîpemonnum, ond hy: hine gesealdon in Êgypta lond#, *They took Joseph, and sold him to merchants, and they sold him into Egypt* (literally, *They took Joseph, and him sold to merchants, and they him sold into Egyptians' land*).

NOTE.--The same order prevails in the case of pronominal nominatives used as predicate nouns: #Ic hit eom#, *It is I* (literally, *I it am*); #Ðû hit eart#, *It is thou* (literally, *Thou it art*).

(2) The attributive genitive, whatever relationship it expresses, usually precedes the noun which it qualifies: #Breoton is gârsecges îgland#, *Britain is an island of the ocean* (literally, *ocean's island*); #Swilce hit is êac berende on wecga ôrum#, *Likewise it is also rich in ores of metals* (literally, *metals' ores*); #Cyninga cyning#, *King of kings* (literally, *Kings' king*); #Gê witon Godes rîces gery:ne#, *Ye know the mystery of the kingdom of God* (literally, *Ye know God's kingdom's mystery*).

A preposition governing the word modified by the genitive, precedes the genitive:[2] #On ealdra manna sægenum#, *In old men's sayings*; #Æt ðæ:ra stræ:ta endum#, *At the ends of the streets* (literally, *At the streets' ends*); #For ealra ðînra hâlgena lufan#, *For all thy saints' love.* See, also, § 94, (5).

[Footnote 2: The positions of the genitive are various. It frequently follows its noun: #þâ bearn þâra Aðeniensa#, *The children of the Athenians.* It may separate an adjective and a noun: #Ân ly:tel sæ:s earm#, *A little arm of (the) sea.* The genitive may here be construed as an adjective, or part of a compound = *A little sea-arm*; #Mid monegum Godes gifum#, *With many God-gifts = many divine gifts.*]

CHAPTER V.

PRACTICAL SUGGESTIONS.

22. In the study of Old English, the student must remember that he is dealing not with a foreign or isolated language but with the earlier forms of his own mother tongue. The study will prove profitable and stimulating in proportion as close and constant comparison is made of the old with the new. The guiding principles in such a comparison are reducible chiefly to two. These are (1) the regular operation of phonetic laws, resulting especially in certain Vowel Shiftings, and (2) the alterations in form and syntax that are produced by Analogy.

(1) "The former of these is of physiological or *natural* origin, and is perfectly and inflexibly regular throughout the same period of the same language; and even though different languages show different phonetic habits and predilections, there is a strong general resemblance between the changes induced in one language and in another; many of the particular laws are true for many languages.

(2) "The other principle is psychical, or mental, or *artificial*, introducing various more or less capricious changes that are supposed to be emendations; and its operation is, to some extent, uncertain and fitful."[1]

[Footnote 1: Skeat, *Principles of English Etymology*, Second Series, § 342. But Jespersen, with Collitz and others, stoutly contests "the theory of sound laws and analogy sufficing between them to explain everything in linguistic development."]

(1) #Vowel-Shiftings.#

23. It will prove an aid to the student in acquiring the inflections and vocabulary of Old English to note carefully the following shiftings that have taken place in the gradual growth of the Old English vowel system into that of Modern English.

(1) As stated in § 3, the Old English inflectional vowels, which were all short and unaccented, weakened in early Middle English to *e*. This *e* in

Modern English is frequently dropped:

OLD ENGLISH. MIDDLE ENGLISH. MODERN ENGLISH. stân-as ston-es stones sun-u sun-e son sun-a sun-e sons ox-an ox-en oxen swift-ra swift-er swifter swift-ost swift-est swiftest lôc-ode lok-ede looked

(2) The Old English long vowels have shifted their phonetic values with such uniform regularity that it is possible in almost every case to infer the Modern English sound; but our spelling is so chaotic that while the student may infer the modern sound, he cannot always infer the modern symbol representing the sound.

OLD MODERN ENGLISH. ENGLISH.

â *o*[2] { nâ = *no*; stân = *stone*; bân = *bone*; (as in *no*) { râd = *road*; âc = *oak*; hâl = *whole*; { hâm = *home*; sâwan = *to sow*; gâst = { *ghost.*

ê *e* { hê = *he*; wê = *we*; ðê = *thee*; mê = (as in *he*) { *me*; gê = *ye*; hêl = *heel*; wêrig = { *weary*; gelêfan = *to believe*; gês = { *geese.*

î (y:) *i* (*y*) { mîn = *mine*; ðîn = *thine*; wîr = *wire*; (as in *mine*) { my:s = *mice*; rîm = *rime* (wrongly spelt { *rhyme*); ly:s = *lice*; bî = *by*; { scînan = *to shine*; stig-râp = *sty-rope* { (shortened to *stirrup*, stîgan meaning { *to mount*).

ô *o* { dô = *I do*; tô = *too, to*; gôs = *goose*; (as in *do*) { tôð = *tooth*; môna = *moon*; ðôm = { *doom*; môd = *mood*; wôgian = *to woo*; { slôh = *I slew.*

û *ou* (*ow*) { ðû = *thou*; fûl = *foul*; hûs = *house*; (as in *thou*) { nû = *now*; hû = *how*; tûn = *town*; { ûre = our; ût = *out*; hlûd = *loud*; { ðûsend = *thousand.*

æ:, *ea* { æ:: sæ: = *sea*; mæ:l = *meal*; dæ:lan = êa, (as in *sea*) { *to deal*; clæ:ne = *clean*; græ:dig = êo { *greedy*. { { êa: êare = *ear*, êast = *east*; drêam = { *dream*; gêar = *year*; bêatan = { *to beat*. { { êo: ðrêo = *three*; drêorig = *dreary*; { sêo = *she*, hrêod = *reed*; dêop = { *deep.*

[Footnote 2: But Old English â preceded by w sometimes gives Modern English *o* as in *two*: #twâ# = *two*; #hwâ# = *who*; #hwâm# = *whom*.]

(2) #Analogy.#

24. But more important than vowel shifting is the great law of Analogy, for Analogy shapes not only words but constructions. It belongs, therefore, to Etymology and to Syntax, since it influences both form and function. By this law, minorities tend to pass over to the side of the majorities. "The greater mass of cases exerts an assimilative influence upon the smaller."[3] The effect of Analogy is to simplify and to regularize. "The main factor in getting rid of irregularities is group-influence, or Analogy--the influence exercised by the members of an association-group on one another.... Irregularity consists in partial isolation from an association-group through some formal difference."[4]

Under the influence of Analogy, entire declensions and conjugations have been swept away, leaving in Modern English not a trace of their former existence. There are in Old English, for example, five plural endings for nouns, -as, -a, -e, -u, and -an. No one could well have predicted[5] that -as (Middle English -*es*) would soon take the lead, and become the norm to which the other endings would eventually conform, for there were more an-plurals than as-plurals; but the as-plurals were doubtless more often employed in everyday speech. *Oxen* (Old English #oxan#) is the sole pure survival of the hundreds of Old English an-plurals. No group of feminine nouns in Old English had -es as the genitive singular ending; but by the close of the Middle English period all feminines formed their genitive singular in -*es* (or -*s*, Modern English *'s*) after the analogy of the Old English masculine and neuter nouns with es-genitives. The weak preterits in -ode have all been leveled under the ed-forms, and of the three hundred strong verbs in Old English more than two hundred have become weak.

These are not cases of derivation (as are the shifted vowels): Modern English -*s* in *sons*, for example, could not possibly be derived from Old English -a in #suna#, or Middle English -*e* in *sune* (§ 23, (1)). They are cases of replacement by Analogy.

A few minor examples will quicken the student's appreciation of the nature of the influence exercised by Analogy:

(*a*) The intrusive *l* in *could* (Chaucer always wrote *coud* or *coude*) is due to association with *would* and *should*, in each of which *l* belongs by etymological right.

(*b*) *He need not* (for *He needs not*) is due to the assimilative influence of the auxiliaries *may*, *can*, etc., which have never added -*s* for their third person singular (§ 137).

(*c*) *I am friends with him*, in which *friends* is a crystalized form for *on good terms*, may be traced to the influence of such expressions as *He and I are friends*, *They are friends*, etc.

(*d*) Such errors as are seen in *runned*, *seed*, *gooses*, *badder*, *hisself*, *says I* (usually coupled with *says he*) are all analogical formations. Though not sanctioned by good usage, it is hardly right to call these forms the products of "false analogy." The grammar involved is false, because unsupported by literary usages and traditions; but the analogy on which these forms are built is no more false than the law of gravitation is false when it makes a dress sit unconventionally.

[Footnote 3: Whitney, *Life and Growth of Language*, Chap. IV.]

[Footnote 4: Sweet, *A New English Grammar*, Part I., § 535.]

[Footnote 5: As Skeat says (§ 22, (2)), Analogy is "fitful." It enables us to explain many linguistic phenomena, but not to anticipate them. The multiplication of books tends to check its influence by perpetuating the forms already in use. Thus Chaucer employed nine *en*-plurals, and his influence served for a time to check the further encroachment of the *es*-plurals. As soon as there is an acknowledged standard in any language, the operation of Analogy is fettered.]

PART II.

ETYMOLOGY AND SYNTAX.

THE STRONG OR VOWEL DECLENSIONS OF NOUNS.

THE a-DECLENSION.

CHAPTER VI.

(*a*) #Masculine *a*-Stems.#

[O.E., M.E., and Mn.E. will henceforth be used for Old English, Middle English, and Modern English. Other abbreviations employed are self-explaining.]

25. The a-Declension, corresponding to the Second or *o*-Declension of Latin and Greek, contains only (*a*) masculine and (*b*) neuter nouns. To this declension belong most of the O.E. masculine and neuter nouns of the Strong Declension. At a very early period, many of the nouns belonging properly to the i- and u-Declensions began to pass over to the a-Declension. This declension may therefore be considered the *normal declension* for all masculine and neuter nouns belonging to the Strong Declension.

26. Paradigms of #sê mûð#, *mouth*; #sê fiscere#, *fisherman*; #sê hwæl#, *whale*; #sê mearh#, *horse*; #sê finger#, *finger*:

Sing. N.A. mûð fiscer-e hwæl mearh finger *G.* mûð-es fiscer-es hwæl-es mêar-es fingr-es *D.I.* mûð-e fiscer-e hwæl-e mêar-e fingr-e

Plur. N.A. mûð-as fiscer-as hwal-as mêar-as fingr-as *G.* mûð-a fiscer-a hwal-a mêar-a fingr-a *D.I.* mûð-um fiscer-um hwal-um mêar-um fingr-um

NOTE.--For meanings of the cases, see § 12. The dative and instrumental are alike in all nouns.

27. The student will observe (1) that nouns whose nominative ends in -e (#fiscere#) drop this letter before adding the case endings; (2) that æ before a consonant (#hwæl#) changes to a in the plural;[1] (3) that h, preceded by r (#mearh#) or l (#seolh#, *seal*), is dropped before an inflectional vowel, the stem diphthong being then lengthened by way of compensation; (4) that dissyllables (#finger#) having the first syllable long, usually syncopate the vowel of the second syllable before adding the case endings.[2]

[Footnote 1: Adjectives usually retain æ in closed syllables, changing it to a in open syllables: #hwæt# (*active*), #glæd# (*glad*), #wær# (*wary*) have G. #hwates#, #glades#, #wares#; D. #hwatum#, #gladum#, #warum#; but A. #hwætne#, #glædne#, #wærne#. Nouns, however, change to a only in open syllables followed by a guttural vowel, a or u. The æ in the open syllables of the singular is doubtless due to the analogy of the N.A. singular, both being closed syllables.]

[Footnote 2: *Cf.* Mn.E. *drizz'ling, rememb'ring, abysmal* (*abysm* = *abiz^{u}m*), *sick'ning*, in which the principle of syncopation is precisely the same.]

28. Paradigm of the Definite Article[3] #sê#, #sêo#, #ðæt# = *the*:

Masculine. Feminine. Neuter.

Sing. N. sê (se) sêo ðæt *G.* ðæs ðæ:re ðæs *D.* ðæ:m (ðâm) ðæ:re ðæ:m (ðâm) *A.* ðone ðâ ðæt *I.* ðy:, ðon ---- ðy:, ðon

All Genders.

Plur. N.A. ðâ *G.* ðâra *D.* ðæ:m (ðâm)

[Footnote 3: This may mean four things: (1) *The*, (2) *That* (demonstrative), (3) *He, she, it*, (4) *Who, which, that* (relative pronoun). Mn.E. demonstrative *that* is, of course, the survival of O.E. neuter #ðæt# in its demonstrative sense. Professor Victor Henry (*Comparative Grammar of English and German*, § 160, 3) sees a survival of dative plural demonstrative #ðæ:m# in such an expression as *in them days*. It seems more probable, however, that *them* so used has followed the lead of *this* and *these*, *that* and *those*, in their double function of pronoun and adjective. There was doubtless some such evolution as, *I saw them. Them what? Them boys.*

An unquestioned survival of the dative singular feminine of the article is seen in the *-ter* of *Atterbury* (= #æt ðæ:re byrig#, *at the town*); and #ðæ:m# survives in the *-ten* of *Attenborough*, the word *borough* having become an uninflected neuter. Skeat, *Principles*, First Series, § 185.]

29. VOCABULARY.[4]

sê bôcere, *scribe* [bôc]. sê cyning, *king.* sê dæg, *day.* sê ende, *end.* sê engel, *angel* [angelus]. sê frêodôm, *freedom.* sê fugol (G. sometimes #fugles#), *bird* [fowl]. sê gâr, *spear* [gore, gar-fish]. sê heofon, *heaven.* sê hierde, *herdsman* [shep-herd]. ond (and), *and.* sê secg, *man, warrior.* sê seolh, *seal.* sê stân, *stone.* sê wealh, *foreigner, Welshman* [wal-nut]. sê weall, *wall.* sê wîsdôm, *wisdom.* sê wulf, *wolf.*

[Footnote 4: The brackets contain etymological hints that may help the student to discern relationships otherwise overlooked. The genitive is given only when not perfectly regular.]

30. EXERCISES.

I. 1. Ðâra wulfa mûðas. 2. Ðæs fisceres fingras. 3. Ðâra Wêala cyninge. 4. Ðæ:m englum ond ðæ:m hierdum. 5. Ðâra daga ende. 6. Ðæ:m bôcerum ond ðæ:m secgum ðæs cyninges. 7. Ðæ:m sêole ond ðæ:m fuglum. 8. Ðâ stânas ond ðâ gâras. 9. Hwala ond mêara. 10. Ðâra engla wîsdôm. 11. Ðæs cyninges bôceres frêodôm. 12. Ðâra hierda fuglum. 13. Ðy: stâne. 14. Ðæ:m wealle.

II. 1. For the horses and the seals. 2. For the Welshmen's freedom. 3. Of the king's birds. 4. By the wisdom of men and angels. 5. With the spear and the stone. 6. The herdsman's seal and the warriors' spears. 7. To the king of heaven. 8. By means of the scribe's wisdom. 9. The whale's mouth and the foreigner's spear. 10. For the bird belonging to (= of) the king's scribe. 11. Of that finger.

CHAPTER VII.

(b) #Neuter a-Stems.#

31. The neuter nouns of the a-Declension differ from the masculines only in the N.A. plural.

32. Paradigms of #ðæt hof#, *court, dwelling*; #ðaet bearn#, *child*; #ðæt bân#, *bone*; #ðæt rîce#, *kingdom*; #ðæt spere#, *spear*; #ðæt werod#, *band of men*; #ðæt tungol#, *star*:

Sing. N.A. hof bearn bân rîc-e *G.* hof-es bearn-es bân-es rîc-es *D.I.* hof-e bearn-e bân-e rîc-e

Plur. N.A. hof-u bearn bân rîc-u *G.* hof-a bearn-a bân-a rîc-a *D.I.* hof-um bearn-um bân-um rîc-um

Sing. N.A. sper-e werod tungol *G.* sper-es werod-es tungl-es *D.I.* sper-e werod-e tungl-e

Plur. N.A. sper-u werod tungl-u *G.* sper-a werod-a tungl-a *D.I.* sper-um werod-um tungl-um

33. The paradigms show (1) that monosyllables with short stems (#hof#) take -u in the N.A. plural; (2) that monosyllables with long stems (#bearn#, #bân#) do not distinguish the N.A. plural from the N.A. singular;[1] (3) that dissyllables in -e, whether the stem be long or short (#rîce#, #spere#), have -u in the N.A. plural; (4) that dissyllables ending in a consonant and having the first syllable short[2] (#werod#) do not usually distinguish the N.A. plural from the N.A. singular; (5) that dissyllables ending in a consonant and having the first syllable long (#tungol#) more frequently take -u in the N.A. plural.

NOTE.--Syncopation occurs as in the masculine a-stems. See § 27, (4).

[Footnote 1: Note the many nouns in Mn.E. that are unchanged in the plural. These are either survivals of O.E. long stems, *swine, sheep, deer, folk*, or analogical forms, *fish, trout, mackerel, salmon*, etc.]

[Footnote 2: Dissyllables whose first syllable is a prefix are, of course, excluded. They follow the declension of their last member: #gebed#, *prayer*, #gebedu#, *prayers*; #gefeoht#, *battle*, #gefeoht#, *battles*.]

34. Present and Preterit Indicative of #habban#, *to have*:

PRESENT.

Sing. 1. Ic hæbbe, *I have*, or *shall have*.[3] 2. ðû hæfst (hafast), *thou hast*, or *wilt have*. 3. hê, hêo, hit hæfð (hafað), *he, she, it has*, or *will have*.

Plur. 1. wê habbað, *we have*, or *shall have*. 2. gê habbað, *ye have*, or *will have*. 3. hîe habbað, *they have*, or *will have*.

PRETERIT.

Sing. 1. Ic hæfde *I had*. 2. ðû hæfdest, *thou hadst*. 3. hê, hêo, hit hæfde, *he, she, it had*.

Plur. 1. wê hæfdon, *we had*. 2. gê hæfdon, *ye had*. 3. hîe hæfdon, *they had*.

NOTE.--The negative #ne#, *not*, which always precedes its verb, contracts with all the forms of #habban#. The negative loses its e, #habban# its h. #Ne# + #habban# = #nabban#; #Ic ne hæbbe = Ic næbbe#; #Ic ne hæfde = Ic næfde#, etc. The negative forms may be got, therefore, by simply substituting in each case n for h.

[Footnote 3: See § 17, Note 1. Note that (as in #hwæl#, § 27, (2)) æ changes to a when the following syllable contains a: #hæbbe#, but #hafast#.]

35. VOCABULARY.

ðæt dæl, *dale*. ðæt dêor, *animal* [deer[4]]. ðæt dor, *door*. ðæt fæt, *vessel* [vat]. ðæt fy:r, *fire*. ðæt gêar, *year*. ðæt geoc, *yoke*. ðæt geset, *habitation* [settlement]. ðæt hêafod, *head*. ðæt hûs, *house*. ðæt lîc, *body* [lich-gate]. ðæt lim, *limb*. on (with dat.) *in*. ðæt spor, *track*. ðæt wæ:pen, *weapon.* ðæt wîf, *wife, woman.* ðæt wîte, *punishment.* ðæt word, *word.*

[Footnote 4: The old meaning survives in Shakespeare's "Rats and mice and such small deer," *King Lear*, III, iv, 144.]

36. EXERCISES.

I. 1. Hê hafað ðæs cyninges bearn. 2. Ðâ Wêalas habbað ðâ speru. 3. Ðâ wîf habbað ðâra secga wæ:pnu. 4. Ðû hæfst ðone fugol ond ðæt hûs ðæs hierdes. 5. Hæfð[5] hêo ðâ fatu[6]? 6. Hæfde hê ðæs wîfes lîc on ðæ:m hofe? 7. Hê næfde ðæs wîfes lîc; hê hæfde ðæs dêores hêafod. 8. Hæfð sê cyning gesetu on ðæ:m dæle? 9. Sê bôcere hæfð ðâ sêolas on ðæ:m hûse. 10. Gê habbað frêodôm.

II. 1. They have yokes and spears. 2. We have not the vessels in the house. 3. He had fire in the vessel. 4. Did the woman have (= Had the woman) the children? 5. The animal has the body of the woman's child. 6. I shall have the heads of the wolves. 7. He and she have the king's houses. 8. Have not (= #Nabbað#) the children the warrior's weapons?

[Footnote 5: See § 20, (2), (b).]

[Footnote 6: See § 27, (2).]

CHAPTER VIII.

THE ô-DECLENSION.

37. The ô-Declension, corresponding to the First or â-Declension of Latin and Greek, contains only feminine nouns. Many feminine i-stems and u-stems soon passed over to this Declension. The ô-Declension may, therefore, be considered the *normal declension* for all strong feminine nouns.

38. Paradigms of #sêo giefu#, *gift*; #sêo wund#, *wound*; #sêo rôd#, *cross*; #sêo leornung#, *learning*; #sêo sâwol#, *soul*:

Sing. N. gief-u wund rôd leornung sâwol *G.* gief-e wund-e rôd-e leornung-a (e) sâwl-e *D.I.* gief-e wund-e rôd-e leornung-a (e) sâwl-e *A.* gief-e wund-e rôd-e leornung-a (e) sâwl-e

Plur. N.A. gief-a wund-a rôd-a leornung-a sâwl-a *G.* gief-a wund-a rôd-a leornung-a sâwl-a *D.I.* gief-um wund-um rôd-um leornung-um sâwl-um

39. Note (1) that monosyllables with short stems (#giefu#) take u in the nominative singular; (2) that monosyllables with long stems (#wund#, #rôd#) present the unchanged stem in the nominative singular; (3) that dissyllables are declined as monosyllables, except that abstract nouns in -ung prefer a to e in the singular.

NOTE.--Syncopation occurs as in masculine and neuter a-stems. See § 27, (4).

40. Present and Preterit Indicative of #bêon# (#wesan#) *to be*:

PRESENT (first form). PRESENT PRETERIT. (second form).

Sing. 1. Ic eom 1. Ic bêom 1. Ic wæs 2. ðû eart 2. ðû bist 2. ðû wæ:re 3. hê is 3. hê bið 3. hê wæs

Plur. 1. wê } 1. wê } 1. wê } 2. gê } sind(on), sint 2. gê } bêoð 2. gê } wæ:ron 3. hîe } 3. hîe } 3. hîe }

NOTE 1.--The forms #bêom#, #bist#, etc. are used chiefly as future tenses in O.E. They survive to-day only in dialects and in poetry. Farmer Dobson, for example, in Tennyson's *Promise of May*, uses *be* for all persons of the present indicative, both singular and plural; and *there be* is frequent in Shakespeare for *there are*. The Northern dialect employed #aron# as well as #sindon# and #sind# for the present plural; hence Mn.E. *are*.

NOTE 2.--Fusion with #ne# gives #neom#, #neart#, #nis# for the present; #næs#, #næ:re#, #næ:ron# for the preterit.

NOTE 3.--The verb *to be* is followed by the nominative case, as in Mn.E.; but when the predicate noun is plural, and the subject a neuter pronoun in the singular, the verb agrees in number with the predicate noun. The neuter singular #ðæt# is frequently employed in this construction: #Ðaet wæ:ron eall Finnas#, *They were all Fins*; #Ðæt sind englas#, *They are angels*; #Ðæ:t wæ:ron engla gâstas#, *They were angels' spirits*.

Notice, too, that O.E. writers do not say *It is I*, *It is thou*, but *I it am*, *Thou it art*: #Ic hit eom#, #ðû hit eart#. See § 21, (1), Note 1.

41. VOCABULARY.

sêo brycg, *bridge*. sêo costnung, *temptation*. sêo cwalu, *death* [quail, quell]. sêo fôr, *journey* [faran]. sêo frôfor, *consolation, comfort*. sêo geoguð, *youth*. sêo glôf, *glove*. sêo hâlignes[1], *holiness*. sêo heall, *hall*. hêr, *here*. hwâ, *who*? hwæ:r, *where*? sêo lufu, *love*. sêo mearc, *boundary* [mark, marches[2]]. sêo mêd, *meed, reward*. sêo mildheortnes, *mild-heartedness, mercy*. sêo stôw, *place* [stow away]. ðæ:r, *there*. sêo ðearf, *need*. sêo wylf, *she wolf*.

[Footnote 1: All words ending in -nes double the -s before adding the case endings.]

[Footnote 2: As in *warden of the marches*.]

42. EXERCISES.

I. 1. Hwæ:r is ðæ:re brycge ende? 2. Hêr sind ðâra rîca mearca.
3. Hwâ hæfð þâ glôfa? 4. Ðæ:r bið ðæ:m cyninge frôfre ðearf. 5. Sêo
wund is on ðæ:re wylfe hêafde. 6. Wê habbað costnunga. 7. Hîe
næ:ron on ðæ:re healle. 8. Ic hit neom. 9. Ðæt wæ:ron Wêalas.
10. Ðæt sind ðæs wîfes bearn.

II. 1. We shall have the women's gloves. 2. Where is the place? 3. He
will be in the hall. 4. Those (#Ðæt#) were not the boundaries of the
kingdom. 5. It was not I. 6. Ye are not the king's scribes. 7. The
shepherd's words are full (#full# + gen.) of wisdom and comfort.
8. Where are the bodies of the children? 9. The gifts are not here.
10. Who has the seals and the birds?

CHAPTER IX.

THE i-DECLENSION AND THE u-DECLENSION.

#The *i*-Declension.# (See § 58.)

43. The i-Declension, corresponding to the group of *i*-stems in the classical Third Declension, contains chiefly (*a*) masculine and (*b*) feminine nouns. The N.A. plural of these nouns ended originally in -e (from older i).

(*a*) #Masculine *i*-Stems.#

44. These stems have almost completely gone over to the a-Declension, so that -as is more common than -e as the N.A. plural ending, whether the stem is long or short. The short stems all have -e in the N.A. singular.

45. Paradigms of #sê wyrm#, *worm*; #sê wine#, *friend*.

Sing. N.A. wyrm win-e *G.* wyrm-es win-es *D.I.* wyrm-e win-e

Plur. N.A. wyrm-as win-as (e) *G.* wyrm-a win-a *D.I.* wyrm-um win-um

#Names of Peoples.#

46. The only i-stems that regularly retain -e of the N.A. plural are certain names of tribes or peoples used only in the plural.

47. Paradigms of #ðâ Engle#, *Angles*; #ðâ Norðymbre#, *Northumbrians*; #ðâ lêode#, *people*:

Plur. N.A. Engle Norðymbre lêode *G.* Engla Norðymbra lêoda *D.I.* Englum Norðymbrum lêodum

(*b*) #Feminine *i*-Stems.#

48. The short stems (#frem-u#) conform entirely to the declension of short ô-stems; long stems (#cwên#, #wyrt#) differ from long ô-stems in

duru) nis hêr.

II. 1. His friends have the bones of the seals and the bodies of the Danes. 2. Art thou the king's son? 3. Has she her[3] gifts in her[3] hands? 4. Here are the fields of the natives. 5. Who had the bird? 6. I had it.[2] 7. The child had the worm in his[3] fingers. 8. The Mercians were here during (the) summer (#on# + dat.).

[Footnote 1: See § 21, (1).]

[Footnote 2: Pronouns agree in gender with the nouns for which they stand. #Hit#, however, sometimes stands for inanimate things of both masculine and feminine genders. See Wülfing (*l.c.*) I, § 238.]

[Footnote 3: See § 76 (last sentence).]

CHAPTER X.

PRESENT INDICATIVE ENDINGS OF STRONG VERBS.

56. The unchanged stem of the present indicative may always be found by dropping -an of the infinitive: #feall-an#, *to fall*; #cêos-an#, *to choose*; #bîd-an#, *to abide*.

57. The personal endings are:

Sing. 1. -e *Plur.* 1. } 2. -est 2. } -að 3. -eð 3. }

#*i*-Umlaut.#

58. The 2d and 3d singular endings were originally not -est and -eð, but -is and -ið; and the i of these older endings has left its traces upon almost every page of Early West Saxon literature. This i, though unaccented and soon displaced, exerted a powerful back influence upon the vowel of the preceding accented syllable. This influence, a form of regressive assimilation, is known as i-umlaut (pronounced *oóm-lowt*). The vowel i or j (= *y*), being itself a palatal, succeeded in palatalizing every guttural vowel that preceded it, and in imposing still more of the i-quality upon diphthongs that were already palatal.[1] The changes produced were these:

a became e (æ): menn (< *mann-iz), *men.* â " æ: æ:nig (< *ân-ig), *any.* u " y wyllen (< *wull-in), *woollen.* û " y: my:s (< *mûs-iz), *mice.* o " e dehter (< *dohtr-i), *to or for the daughter.* ô " ê fêt (< *fôt-iz), *feet.* ea " ie wiexð (< *weax-ið), *he grows* (weaxan = *to grow*). êa " îe hîewð (< *hêaw-ið), *he hews* (hêawan = to *hew*). eo " ie wiercan (< *weorc-jan), *to work.* êo " îe lîehtan (< *lêoht-jan), *to light.*

[Footnote 1: The *palatal* vowels and diphthongs were long or short æ, e, i, (ie), y, ea, eo; the *guttural* vowels were long or short a, o, u.]

#The Unchanged Present Indicative.#

59. In the Northumbrian and Mercian dialects, as well as in the dialect of Late West Saxon, the 2d and 3d singular endings were usually

joined to the present stem without modification either of the stem itself or of the personal endings. The complete absence of umlauted forms in the present indicative of Mn.E. is thus accounted for.

In Early West Saxon, however, such forms as the following are comparatively rare in the 2d and 3d singular:

Sing. 1. Ic feall-e cêos-e bîd-e (*I fall*) (*I choose*) (*I abide*) 2. ðû feall-est cêos-est bîd-est 3. hê feall-eð cêos-eð bîd-eð

Plur. 1. wê } 2. gê } feall-að cêos-að bîd-að 3. hîe }

#The Present Indicative with i-Umlaut and Contraction.#

60. The 2d and 3d persons singular are distinguished from the other forms of the present indicative in Early West Saxon by (1) i-umlaut of the vowel of the stem, (2) syncope of the vowel of the ending, giving -st and -ð for -est and -eð, and (3) contraction of -st and -ð with the final consonant or consonants of the stem.

#Contraction.#

61. The changes produced by i-umlaut have been already discussed. By these changes, therefore, the stems of the 2d and 3d singular indicative of such verbs as (1) #stondan# (= #standan#), *to stand*, (2) #cuman#, *to come*, (3) #grôwan#, *to grow*, (4) #brûcan#, *to enjoy*, (5) #blâwan#, *to blow*, (6) #feallan#, *to fall*, (7) #hêawan#, *to hew*, (8) #weorpan#, *to throw*, and (9) #cêosan#, *to choose*, become respectively (1) #stend-#,[2] (2) #cym-#, (3) #grêw-#, (4) #bry:c-#, (5) #blæ:w-#, (6) #fiell-#, (7) #hîew-#, (8) #wierp-#, and (9) #cîes-#.

If the unchanged stem contains the vowel e, this is changed in the 2d and 3d singular to i (ie): #cweðan# *to say*, stem #cwið-#; #beran# *to bear*, stem #bier-#. But this mutation[3] had taken place long before the period of O.E., and belongs to the Germanic languages in general. It is best, however, to class the change of e to i or ie with the changes due to umlaut, since it occurs consistently in the 2d and 3d singular stems of Early West Saxon, and outlasted almost all of the umlaut forms proper.

If, now, the syncopated endings -st and -ð are added directly to the umlauted stem, there will frequently result such a massing of consonants as almost to defy pronunciation: #cwið-st#, *thou sayest*; #stend-st#, *thou standest*, etc. Some sort of contraction, therefore, is demanded for the sake of euphony. The ear and eye will, by a little practice, become a sure guide in these contractions. The following rules, however, must be observed. They apply only to the 2d and 3d singular of the present indicative:

(1) If the stem ends in a double consonant, one of the consonants is dropped:

1. feall-e (*I fall*) 1. winn-e (*I fight*) 1. swimm-e (*I swim*) 2. fiel-st 2. win-st 2. swim-st 3. fiel-ð 3. win-ð 3. swim-ð

(2) If the stem ends in -ð, this is dropped:

1. cweð-e (*I say*) 1. weorð-e (*I become*) 2. cwi-st 2. wier-st 3. cwi-ð 3. wier-ð

(3) If the stem ends in -d, this is changed to -t. The -ð of the ending is then also changed to -t, and usually absorbed. Thus the stem of the 2d singular serves as stem and ending for the 3d singular:

1. stond-e (= stand-e) (*I stand*) 1. bind-e (*I bind*) 2. stent-st 2. bint-st 3. stent 3. bint

1. bîd-e (*I abide*) 1. rîd-e (*I ride*) 2. bît-st 2. rît-st 3. bît (-t) 3. rît (-t)

(4) If the stem ends already in -t, the endings are added as in (3), -ð being again changed to -t and absorbed:

1. brêot-e (*I break*) 1. feoht-e (*I fight*) 1. bît-e (*I bite*) 2. brîet-st 2. fieht-st 2. bît-st 3. brîet (-t) 3. fieht 3. bît (-t)

(5) If the stem ends in -s, this is dropped before -st (to avoid -sst), but is retained before -ð, the latter being changed to -t. Thus the 2d and 3d singulars are identical:[4]

1. cêos-e (*I choose*) 1. rîs-e (*I rise*) 2. cîe-st 2. rî-st 3. cîes-t 3. rîs-t

[Footnote 2: The more common form for stems with a is æ rather than e: #faran#, *to go*, 2d and 3d singular stem #fær-#; #sacan#, *to contend*, stem #sæc-#. Indeed, a changes to e *via* æ (Cosijn, *Altwestsächsische Grammatik*, I, § 32).]

[Footnote 3: Umlaut is frequently called Mutation. Metaphony is still another name for the same phenomenon. The term Metaphony has the advantage of easy adjectival formation (metaphonic). It was proposed by Professor Victor Henry (*Comparative Grammar of English and German*, Paris, 1894), but has not been naturalized.]

[Footnote 4: This happens also when the infinitive stem ends in #st#:

1. berst-e (*I burst*) 2. bier-st 3. bierst.]

62. EXERCISES.

I. 1. Sê cyning fielð. 2. Ðâ wîf cêosað ðâ giefa. 3. Ðû stentst on ðæ:m hûse. 4. Hê wierpð ðæt wæ:pen. 5. Sê secg hîewð ðâ lîc. 6. Ðæt sæ:d grêwð ond wiexð (*Mark* iv. 27). 7. Ic stonde hêr, ond ðû stentst ðæ:r. 8. "Ic hit eom," cwið hê. 9. Hîe berað ðæs wulfes bân. 10. Hê hîe bint, ond ic hine binde. 11. Ne rîtst ðû?

II. 1. We shall bind him. 2. Who chooses the child's gifts? 3. "He was not here," says she. 4. Wilt thou remain in the hall? 5. The wolves are biting (= bite) the fishermen. 6. He enjoys[5] the love of his children. 7. Do you enjoy (= Enjoyest thou) the consolation and friendship of the scribe? 8. Will he come? 9. I shall throw the spear, and thou wilt bear the weapons. 10. The king's son will become king. 11. The army (#werod#) is breaking the doors and walls of the house.

[Footnote 5: #Brûcan#, *to enjoy*, usually takes the genitive case, not the accusative. It means "to have joy of any thing."]

CHAPTER XI.

THE CONSONANT DECLENSIONS OF NOUNS.

#The Weak or *n*-Declension.#

63. The n-Declension contains almost all of the O.E. nouns belonging to the Consonant Declensions. The stem characteristic n has been preserved in the oblique cases, so that there is no difficulty in distinguishing n-stems from the preceding vowel stems.

The n-Declension includes (*a*) masculines, (*b*) feminines, and (*c*) neuters. The masculines far outnumber the feminines, and the neuters contain only #êage#, *eye* and #êare#, *ear.* The masculines end in -a, the feminines and neuters in -e.

64. Paradigms of (*a*) #sê hunta#, *hunter;* (*b*) #sêo tunge#, *tongue;* (*c*) #ðæt êage#, *eye*:

Sing. N. hunt-a tung-e êag-e *G.D.I.* hunt-an tung-an êag-an *A.* hunt-an tung-an êag-e

Plur. N.A. hunt-an tung-an êag-an *G.* hunt-ena tung-ena êag-ena *D.I.* hunt-um tung-um êag-um

65. VOCABULARY.

sê adesa, *hatchet, adze.* sê æ:metta, *leisure* [empt-iness]. sê bona (bana), *murderer* [bane]. sêo cirice, *church* [Scotch kirk]. sê cnapa (later, #cnafa#), *boy* [knave]. sê cuma, *stranger* [comer]. ðæt êare, *ear.* sêo eorðe, *earth.* sê gefêra, *companion* [co-farer]. sê guma, *man* [bride-groom[1]]. sêo heorte, *heart.* sê môna, *moon.* sêo næ:dre, *adder* [a nadder > an adder[2]]. sê oxa, *ox.* sê scêowyrhta, *shoe-maker* [shoe-wright]. sêo sunne, *sun.* sê têona, *injury* [teen]. biddan (with dat. of person and gen. of thing[3]), *to request, ask for.* cwelan, *to die* [quail]. gescieppan, *to create* [shape, land-scape, friend-ship]. giefan (with dat. of indirect object), *to give.* healdan, *to hold.* helpan (with dat.), *to help.* sceððan[4] (with dat.), *to injure* [scathe]. wiðstondan (-standan) (with dat.), *to withstand.* wrîtan, *to write.*

[Footnote 1: The *r* is intrusive in *-groom*, as it is in *cart-r-idge*, *part-r-idge*, *vag-r-ant*, and *hoa-r-se*.]

[Footnote 2: The *n* has been appropriated by the article. Cf. *an apron* (< *a napron*), *an auger* (< *a nauger*), *an orange* (< *a norange*), *an umpire* (< *a numpire*).]

[Footnote 3: In Mn.E. we say "I request a favor of you"; but in O.E. it was "I request you (dative) of a favor" (genitive). Cf. *Cymbeline*, III, vi, 92: "We'll mannerly demand thee of thy story." See Franz's *Shakespeare-Grammatik*, § 361 (1900).]

[Footnote 4: #Sceððan# is conjugated through the present indicative like #fremman#. See § 129.]

66. EXERCISES.

I. 1. Sê scêowyrhta bry:cð his æ:mettan. 2. Ðâ guman biddað ðæ:m cnapan ðæs adesan. 3. Hwâ is sê cuma? 4. Hielpst ðû ðæ:m bonan? 5. Ic him ne helpe. 6. Ðâ bearn sceððað ðæs bonan êagum ond êarum. 7. Sê cuma cwielð on ðæ:re cirican. 8. Sê hunta wiðstent ðæ:m wulfum. 9. Ðâ oxan berað ðæs cnapan gefêran. 10. Sê môna ond ðâ tunglu sind on ðæ:m heofonum. 11. Ðâ huntan healdað ðæ:re næ:dran tungan. 12. Hê hiere giefð ðâ giefa. 13. Ðâ werod sceððað ðæs cyninges feldum.

II. 1. Who will bind the mouths of the oxen? 2. Who gives him the gifts? 3. Thou art helping him, and I am injuring him. 4. The boy's companion is dying. 5. His nephew does not enjoy his leisure. 6. The adder's tongue injures the king's companion. 7. The sun is the day's eye. 8. She asks the strangers for the spears. 9. The men's bodies are not here. 10. Is he not (#Nis hê#) the child's murderer? 11. Who creates the bodies and the souls of men? 12. Thou withstandest her. 13. He is not writing.

CHAPTER XII.

#Remnants of Other Consonant Declensions.#

67. The nouns belonging here are chiefly masculines and feminines. Their stem ended in a consonant other than n. The most important of them may be divided as follows: (1) The *foot* Declension, (2) r-Stems, and (3) nd-Stems. These declensions are all characterized by the prevalence, wherever possible, of i-umlaut in certain cases, the case ending being then dropped.

68. (1) The nouns belonging to the *foot* Declension exhibit umlaut most consistently in the N.A. plural.

Sing. N.A. sê fôt sê mon sê tôð sêo cû *Sing. N.A.* (*foot*) (*man*) (*tooth*) (*cow*) *Plur. N.A.* fêt men têð cy:

NOTE.--The dative singular usually has the same form as the N.A. plural. Here belong also #sêo bôc# (*book*), #sêo burg# (*borough*), #sêo gôs# (*goose*), #sêo lûs# (*louse*), and #sêo mûs# (*mouse*), all with umlauted plurals. Mn.E. preserves only six of the *foot* Declension plurals: *feet, men, teeth, geese, lice,* and *mice.* The *c* in the last two is an artificial spelling, intended to preserve the sound of voiceless *s.* Mn.E. *kine* (= *cy-en*) is a double plural formed after the analogy of weak stems; Burns in *The Twa Dogs* uses *kye.*

No umlaut is possible in #sêo niht# (*night*) and #sê mônað# (*month*), plural #niht# and #mônað# (preserved in Mn.E. *twelvemonth* and *fortnight*).

(2) The r-Stems contain nouns expressing kinship, and exhibit umlaut of the dative singular.

Sing. N.A. sê fæder sê brôðor sêo môdor (*father*) (*brother*) (*mother*) *D.* fæder brêðer mêder

Sing. N.A. sêo dohtor (*daughter*) sêo swuster (*sister*) *D.* dehter swyster

NOTE.--The N.A. plural is usually the same as the N.A. singular. These umlaut datives are all due to the presence of a former i. Cf. Lat. dative singular *patri, frâtri, mâtri, sorori* (< **sosori*), and Greek +thugatri+.

(3) The nd-Stems show umlaut both in the N.A. plural and in the dative singular:

Sing. N.A. sê frêond (*friend*) sê fêond (*enemy*) *D.* frîend fîend

Plur. N.A. frîend fîend

NOTE.--Mn.E. *friend* and *fiend* are interesting analogical spellings. When s had been added by analogy to the O.E. plurals #frîend# and #fîend#, thus giving the double plurals *friends* and *fiends*, a second singular was formed by dropping the s. Thus *friend* and *fiend* displaced the old singulars *frend* and *fend*, both of which occur in the M.E. *Ormulum*, written about the year 1200.

#Summary of O.E. Declensions.#

69. A brief, working summary of the O.E. system of declensions may now be made on the basis of gender.

All O.E. nouns are (1) masculine, (2) feminine, or (3) neuter.

(1) The masculines follow the declension of #mûð# (§ 26), except those ending in -a, which are declined like #hunta# (§ 64):

Sing. N.A. mûð *N.* hunta *G.* mûðes *G.D.A.* huntan *D.I.* mûðe *I.* huntan

Plur. N.A. mûðas huntan *G.* mûða huntena *D.I.* mûðum huntum

(2) The short-stemmed neuters follow the declension of #hof# (§ 32); the long-stemmed, that of #bearn# (§ 32):

Sing. N.A. hof bearn *G.* hofes bearnes *D.I.* hofe bearne

Plur. N.A. hofu bearn *G.* hofa bearna *D.I.* hofum bearnum

(3) The feminines follow the declensions of #giefu# and #wund# (§ 38) (the only difference being in the N. singular), except those ending in -e, which follow the declension of #tunge# (§ 64):

Sing. N. giefu wund tunge *G.* giefe wunde tungan *D.I.* giefe wunde tungan *A.* giefe wunde tungan

Plur. N.A. giefa wunda tungan *G.* giefa wunda tungena *D.I.* giefum wundum tungum

70. VOCABULARY.

ac, *but.* bûtan (with dat.), *except, but, without.* sê Crîst, *Christ.* sê eorl, *earl, alderman, warrior.* ðæt Englalond, *England* [Angles' land]. faran, *to go* [fare]. findan, *to find.* sê God, *God.* hâtan, *to call, name.* sê hlâford, *lord* [#hlâf-weard#]. mid (with dat.), *with.* on (with acc.), *on, against, into.* tô (with dat.), *to.* uton (with infin.), *let us.*

NOTE.--O.E. #mon# (#man#) is frequently used in an indefinite sense for *one, people, they.* It thus takes the place of a passive construction proper: #And man nam þâ gebrotu þe þâr belifon, twelf cy:pan fulle#, *And there were taken up of fragments that remained there twelve baskets full*; but more literally, *And one* (or *they) took the fragments,* etc.; #Ond Hæstenes wîf ond hîs suna twêgen mon brôhte tô ðæ:m cyninge#, *And Hæsten's wife and his two sons were brought to the king.*

71. EXERCISES.

I. 1. Môn hine hæ:t Ælfred. 2. Uton faran on ðæt scip. 3 God is cyninga cyning ond hlâforda hlâford. 4. Sê eorl ne giefð giefa his fîend. 5. Ic næs mid his frîend. 6. Sêo môdor færð mid hiere dehter on ðâ burg. 7. Fintst ðû ðæs bôceres bêc? 8. Hê bint ealle (all) ðâ dêor bûtan ðæ:m wulfum. 9. Ðû eart Crîst, Godes sunu. 10. "Uton bindan ðæs bonan fêt," cwið hê.

II. 1. Christ is the son of God. 2. Let us call him Cædmon. 3. He throws his spear against the door. 4. Thou art not the earl's brother. 5. He will go with his father to England, but I shall remain (abide) here. 6. Gifts are not given to murderers. 7. Who will find the tracks of the animals? 8. They ask their lord for his weapons (§ 65, Note 3).

CHAPTER XIII.

PRONOUNS.

(1) #Personal Pronouns.#

72. Paradigms of #ic#, *I*; #ðû#, *thou.* For #hê#, #hêo#, #hit#, see § 53.

Sing. N. ic ðû *G.* mîn ðîn *D.* mê ðê *A.* mê (mec) ðê (ðec)

Dual N. wit (*we two*) git (*ye two*) *G.* uncer (*of us two*) incer (*of you two*) *D.* unc (*to* or *for us two*) inc (*to* or *for you two*) *A.* unc (*us two*) inc (*you two*)

Plur. N. wê gê *G.* ûser (ûre) êower *D.* ûs êow *A.* ûs (ûsic) êow (êowic)

NOTE 1.--The dual number was soon absorbed by the plural. No relic of it now remains. But when two and only two are referred to, the dual is consistently used in O.E. An example occurs in the case of the two blind men (*Matthew* ix. 27-31): #Gemiltsa unc, Davîdes sunu!# *Pity us, (thou) Son of David!* #Sîe inc æfter incrum gelêafan#, *Be it unto you according to your faith.*

NOTE 2.--Mn.E. *ye* (< gê), the nominative proper, is fast being displaced by *you* (< #êow#), the old objective. The distinction is preserved in the King James's version of the Bible: *Ye in me, and I in you* (*John* xiv. 20); but not in Shakespeare and later writers.

(2) #Demonstrative Pronouns.#

73. Paradigm of #ðés#, #ðêos#, #ðis#, *this.* For the Definite Article as a demonstrative, meaning *that*, see § 28, Note 3.

Masculine. Feminine. Neuter. Sing. N. ðês ðêos ðis *G.* ðisses ðisse ðisses *D.* ðissum ðisse ðissum *A.* ðisne ðâs ðis *I.* ðy:s ---- ðy:s

All Genders. Plur. N.A. ðâs *G.* ðissa *D.* ðissum

(3) #The Interrogative Pronoun.#

74. Paradigm of #hwâ#, #hwæt#, *who, what?*

Masculine. Neuter. Sing. N. hwâ hwæt *G.* hwæs hwæs *D.* hwæ:m hwæ:m *A.* hwone hwæt *I.* ---- hwy:

NOTE 1.--The derivative interrogatives, #hwæðer# (< #*hwâ-ðer#), *which of two?* and #hwilc# (< #*hwâ-lîc#), *which?* are declined as strong adjectives (§§ 79-82).

NOTE 2.--The instrumental case of #hwâ# survives in Mn.E. *why = on what account*; the instrumental of the definite article is seen in the adverbial *the: The sooner, the better = by how much sooner, by so much better.*

NOTE 3.--How were the Mn.E. relative pronouns, *who* and *which*, evolved from the O.E. interrogatives? The change began in early West Saxon with #hwæt# used in indirect questions (Wülfing, *l.c.* § 310, [beta]): #Nû ic wât eall hwæt ðû woldest#, *Now I know all that thou desiredst.* The direct question was, #Hwæt woldest ðû?# But the presence of #eall# shows that in Alfred's mind #hwæt# was, in the indirect form, more relative than interrogative.

(4) #Relative Pronouns.#

75. O.E. had no relative pronoun proper. It used instead (1) the Indeclinable Particle #ðe#, *who, whom, which, that*, (2) the Definite Article (§ 28), (3) the Definite Article with the Indeclinable Particle, (4) the Indeclinable Particle with a Personal Pronoun.

The Definite Article agrees in gender and number with the antecedent. The case depends upon the construction. *The bird which I have* may, therefore, be:--

(1) #Sê fugol ðe ic hæbbe#; (2) #Sê fugol ðone ic hæbbe#; (3) #Sê fugol ðone ðe# (= *the which*) #ic hæbbe#; (4) #Sê fugol ðe hine ic hæbbe#.

NOTE.--O.E. #ðe# agrees closely in construction with Mn.E. relative *that*: (1) Both are indeclinable. (2) Both refer to animate or inanimate objects. (3) Both may be used with phrasal value: #ðy: ylcan dæge ðe hî hine tô ðæ:m âde beran wyllað#, *On the same day that* (= *on which*) *they intend to bear him to the funeral pile.* (4) Neither can be preceded by a preposition.

(5) #Possessive Pronouns.#

76. The Possessive Pronouns are #mîn#, *mine*; #ðîn#, *thine*; #ûre#, *our*; #êower#, *your*; [#sîn#, *his, her, its*]; #uncer#, *belonging to us two*; #incer#, *belonging to you two.* They are declined as strong adjectives. The genitives of the Third Personal Pronoun, #his#, *his*, #hiere#, *her*, #hiera#, *their*, are indeclinable.

(6) #Indefinite Pronouns.#

77. These are #æ:lc#, *each, every*; #ân#, *a, an, one*; #æ:nig# (< #ân-ig#), *any*; #næ:nig# (< #ne-æ:nig#), *none*; #ôðer#, *other*; #sum#, *one, a certain one*; #swilc#, *such.* They are declined as strong adjectives.

NOTE.--O.E. had three established methods of converting an interrogative pronoun into an indefinite: (1) By prefixing #ge#, (2) by prefixing #æ:g#, (3) by interposing the interrogative between #swâ ... swâ#: (1) #gehwâ#, *each*; #gehwæðer#, *either*; #gehwilc#, *each*; (2) #æ:ghwâ#, *each*; #æ:ghwæðer#, *each*; #æ:ghwilc#, *each*; (3) #swâ hwâ swâ#, *whosoever*; #swâ hwæðer swâ#, *whichsoever of two*; #swâ hwilc swâ#, *whosoever.*

CHAPTER XIV.

ADJECTIVES, STRONG AND WEAK.

78. The declension of adjectives conforms in general to the declension of nouns, though a few pronominal inflections have influenced certain cases. Adjectives belong either to (1) the Strong Declension or to (2) the Weak Declension. The Weak Declension is employed when the adjective is preceded by #sê# or #ðês#, *the*, *that*, or *this*; otherwise, the Strong Declension is employed: #ðâ gôdan cyningas#, *the good kings*; #ðês gôda cyning#, *this good king*; but #gôde cyningas#, *good kings*.

NOTE.--The Weak Declension is also frequently used when the adjective is employed in direct address, or preceded by a possessive pronoun: #Dryhten, ælmihtiga God ... ic bidde ðê for ðînre miclan mildheortnesse#, *Lord, almighty God, I pray thee, for thy great mercy*.

(1) #Strong Declension of Adjectives.#

(a) *Monosyllables.*

79. The strong adjectives are chiefly monosyllabic with long stems: #gôd#, *good*; #eald#, *old*; #long#, *long*; #swift#, *swift*. They are declined as follows.

80. Paradigm of #gôd#, *good*:

Masculine. Feminine. Neuter.

Sing. N. gôd gôd gôd *G.* gôdes gôdre gôdes *D.* gôdum gôdre gôdum *A.* gôdne gôde gôd *I.* gôde ---- gôde

Plur. N.A. gôde gôda gôd *G.* gôdra gôdra gôdra *D.I.* gôdum gôdum gôdum

81. If the stem is short, -u is retained as in #giefu# (§ 39, (1)) and #hofu# (§ 33, (1)). Thus #glæd# (§ 27, Note 1), *glad*, and #til#, *useful*, are inflected:

Masculine. Feminine. Neuter. Sing. N. { glæd gladu glæd { til tilu til

Plur. N.A. { glade glada gladu { tile tila tilu

(b) *Polysyllables.*

82. Polysyllables follow the declension of short monosyllables. The most common terminations are #-en#, *-en*; #-fæst#, *-fast*; #-full#, *-ful*; #-lêas#, *-less*; #-lîc#, *-ly*; #-ig#, *-y*: #hæ:ð-en# (#hæ:ð# = *heath*), *heathen*; #stede-fæst# (#stede# = *place*), *steadfast*; #sorg-full# (#sorg# = *sorrow*), *sorrowful*; #cyst-lêas# (#cyst# = *worth*), *worthless*; #eorð-lîc# (#eorðe# = *earth*), *earthly*; #blôd-ig# (#blôd# = *blood*), *bloody*. The present and past participles, when inflected and not as weak adjectives, may be classed with the polysyllabic adjectives, their inflection being the same.

Syncopation occurs as in a-stems (§ 27, (4)). Thus #hâlig#, *holy*, #blîðe#, *blithe*, #berende#, *bearing*, #geboren#, *born*, are thus inflected:

Masculine. Feminine. Neuter. Sing. N. { hâlig hâlgu hâlig { blîðe blîðu blîðe { berende berendu berende { geboren geborenu geboren

Plur. N.A. { hâlge hâlga hâlgu { blîðe blîða blîðu { berende berenda berendu { geborene geborena geborenu

(2) #Weak Declension of Adjectives.#

83. The Weak Declension of adjectives, whether monosyllabic or polysyllabic, does not differ from the Weak Declension of nouns, except that -ena of the genitive plural is usually replaced by -ra of the strong adjectives.

Masculine. Feminine. Neuter. 84. *Sing. N.* gôda gôde gôde *G.* gôdan gôdan gôdan *D.I.* gôdan gôdan gôdan *A.* gôdan gôdan gôde

All Genders. Plur. N.A. gôdan *G.* gôdra (gôdena) *D.I.* gôdum

85. RULE OF SYNTAX.

Adjectives agree with their nouns in gender, number, and case; but participles, when used predicatively, may remain uninflected (§ 139, § 140).

86. VOCABULARY.

dêad, *dead.* eall, *all.* hâl,[1] *whole, hale.* heard, *hard.* ðæt hors, *horse.* lêof, *dear* [as lief]. ly:tel, *little.* micel, *great, large.* monig, *many.* niman, *to take* [nimble, numb]. nîwe, *new.* rîce, *rich, powerful.* sôð, *true* [sooth-sayer]. stælwierðe,[2] *serviceable* [stalwart]. swîðe, *very.* sê tûn, *town, village.* sê ðegn, *servant, thane, warrior.* ðæt ðing, *thing.* sê weg, *way.* wîs, *wise.* wið (with acc.), *against,* in a hostile sense [with-stand]. sê ilca, *the same* [of that ilk].

[Footnote 1: #Hâlig#, *holy*, contains, of course, the same root. "I find," says Carlyle, "that you could not get any better definition of what 'holy' really is than 'healthy--completely healthy.'"]

[Footnote 2: This word has been much discussed. The older etymologists explained it as meaning *worth stealing.* A more improbable conjecture is that it means *worth a stall* or *place.* It is used of ships in the *Anglo-Saxon Chronicle.* As applied to men, Skeat thinks it meant *good* or *worthy at stealing*; but the etymology is still unsettled.]

87. EXERCISES.

I. 1. Ðâs scipu ne sind swîðe swift, ac hîe sind swîðe stælwierðu. 2. Sêo gôde cwên giefð æ:lcum ðegne moniga giefa. 3. Ðês wîsa cyning hæfð monige micele tûnas on his rîce. 4. Næ:nig mon is wîs on eallum ðingum. 5. Ðy: ilcan dæge (§ 98, (2)) mon fond (found) ðone ðegn ðe mînes wines bêc hæfde. 6. Ealle ðâ secgas ðâ ðe swift hors habbað rîdað wið ðone bonan. 7. Ðîne fîend sind mîne frîend. 8. Sê micela stân ðone ðe ic on mînum hondum hæbbe is swîðe heard. 9. Hîe sceððað ðæ:m ealdum horsum. 10. Uton niman ðâs tilan giefa ond hîe beran tô ûrum lêofum bearnum.

II. 1. These holy men are wise and good. 2. Are the little children very dear to the servants (dat. without #tô#)? 3. Gifts are not given (§ 70, Note 1) to rich men. 4. All the horses that are in the king's fields are swift. 5. These stones are very large and hard. 6. He takes the dead man's spear and fights against the large army. 7. This new house has many doors. 8. My ways are not your ways. 9. Whosoever chooses me, him I also (#êac#) choose. 10. Every man has many friends that are not wise.

CHAPTER XV.

NUMERALS.

88. Numerals are either (*a*) Cardinal, expressing pure number, *one*, *two*, *three*; or (*b*) Ordinal, expressing rank or succession, *first*, *second*, *third*.

(*a*) #Cardinals.#

89. The Cardinals fall into the three following syntactic groups:

GROUP I.

1. ân 2. twêgen [twain] 3. ðrîe

These numerals are inflected adjectives. #Ân#, *one*, *an*, *a*, being a long stemmed monosyllable, is declined like #gôd# (§ 80). The weak form, #âna#, means *alone*.

#Twêgen# and #ðrîe#, which have no singular, are thus declined:

Masc. Fem. Neut. Masc. Fem. Neut. Plur. N.A. twêgen twâ twâ (tû) ðrîe ðrêo ðrêo *G.* twêgra twêgra twêgra ðrêora ðrêora ðrêora *D.* { twæ:m twæ:m twæ:m ðrîm ðrîm ðrîm { (twâm) (twâm) (twâm)

90. GROUP II.

4. fêower 5. fîf 6. siex 7. seofon 8. eahta 9. nigon 10. tîen 11. endlefan 12. twelf 13. ðrêotîene 14. fêowertîene 15. fîftîene 16. siextîene 17. seofontîene 18. eahtatîene 19. nigontîene

These words are used chiefly as uninflected adjectives: #on gewitscipe ðrêora oþþe fêower bisceopa#, *on testimony of three or four bishops*; #on siex dagum#, *in six days*; #ân næ:dre ðe hæfde nigon hêafdu#, *a serpent which had nine heads*; #æðeling eahtatîene wintra#, *a prince of eighteen winters*.

91. GROUP III.

20. twêntig 21. ân ond twêntig 30. ðrîtig 40. fêowertig 50. fîftig 60. siextig 70. hundseofontig 80. hundeahtatig 90. hundnigontig 100. hund 200. twâ hund 1000. ðûsend 2000. twâ ðûsend

All these numbers are employed as neuter singular nouns, and are followed by the genitive plural: #Næfde hê þeah mâ ðonne twêntig hry:ðera, and twêntig scêapa, and twêntig swy:na#, *He did not have, however, more than twenty (of) cattle, and twenty (of) sheep, and twenty (of) swine*; #Hîe hæfdon hundeahtatig scipa#, *They had eighty ships*; #twâ hund mîla brâd#, *two hundred miles broad*; #ðæ:r wæ:ron seofon hund gûðfanena genumen#, *there were seven hundred standards captured*; #ân ðûsend monna#, *a thousand men*; #Hannibales folces wæs twâ ðûsend ofslagen#, *Of Hannibal's men there were two thousand slain*; #Hîe âcuron endlefan ðûsend monna#, *They chose eleven thousand men.*

NOTE 1.--Group III is rarely inflected. Almost the only inflectional endings that are added are (1) -es, a genitive singular termination for the numerals in #-tig#, and (2) -e, a dative singular for #hund#. (1) The first is confined to adjectives expressing extent of space or time, as, #eald#, *old*; #brâd#, *broad*; #hêah#, *high*; and #long#, *long*: #ðæt is ðrîtiges mîla long#, *that is thirty miles long*; #Hê wæs ðrîtiges gêara eald#, *He was thirty years old.* (2) The second is employed after #mid#: #mid twæ:m hunde scipa#, *with two hundred ships*; #mid ðrîm hunde monna#, *with three hundred men*; #Ðæ:r wearð ... Regulus gefangen mid V hunde monna#, *There was Regulus captured with five hundred men.*

The statement made in nearly all the grammars that #hunde# occurs as a nominative and accusative plural is without foundation.

NOTE 2.--Many numerals, otherwise indeclinable, are used in the genitive plural with the indefinite pronoun #sum#, which then means *one of* a certain number. In this peculiar construction, the numeral always precedes #sum#: #fêowera sum#, *one of four* (= *with three others*); #Hê sæ:de þæt hê syxa sum ofslôge syxtig#, *He said that he, with five others, slew sixty* (*whales*); #Hê wæs fêowertigra sum#, *He was one of forty.*

NOTE 3.--These are the most common constructions with the Cardinals. The forms in #-tig# have only recently been investigated. A study of Wülfing's citations shows that Alfred occasionally uses the forms in #-tig# (1) as adjectives with plural inflections: #mid XXXgum cyningum#, *with thirty kings*; and (2) as nouns with plural inflections: #æfter siextigum daga#, *after sixty days*. But both constructions are rare.

(b) #Ordinals.#

92. The Ordinals, except the first two, are formed from the Cardinals. They are:

1. forma, æ:resta, fyrsta 2. ôðer, æfterra 3. ðridda 4. fêorða 5. fîfta 6. siexta 7. seofoða 8. eahtoða 9. nigoða 10. têoða 11. endlefta 12. twelfta 13. ðrêotêoða 14. fêowertêoða 15. fîftêoða etc. 20. twêntigoða 21. ân ond twêntigoða 30. ðrîtigoða etc.

NOTE.--There are no Ordinals corresponding to #hund# and #ðûsend#.

With the exception of #ôðer# (§ 77), all the Ordinals are declined as Weak Adjectives; the article, however, as in Mn.E., is frequently omitted: #Brûtus wæs sê forma consul#, *Brutus was the first consul*; #Hêr endað sêo æ:reste bôc, ond onginneð sêo ôðer#, *Here the first book ends, and the second begins*; #ðy: fîftan dæge#, *on the fifth day*; #on ðæ:m têoðan gêare hiera gewinnes#, *in the tenth year of their strife*; #Hêo wæs twelfte#, *She was twelfth*; #Sê wæs fêorða from Agusto#, *He was fourth from Augustus*.

CHAPTER XVI.

ADVERBS, PREPOSITIONS, AND CONJUNCTIONS.

#Adverbs.#

93. (1) Adverbs are formed by adding -e or #-lîce# to the corresponding adjectives: #sôð#, *true*; #sôðe# or #sôðlîce#, *truly*; #earmlîc#, *wretched*; #earmlîce#, *wretchedly*; #wîd#, *wide*; #wîde#, *widely*; #micel#, *great*; #micle# (#micele#), *greatly, much*.

(2) The terminations -e and #-lîce# are replaced in some adverbs by #-(l)unga# or #-(l)inga#: #eallunga#, *entirely*; #fæ:ringa#, *suddenly*; #grundlunga#, *from the ground, completely*.

NOTE 1.--In Mn.E. *headlong, darkling*, and *groveling*, originally adverbs, we have survivals of these endings.

(3) The genitive case is frequently used adverbially: #sûðeweardes#, *southwards*; #ealles#, *altogether, entirely*; #dæges#, *by day*; #nihtes#, *by night*; #ðæs#, *from that time, afterwards*. Cf. #hys# (= #his#) #weges# in #Ðonne rîdeð æ:lc hys weges#, *Then rides each his way*.

NOTE 2.--The adverbial genitive is abundantly preserved in Mn.E. *Always, crossways, sideways, needs* (= *necessarily*), *sometimes*, etc., are not plurals, but old genitive singulars. The same construction is seen in *of course, of a truth, of an evening, of old, of late*, and similar phrases.

(4) Dative and instrumental plurals may be used as adverbs: #hwîlum#, *at times, sometimes* [whilom]; #stundum# (#stund# = *period*), *from time to time*; #miclum#, *greatly*. Especially common is the suffix #-mæ:lum# (#mæ:l# = *time, #measure#* [meal]), preserved adverbially in Mn.E. *piecemeal*: #dropmæ:lum#, *drop by drop*; #styccemæ:lum# (#stycce# = *piece*), *piecemeal, here and there*.

(5) The suffix -an usually denotes motion from:

hêr, *here.* hider, *hither.* heonan, *hence.* ðæ:r, *there.* ðider, *thither.*
ðonan, *thence.* hwæ:r, *where?* hwider, *whither?* hwonan, *whence?*
norðan, *from the north.* êastan, *from the east.* hindan, *from behind.*
feorran, *from far.* ûtan, *from without.*

(6) The adverb #rihte# (#riht# = *right, straight*) denotes *motion toward*
in #norðrihte#, *northward, due north*; #êastrihte#, *due east*; #sûðrihte#,
due south; #westrihte#, *due west.*

#Prepositions.#

94. The nominative is the only case in O.E. that is never governed by a
preposition. Of the other cases, the dative and accusative occur most
frequently with prepositions.

(1) The prepositions that are most frequently found with the dative are:

æfter, *after.* æ:t, *at.* be (bî), *by, near, about.* betwêonan (betuh),
between. bûtan (bûton), *except.* for, *for.* from (fram), *from, by.* mid,
with. of, *of, from.* tô, *to.* tôforan, *before.* tôweard, *toward.*

(2) The following prepositions require the accusative:

geond, *throughout* [be-yond]. ofer, *over, upon.* oð, *until, up to.* ðurh,
through. ymbe, *about, around* [um-while, ember-days].

(3) The preposition #on# (rarely #in#), meaning *into*, is usually followed
by the accusative; but meaning *in, on*, or *during*, it takes the dative or
instrumental. The preposition #wið#, meaning *toward*, may be followed
by the genitive, dative, or accusative; but meaning *against*, and
implying *motion* or *hostility*, the accusative is more common.

(4) The following phrases are used prepositionally with the dative:

be norðan, *north of.* be êastan, *east of.* be sûðan, *south of.* be westan,
west of. tô êacan, *in addition to.* on emnlange (efn-lang = *evenly long*),
along. tô emnes, *along.*

(5) Prepositions regularly precede the noun or pronoun that they introduce; but by their adverbial nature they are sometimes drawn in front of the verb: #And him wæs mycel menegu tô gegaderod#, *And there was gathered unto him a great multitude*. In relative clauses introduced by #ðe#, the preceding position is very common: #sêo scîr ... ðe hê on bûde#, *the district, ... which he dwelt in* (= *which he in-habited*); #Hê wæs swy:ðe spêdig man on ðæ:m æ:htum ðe hiera spêda on bêoð#, *He was a very rich man in those possessions which their riches consist in*; #ny:hst ðæ:m tûne ðe sê dêada man on lîð#, *nearest the town that the dead man lies in*.

#Conjunctions.#

95. (1) The most frequently occurring conjunctions are:

#ac, *but.* æ:r, *before, ere.* bûtan (bûton), *except that, unless.* êac, *also* [eke]. for ðæ:m, } for ðæ:m ðe, } *because.* for ðon, } for ðon ðe, } for ðy:, *therefore.* gif, *if.* hwæðer, *whether.* ond (and), *and.* oððe, *or.* ðæt, *that, so that.* ðêah, *though, however.*

(2) The correlative conjunctions are:

æ:gðer ge ... ge, *both ...... and.* æ:gðer ...... ôðer } *either .... or.* oððe .... oððe } nê .... nê, *neither ... nor.* sam .... sam, *whether ... or.* swâ .... swâ { *the .... the.* { *as .... as.* ðâ ....,, ðâ } *when ...... then.* ðonne ...... ðonne }

CHAPTER XVII.

COMPARISON OF ADJECTIVES AND ADVERBS.

#Adjectives#.

96. (1) Adjectives are regularly compared by adding -ra for the comparative, and -ost (rarely -est) for the superlative:

Positive. Comparative. Superlative. earm, *poor* earmra earmost rîce, *rich* rîcra rîcost smæl, *narrow* smælra smalost brâd, *broad* brâdra (bræ:dra) brâdost swift, *swift* swiftra swiftost

(2) Forms with i-umlaut usually have superlative in -est:

Positive. Comparative. Superlative. eald, *old* ieldra ieldest long, *long* lengra lengest strong, *strong* strengra strengest geong, *young* giengra giengest hêah, *high* hîerra hîehst

(3) The following adjectives are compared irregularly:

Positive. Comparative. Superlative. gôd, *good* betra betst ly:tel, *little, small* læ:ssa læ:st micel, *great, much* mâra mæ:st yfel, *bad* wiersa wierst

(4) The positive is sometimes supplied by an adverb:

Positive. Comparative. Superlative. feor, *far* fierra fierrest nêah, *near* nêarra nîehst æ:r, *before* æ:rra, *former* æ:rest, *first*

(5) The comparatives all follow the Weak Declension. The superlatives, when preceded by the definite article, are weak; but when used predicatively they are frequently strong: #sê læ:sta dæ:l#, *the least part*; #Ðonne cymeð sê man sê ðæt swiftoste hors hafað tô ðæ:m æ:restan dæ:le and tô ðæ:m mæ:stan#, *Then comes the man that has the swiftest horse to the first part and to the largest.* But, #ðæt by:ne land is êasteweard brâdost# (not #brâdoste#), *the cultivated land is broadest eastward*; #and# (#hit#) #bið ealra wyrta mæ:st#, *and it is largest of all herbs*; #Ac hyra# (= #hiera#) #âr is mæ:st on ðæ:m gafole

ðe ðâ Finnas him gyldað#, *But their income is greatest in the tribute that the Fins pay them.*

(6) The comparative is usually followed by #ðonne# and the nominative case: #Sê hwæl bið micle læ:ssa ðonne ôðre hwalas#, *That whale is much smaller than other whales*; #Ðâ wunda ðæs môdes bêoð dîgelran ðonne ðâ wunda ðæs lîchaman#. *The wounds of the mind are more secret than the wounds of the body.*

But when #ðonne# is omitted, the comparative is followed by the dative: #Ûre Âlîesend, ðe mâra is ond mæ:rra eallum gesceaftum#, *Our Redeemer, who is greater and more glorious than all created things*; #nê ongeat hê nô hiene selfne betran ôðrum gôdum monnum#, *nor did he consider himself better than other good men.*

#Adverbs.#

97. (1) Adverbs are regularly compared by adding -or for the comparative and -ost (rarely -est) for the superlative:

Positive. Comparative. Superlative. georne, *willingly* geornor geornost swîðe, *very, swîðor, more swîðost,* most, chiefly *severely* æ:r, *before* æ:ror, *formerly* æ:rest, *first* norð, *northwards* norðor norðmest[1]

(2) The comparatives of a few adverbs may be found by dropping -ra of the corresponding adjective form:

Positive. Comparative. Superlative. longe, *long* leng lengest micle, *much* mâ mæ:st wel, *well* bet betst

[Footnote 1: This is really a double superlative, m being itself an old superlative suffix. Cf. Latin *opti-m-us.* In Mn.E. *northmost* and *hindmost,* *-m-est* has been confused with *-most,* with which etymologically it has nothing to do.]

#Expressions of Time.#

98. (1) Duration of time and extent of space are usually expressed by the accusative case: #Ealle ðâ hwîle ðe ðæt lîc bið inne#, *All the time*

that the body is within; #twêgen dagas#, *for two days*; #ealne weg#, *all the way, always.*

(2) Time when is more often expressed by the instrumental case when no preposition is used: #ðy: ilcan dæge#, *the same day*; #æ:lce gêare#, *each year*; #ðy: gêare#, *that year*; #æ:lce dæge#, *each day*.

(3) Time or space within which is expressed by #on# and the dative: #on sumera#, *in summer*; #on wintra#, *in winter*; #on fîf dagum#, *in five days*; #on fîf mîlum#, *in five miles*; #on ðissum gêare#, *in this year*; #on ðæ:m tîman#, *in those times.* Sometimes by the genitive without a preceding preposition: #ðæ:s gêares#, *in that year.*

99. VOCABULARY.

ðæt gefylce [folc], *troop, division.* ðæt lond (land), *land.* sêo mîl, *mile.* ôðer ... ôðer, *the one ... the other; the former ... the latter.* sê sige, *victory.* sige[2] habban, *to win (the) victory.* sprecan, *to speak.* ðæt swîn (swy:n), *swine, hog.* wêste, *waste.*

[Footnote 2: #Sige# usually, but not invariably, precedes #habban#.]

100. EXERCISES.

I. 1. Hê hæfð ðrêo swîðe swift hors. 2. Ic hæbbe nigontîene scêap ond mâ ðonne twêntig swîna. 3. Sêo gôde cwên cîest twâ hund monna. 4. Uton feohtan wið ðâ Dene mid ðrîm hunde scipa. 5. Ond hîe wæ:ron on twæ:m gefylcum: on ôðrum wæs[3] Bâchsecg ond Halfdene ðâ hæ:ðnan cyningas, ond on ôðrum wæ:ron ðâ eorlas. 6. Ðû spricst sôðlîce. 7. Ðonne rît æ:lc mon his weges. 8. Æfter monigum dagum, hæfde Ælfred cyning[4] sige. 9. Ðis lond is wêste styccemæ:lum. 10. Ðês feld is fîftiges mîla brâd. 11. Ælfred cyning hæfde monige frîend, for ðæ:m ðe hê wæs æ:gðer ge wîs ge gôd. 12. Ðâ hwalas, ðe ðû ymbe spricst, sind micle læ:ssan ôðrum hwalum. 13. Hêo is ieldre ðonne hiere swuster, ac mîn brôðor is ieldra ðonne hêo. 14. Wê cumað tô ðæ:m tûne æ:lce gêare. 15. Ðâ men ðe ðâ swiftostan hors hæ:fdon wæ:ron mid ðæ:m Denum fêower dagas.

II. 1. Our army (#werod#) was in two divisions: one was large, the other was small. 2. The richest men in the kingdom have more (#mâ#) than thirty ships. 3. He was much wiser than his brother. 4. He fights against the Northumbrians with two ships. 5. After three years King Alfred gained the victory. 6. Whosoever chooses these gifts, chooses well. 7. This man's son is both wiser and better than his father. 8. When the king rides, then ride his thanes also. 9. The richest men are not always (â) the wisest men.

[Footnote 3: See p. 100, note on #gefeaht#.] [[Linenote 100.8]]

[Footnote 4: The proper noun comes first in appositive expressions: #Ælfred cyning#, #Sidroc eorl#, #Hêahmund bisceop#.]

CHAPTER XVIII.

STRONG VERBS: CLASS I. (See § 17.)

#Syntax of Moods.#

101. Of the three hundred simple verbs belonging to the O.E. Strong Conjugation, it is estimated[1] that seventy-eight have preserved their strong inflections in Mn.E., that eighty-eight have become weak, and that the remaining one hundred and thirty-four have entirely disappeared, their places being taken in most cases by verbs of Latin origin introduced through the Norman-French.

NOTE.--Only the simple or primitive verbs, not the compound forms, are here taken into consideration. The proportionate loss, therefore, is really much greater. O.E. abounded in formative prefixes. "Thus from the Anglo-Saxon #flôwan#, *to flow*, ten new compounds were formed by the addition of various prefixes, of which ten, only one, #oferflôwan#, *to overflow*, survives with us. In a similar manner, from the verb #sittan#, *to sit*, thirteen new verbs were formed, of which not a single one is to be found to-day." Lounsbury, *ib.* Part I, p. 107.

[Footnote 1: Lounsbury, *English Language*, Part II, § 241.]

102. #Class I: The "Drive" Conjugation.#

Vowel Succession: î, â, i, i.

INFINITIVE. PRETERIT SING. PRETERIT PLUR. PAST PART.

Drîf-an drâf drif-on gedrif-en, *to drive.*

#Indicative.# #Subjunctive.#

PRESENT. PRESENT.

Sing. 1. Ic drîf-e *Sing.* 1. Ic } 2. ðû drîf-st (drîf-est) 2. ðû } drîf-e 3. hê drîf-ð (drîf-eð) 3. hê }

Plur. 1. wê } *Plur.* 1. wê } 2. gê } (drîf-að) 2. gê } drîf-en 3. hîe } 3. hîe }

PRETERIT. PRETERIT.

Sing. 1. Ic drâf *Sing.* 1. Ic } 2. ðû drif-e 2. ðû } drif-e 3. hê drâf 3. hê }

Plur. 1. wê } *Plur.* 1. wê } 2. gê } drif-on 2. gê } drif-en 3. hîe } 3. hîe }

#Imperative.# #Infinitive.# #Present Participle.#

Sing. 2. drîf drîf-an drîf-ende *Plur.* 1. drîf-an 2. drîf-að

#Gerund.# #Past Participle.#

tô drîf-anne (-enne) gedrif-en

#Tense Formation of Strong Verbs.#

103. (1) It will be seen from the conjugation of #drîfan# that the *present stem* in all strong verbs is used throughout the present indicative, the present subjunctive, the imperative, the infinitive, the gerund, and the present participle. More than half of the endings, therefore, of the Strong Conjugation are added directly to the present stem.

(2) That the *preterit singular stem* is used in only two forms of the verb, the 1st and 3d persons singular of the preterit indicative: #Ic drâf#, #hê drâf#.

(3) That the *preterit plural stem* is used in the preterit plural indicative, in the second person of the preterit singular indicative, and in the singular and plural of the preterit subjunctive.

(4) That the *stem of the past participle* (#gedrif-#) is used for no other form.

#Syntax of the Verb.#

104. The Indicative Mood[2] represents the predicate *as a reality*. It is used both in independent and in dependent clauses, its function in

O.E. corresponding with its function in Mn.E.

[Footnote 2: Usage sanctions *mood*, but the better spelling would be *mode*. It is from the Lat. *modus*, whereas *mood* (= *temper*) is O.E. *môd*.]

105. The Subjunctive Mood represents the predicate *as an idea*.[3] It is of far more frequent occurrence in O.E. than in Mn.E.

1. When used in independent clauses it denotes desire, command, or entreaty, and usually precedes its subject: #Sîe ðîn nama gehâlgod#, *Hallowed be Thy name*; #Ne swerigen gê#, *Do not swear*.

2. In dependent clauses it denotes uncertainty, possibility, or mere futurity.[4] (*a*) Concessive clauses (introduced by #ðêah#, *though*) and (*b*) temporal clauses (introduced by #æ:r#, #æ:r ðæ:m ðe#, *before*) are rarely found with any other mood than the subjunctive. The subjunctive is also regularly used in Alfredian prose (*c*) after verbs of saying, even when no suggestion of doubt or discredit attaches to the narration.[5] "Whether the statement refer to a fact or not, whether the subject-matter be vouched for by the reporter, as regards its objective reality and truth, the subjunctive does not tell. It simply represents a statement as reported"[6]: #ðêah man âsette twêgen fæ:tels full ealað oððe wæteres#, *though one set two vessels full of ale or water*; #æ:r ðæ:m ðe hit eall forhergod wæ:re#, *before it was all ravaged*; #Hê sæ:de ðæt Norðmanna land wæ:re swy:ðe lang and swy:ðe smæl#, *He said that the Norwegians' land was very long and very narrow.*

[Footnote 3: Gildersleeve's *Latin Grammar*, § 255.]

[Footnote 4: Thus when Alfred writes that an event took place *before* the founding of Rome, he uses the subjunctive: #æ:r ðæ:m ðe Rômeburh getimbrod wæ:re# = *before Rome were founded*; but, #æfter ðæ:m ðe Rômeburh getimbrod wæs# = *after Rome was founded*.]

[Footnote 5: "By the time of Ælfric, however, the levelling influence of the indicative [after verbs of saying] has made considerable progress."--Gorrell, *Indirect Discourse in Anglo-Saxon* (Dissertation,

1895), p. 101.]

[Footnote 6: Hotz, *On the Use of the Subjunctive Mood in Anglo-Saxon* (Zürich, 1882).]

106. The Imperative is the mood of command or intercession: #Iôhannes, cum tô mê#, *John, come to me*; #And forgyf ûs ûre gyltas#, *And forgive us our trespasses*; #Ne drîf ûs fram ðê#, *Do not drive us from thee.*

107. (1) The Infinitive and Participles are used chiefly in verb-phrases (§§ 138-141); but apart from this function, the Infinitive, being a neuter noun, may serve as the subject or direct object of a verb. #Hâtan# (*to command, bid*), #læ:tan# (*to let, permit*), and onginnan (*to begin*) are regularly followed by the Infinitive: #Hine rîdan lyste#, *To ride pleased him*; #Hêt ðâ bæ:re settan#, *He bade set down the bier*;[7] #Læ:tað ðâ ly:tlingas tô mê cuman#, *Let the little ones come to me*; #ðâ ongann hê sprecan#, *then began he to speak.*

(2) The Participles may be used independently in the dative absolute construction (an imitation of the Latin ablative absolute), usually for the expression of time:[8] #Him ðâ gy:t sprecendum#, *While he was yet speaking*; #gefylledum dagum#, *the days having been fulfilled.*

[Footnote 7: Not, *He commanded the bier to be set down.* The Mn.E. passive in such sentences is a loss both in force and directness.]

[Footnote 8: Callaway, *The Absolute Participle in Anglo-Saxon* (Dissertation, 1889), p. 19.]

108. The Gerund, or Gerundial Infinitive, is used:

(1) To express purpose: #Ût êode sê sâwere his sæ:d tô sâwenne#, *Out went the sower his seed to sow.*

(2) To expand or determine the meaning of a noun or adjective: #Sy:môn, ic hæbbe ðê tô secgenne sum ðing#, *Simon, I have something to say to thee*; #Hit is scondlîc ymb swelc tô sprecanne#, *It is shameful to speak about such things.*

(3) After #bêon# (#wesan#) to denote duty or necessity: #Hwæt is nû mâ ymbe ðis tô sprecanne#, *What more is there now to say about this*? #ðonne is tô geðencenne hwaet Crîst self cwæð#, *then it behooves to bethink what Christ himself said.*

NOTE.--The Gerund is simply the dative case of the Infinitive after #tô#. It began very early to supplant the simple Infinitive; hence the use of *to* with the Infinitive in Mn.E. As late as the Elizabethan age the Gerund sometimes replaced the Infinitive even after the auxiliary verbs:

"Some pagan shore, Where these two Christian armies *might combine* The blood of malice in a vein of league, And not *to spend* it so unneighbourly." *--King John*, V, ii, 39.

When *to* lost the meaning of purpose and came to be considered as a merely formal prefix, *for* was used to supplement the purpose element: *What went ye out for to see?*[9]

[Footnote 9: This is not the place to discuss the Gerund in Mn.E., the so-called "infinitive in *-ing*." The whole subject has been befogged for the lack of an accepted nomenclature, one that shall do violence neither to grammar nor to history.]

CHAPTER XIX.

STRONG VERBS: CLASSES II AND III.

109. #Class II: The "Choose" Conjugation.#

Vowel Succession: êo, êa, u, o.

INFINITIVE.[1] PRET. SING. PRET. PLUR.[2] PAST PART.[2]

cêos-an, cêas, cur-on gecor-en, *to choose*.

#Indicative.# #Subjunctive#.

PRESENT. PRESENT.

Sing. 1. Ic cêos-e *Sing.* 1. Ic } 2. ðû cîest (cêos-est) 2. ðû } cêos-e 3. hê cîest (cêos-eð) 3. hê }

Plur. 1. wê } *Plur.* 1. wê } 2. gê } cêos-að 2. gê } cêos-en 3. hîe } 3. hîe }

PRETERIT. PRETERIT.

Sing. 1. Ic cêas *Sing.* 1. Ic } 2. ðû cur-e 2. ðû } cur-e 3. hê cêas 3. hê }

Plur. 1. wê } *Plur.* 1. wê } 2. gê } cur-on 2. gê } cur-en 3. hîe } 3. hîe }

#Imperative.# #Infinitive.# #Present Participle.#

Sing. 2. cêos cêos-an cêos-ende *Plur.* 1. cêos-an 2. cêos-að

#Gerund.# #Past Participle.#

tô cêos-anne (-enne) gecor-en

[Footnote 1: A few verbs of Class II have û instead of êo in the infinitive:

brûcan, brêac, brucon, gebrocen, *to enjoy* [brook]. bûgan, bêag, bugon, gebogen, *to bend, bow.*]

[Footnote 2: By a law known as Grammatical Change, final ð, s, and h of strong verbs generally become d, r, and g, respectively, in the preterit plural and past participle.]

110. #Class III: The "Bind" Conjugation.#

Vowel Succession: {i,e}, a, u, {u,o}.

The present stem ends in m, n, l, r, or h, + one or more consonants:

m: belimp-an, { belomp }, belump-on, belump-en, *to belong.* { belamp }

n: bind-an, { bond }, bund-on, gebund-en, *to bind.* { band }

l: help-an, healp, hulp-on, geholp-en, *to help.*

r: weorð-an, wearð, wurd-on, geword-en, *to become.*

h: gefeoht-an, gefeaht, gefuht-on, gefoht-en, *to fight.*

NOTE 1.--If the present stem ends in a nasal (m, n) + a consonant, the past participle retains the u of the pret. plur.; but if the present stem ends in a liquid (l, r) or h, + a consonant, the past participle has o instead of u.

NOTE 2.--Why do we not find #*halp#, #*warð#, and #*faht# in the pret. sing.? Because a before l, r, or h, + a consonant, underwent "breaking" to ea. Breaking also changes every e followed by r or h, + a consonant, to eo: #weorðan# (< #*werðan#), feohtan (< #*fehtan#).

111. #Indicative.# #Subjunctive.#

PRESENT. PRESENT.

Sing. 1. Ic bind-e *Sing.* 1. Ic } 2. ðû bintst (bind-est) 2. ðû } bind-e 3. hê bint (bind-eð) 3. hê }

Plur. 1. wê } Plur. 1. wê } 2. gê } bind-að 2. gê } bind-en 3. hîe } 3. hîe }

PRETERIT. PRETERIT.

Sing. 1. Ic bond Sing. 1. Ic } 2. ðû bund-e 2. ðû } bund-e 3. hê bond 3. hê }

Plur. 1. wê } Plur. 1. wê } 2. gê } bund-on 2. gê } bund-en 3. hîe } 3. hîe }

#Imperative.# #Infinitive.# #Present Participle.#

Sing. 2. bind bind-an bind-ende Plur. 1. bind-an 2. bind-að

#Gerund.# #Past Participle.#

tô bind-anne (-enne) gebund-en

112. VOCABULARY.

ðæt gefeoht, *fight, battle.* sêo gerecednes, *narration* [#reccan#]. ðæt gesceap, *creation* [#scieppan#]. sêo hergung (§ 39, (3)), *harrying, plundering* [#hergian#]. sê medu (medo) (§ 51), *mead.* sêo meolc, *milk.* sê middangeard, *world* [middle-yard]. sê munuc, *monk* [monachus]. sêo my:re, mare [#mearh#]. hê sæ:de, *he said.* hîe sæ:don, *they said.* sêo spêd, *riches* [speed]. spêdig, *rich, prosperous* [speedy]. sêo tîd, *time* [tide]. unspêdig, *poor.* sê westanwind, *west-wind.* ðæt wîn, *wine.*

ârîsan, ârâs, ârison, ârisen, *to arise.* bîdan, bâd, bidon, gebiden, *to remain, expect* (with gen.) drôogan,[3] drêag, drugon, gedrogen, *to endure, suffer.* drincan, dronc, druncon, gedruncen, *to drink.* findan, fond, fundon, gefunden, *to find.* geswîcan geswâc, geswicon, geswicen, *to cease, cease from* (with gen.) iernan (yrnan), orn, urnon, geurnen, *to run.* onginnan, ongonn, ongunnon, ongunnen, *to begin.* rîdan, râd, ridon, geriden, *to ride.* singan, song, sungon, gesungen, *to sing.* wrîtan, wrât, writon, gewriten, *to write.*

[Footnote 3: *Cf.* the Scotch "to *dree* one's weird" = *to endure one's fate.*]

113. EXERCISES.

I. 1. Æfter ðissum wordum, sê munuc wrât ealle ðâ gerecednesse on ânre bêc. 2. Ðâ eorlas ridon ûp æ:r ðæ:m ðe ðâ Dene ðæs gefeohtes geswicen. 3. Cædmon song æ:rest be middangeardes gesceape. 4. Sê cyning ond ðâ rîcostan men drincað my:ran meolc, ond ðâ unspêdigan drincað medu. 5. Ond hê ârâs ond sê wind geswâc. 6. Hîe sæ:don ðæt hîe ðæ:r westwindes biden. 7. Hwæt is nû mâ ymbe ðâs ðing tô sprecanne? 8. Ðâ secgas ongunnon geswîcan ðæ:re hergunga. 9. Ðâ bêag ðæt lond ðæ:r êastryhte, oððe sêo sæ: in on ðæt lond. 10. Ðâs lond belimpað tô, ðæ:m Englum. 11. Ðêah ðâ Dene ealne dæg gefuhten, gîet hæfde Ælfred cyning sige. 12. Ond ðæs (afterwards) ymbe ânne mônað gefeaht Ælfred cyning wið ealne ðone here æt Wiltûne.

II. 1. The most prosperous men drank mare's milk and wine, but the poor men drank mead. 2. I suffered many things before you began to help me (dat.). 3. About two days afterwards (#Ðæs ymbe twêgen dagas#), the plundering ceased. 4. The king said that he fought against all the army (#here#). 5. Although the Danes remained one month (§ 98, (1)), they did not begin to fight. 6. These gifts belonged to my brother. 7. The earls were glad because their lord was (indicative) with them. 8. What did you find? 9. Then wrote he about (#be#) the wise man's deeds. 10. What more is there to endure?

CHAPTER XX.

STRONG VERBS: CLASSES IV, V, VI, AND VII.

CONTRACT VERBS.

[The student can now complete the conjugation for himself (§ 103). Only the principal parts will be given.]

114. #Class IV: The "Bear" Conjugation.#

Vowel Succession: e, æ, æ:, o.

The present stem ends in l, r, or m, no consonant following:

l: hel-an, hæl, hæ:l-on, gehol-en, *to conceal.* r: ber-an, bær, bæ:r-on, gebor-en, *to bear.*

The two following verbs are slightly irregular:

m: { nim-an, nôm (nam), nôm-on (nâm-on), genum-en, *to take.* { cum-an, c(w)ôm, c(w)ôm-on, gecum-en, *to come.*

115. #Class V: The "Give" Conjugation.#

Succession of Vowels: e (ie), æ, æ:, e.

The present stem ends in a single consonant, never a liquid or nasal:

met-an, mæt, mæ:ton, gemet-en, *to measure, mete.* gief-an, geaf, gêaf-on, gegief-en, *to give.*

NOTE 1.--The palatal consonants, g, c, and sc, convert a following e into ie, æ into ea, and æ: into êa. Hence #giefan# (< #*gefan#), #geaf# (< #*gæf#), #gêafon# (< #*gæ:fon#), #gegiefen# (< #*gegefen#). This change is known as Palatalization. See § 8.

NOTE 2.--The infinitives of the following important verbs are only apparently exceptional:

biddan, bæd, bæ:d-on, gebed-en, *to ask for* [bid]. licgan, læg, læ:g-on, geleg-en, *to lie, extend.* sittan, sæt, sæ:t-on, geset-en, *to sit.*

The original e reappears in the participial stems. It was changed to i in the present stems on account of a former -jan in the infinitive (#bid-jan#, etc.). See § 61. To the same cause is due the doubling of consonants in the infinitive. All simple consonants in O.E., with the exception of r, were doubled after a short vowel, when an original j followed.

116. #Class VI: The "Shake" Conjugation.#

Succession of Vowels: a, ô, ô, a.

scac-an, scôc, scôc-on, gescac-en, *to shake.* far-an, fôr, fôr-on, gefar-en, *to go* [fare].

117. #Class VII: The "Fall" Conjugation.#

Vowel Succession: {â,æ:}, ê, ê, {â,æ:}; or {ea,êa,ô}, êo, êo, {ea,êa,ô}.

(1) hât-an, hêt, hêt-on, gehât-en, *to call, name, command.* læ:t-an, lêt, lêt-on, gelæ:t-en, *to let.*

(2) feall-an, fêoll, fêoll-on, gefeall-en, *to fall.* heald-an, hêold, hêold-on, geheald-en, *to hold.* hêaw-an, hêow, hêow-on, gehêaw-en, *to hew.* grôw-an, grêow, grêow-on, gegrôw-en, *to grow.*

NOTE 1.--This class consists of the Reduplicating Verbs; that is, those verbs that originally formed their preterits not by internal vowel change (ablaut), but by prefixing to the present stem the initial consonant + e (*cf.* Gk. #le-loipa# and Lat. *d[)e]-di*). Contraction then took place between the syllabic prefix and the root, the fusion resulting in ê or êo: #*he-hat# > #heht# > #hêt#.

NOTE 2.--A peculiar interest attaches to #hâtan#: the forms #hâtte# and #hâtton# are the sole remains in O.E. of the original Germanic passive. They are used both as presents and as preterits: #hâtte# = *I am* or *was called, he is* or *was called.* No other verb in O.E. could have a passive sense without calling in the aid of the verb *to be* (§ 141).

#Contract Verbs.#

118. The few Contract Verbs found in O.E. do not constitute a new class; they fall under Classes I, II, V, VI, and VII, already treated. The present stem ended originally in h. This was lost before -an of the infinitive, contraction and compensatory lengthening being the result. The following are the most important of these verbs:

Classes.

I. ðêon (< *ðîhan), ðâh, ðig-on, { geðig-en }, *to thrive.* { geðung-en } II. têon (< *têohan), têah, tug-on, getog-en, *to draw, go* [tug]. V. sêon (< *sehwan), seah, sâw-on, gesew-en, *to see.* VI. slêan (< *slahan), slôh, slôg-on, geslæg-en, *to slay.* VII. fôn (< *fôhan), fêng, fêng-on, gefong-en, *to seize* [fang].

119. The Present Indicative of these verbs runs as follows (see rules of i-umlaut, § 58):

Sing. 1. Ic ðêo têo sêo slêa fô 2. ðû ðîhst tîehst siehst sliehst fêhst 3. hê ðîhð tîehð siehð sliehð fêhð

Plur. 1. wê } 2. gê } ðêoð têoð sêoð slêað fôð 3. hîe }

The other tenses and moods are regularly formed from the given stems.

120. VOCABULARY.

sêo æ:ht, *property, possession* [#âgan#]. aweg, *away* [#on weg#]. sêo fierd, *English army* [#faran#]. sê here, *Danish army* [#hergian#]. on gehwæðre hond, *on both sides.* sige niman (= sige habban), *to win (the) victory.* sêo spræ:c, *speech, language.* tô rîce fôn, *to come to the throne.*[1] ðæt wæl [Val-halla] } *slaughter, carnage.* sê wælsliht, } sê weall, *wall, rampart.* ðæt wildor, *wild beast, reindeer.* sê wîngeard, *vineyard.*

âbrecan,[2] âbræc, âbræ:con, âbrocen, *to break down*. cweðan, cwæð, cwæ:don, gecweden, *to say* [quoth]. gesêon, geseah, gesâwon, gesewen, *to see*. grôwan, grêow, grêowon, gegrôwen, *to grow*. ofslêan, ofslôh, ofslôgon, ofslægen, *to slay*. sprecan, spræc, spræ:con, gesprecen, *to speak*. stelan, stæl, stæ:lon, gestolen, *to steal*. stondan, stôd, stôdon, gestonden, *to stand*. weaxan, wêox, wêoxon, geweaxen, *to grow, increase* [wax].

[Footnote 1: Literally, *to take to (the) kingdom. Cf.* "Have you anything to take to?" (*Two Gentlemen of Verona*, IV, i, 42).]

[Footnote 2: #Brecan# belongs properly in Class V, but it has been drawn into Class IV possibly through the influence of the r in the root.]

121. EXERCISES.

I. 1. Æfter ðæ:m sôðlîce (indeed) ealle men spræ:con âne (one) spræ:ce. 2. Ond hê cwæð: "Ðis is ân folc, ond ealle hîe sprecað âne spræ:ce." 3. On sumum stôwum wîngeardas grôwað. 4. Hê hêt ðâ næ:dran ofslêan. 5. Ðâ Engle âbræ:con ðone longan weall, ond sige nômon. 6. Ond ðæt sæ:d grêow ond wêox. 7. Ic ne geseah ðone mon sê ðe ðæs cnapan adesan stæl. 8. Hê wæs swy:ðe spêdig man on ðæ:m æ:htum ðe hiera spêda on[3] bêoð, ðæt is, on wildrum. 9. Ond ðæ:r wearð (was) micel wælsliht on gehwæðre hond. 10. Ond æfter ðissum gefeohte côm Ælfred cyning mid his fierde, ond gefeaht wið ealne ðone here, ond sige nôm. 11. Ðêos burg hâtte[4] Æscesdûn (Ashdown). 12. Ðæ:re cwêne lîc læg on ðæ:m hûse. 13. Ond sê dæ:l ðe ðæ:r aweg côm wæs swy:ðe ly:tel. 14. Ond ðæs ðrêotîene dagas Æðered tô rîce fêng.

II. 1. The men stood in the ships and fought against the Danes. 2. Before the thanes came, the king rode away. 3. They said (#sæ:don#) that all the men spoke one language. 4. They bore the queen's body to Wilton. 5. Alfred gave many gifts to his army (dat. without #tô#) before he went away. 6. These men are called earls. 7. God sees all things. 8. The boy held the reindeer with (#mid#) his hands. 9. About six months afterwards, Alfred gained the victory, and came to the throne. 10. He said that there was very great slaughter on both sides.

[Footnote 3: See § 94, (5).]

[Footnote 4: See § 117, Note 2.]

CHAPTER XXI.

WEAK VERBS (§ 18).

122. The verbs belonging to the Weak Conjugation are generally of more recent origin than the strong verbs, being frequently formed from the roots of strong verbs. The Weak Conjugation was the growing conjugation in O.E. as it is in Mn.E. We instinctively put our newly coined or borrowed words into this conjugation (*telegraphed*, *boycotted*); and children, by the analogy of weak verbs, say *runned* for *ran*, *seed* for *saw*, *teared* for *tore*, *drawed* for *drew*, and *growed* for *grew*. So, for example, when Latin *dictâre* and *breviâre* came into O.E., they came as weak verbs, #dihtian# and #brêfian#.

#The Three Classes of Weak Verbs.#

123. There is no difficulty in telling, from the infinitive alone, to which of the three classes a weak verb belongs. Class III has been so invaded by Class II that but three important verbs remain to it: #habban#, *to have*; #libban#, *to live*; and #secgan#, *to say*. Distinction is to be made, therefore, only between Classes II and I. Class II contains the verbs with infinitive in -ian not preceded by r. Class I contains the remaining weak verbs; that is, those with infinitive in #-r-ian# and those with infinitive in -an (not -ian).

#Class I.#

124. The preterit singular and past participle of Class I end in -ede and -ed, or -de and -ed respectively.

NOTE.--The infinitives of this class ended originally in -jan (= -ian). This accounts for the prevalence of i-umlaut in these verbs, and also for the large number of short-voweled stems ending in a double consonant (§ 115, Note 2). The weak verb is frequently the causative of the corresponding strong verb. In such cases, the root of the weak verb corresponds in form to the preterit singular of the strong verb: Mn.E. *drench* (= to make drink), *lay* (= to make lie), *rear* (= to make rise), and *set* (= to make sit), are the umlauted forms of #dronc# (preterit singular of #drincan#), #læg# (preterit singular of #licgan#),

#râs# (preterit singular of #rîsan#), and #sæt# (preterit singular of #sittan#).

#Preterit and Past Participle in *-ede* and *-ed.*#

125. Verbs with infinitive in -an preceded by ri- or the double consonants mm, nn, ss, bb, cg (= gg), add -ede for the preterit, and -ed for the past participle, the double consonant being always made single:

ri: neri-an, ner-ede, gener-ed, *to save.* mm: fremm-an, frem-ede, gefrem-ed, *to perform* [frame]. nn: ðenn-an, ðen-ede, geðen-ed, *to extend.* ss: cnyss-an, cnys-ede, gecnys-ed, *to beat.* bb: swebb-an, swef-ede, geswef-ed, *to put to sleep.* cg: wecg-an, weg-ede, geweg-ed, *to agitate.*

NOTE.--#Lecgan#, *to lay*, is the only one of these verbs that syncopates the e: #lecgan#, #legde# (#lêde#), #gelegd# (#gelêd#), instead of #legede#, #geleged#.

#Preterit and Past Participle in *-de* and *-ed.*#

126. All the other verbs belonging to Class I. add -de for the preterit and -ed for the past participle. This division includes, therefore, all stems long by nature (§ 10, (3), (*a*)):

dæ:l-an, dæ:l-de, gedæ:l-ed, *to deal out, divide* [dæ:l]. dêm-an, dêm-de, gedêm-ed, *to judge* [dôm]. grêt-an, grêt-te, gegrêt-ed, *to greet.* hîer-an, hîer-de, gehîer-ed, *to hear.* læ:d-an, læ:d-de, gelæ:d-ed, *to lead.*

NOTE 1.--A preceding voiceless consonant (§ 9, Note) changes -de into -te: #*grêt-de# > #grêt-te#; #*mêt-de# > #mêt-te#; #*îec-de# > #îec-te#. Syncope and contraction are also frequent in the participles: #gegrêt-ed# > #*gegrêt-d# > #gegrêt(t)#; #gelæ:d-ed# > #gelæ:d(d)#.

NOTE 2.--#Bûan#, *to dwell, cultivate*, has an admixture of strong forms in the past participle: #bûan#, #bûde#, #gebûd# (#by:n#, #gebûn#). The present participle survives in Mn.E. *husband* = *house-dweller.*

127. It includes, also, all stems long by position (§ 10, (3), (*b*)) except those in mm, nn, ss, bb, and cg (§ 125):

send-an, send-e, gesend-ed, *to send*. sett-an, set-te, geset-ed, *to set* [sittan]. sigl-an, sigl-de, gesigl-ed, *to sail*. spend-an, spend-e, gespend-ed, *to spend*. tredd-an, tred-de, getred-ed, *to tread*.

NOTE.--The participles frequently undergo syncope and contraction: #gesended# > #gesend#; #geseted# > #geset(t)#; #gespended# > #gespend#; #getreded# > #getred(d)#.

#Irregular Verbs of Class I.#

128. There are about twenty verbs belonging to Class I that are irregular in having no umlaut in the preterit and past participle. The preterit ends in -de, the past participle in -d; but, through the influence of a preceding voiceless consonant (§ 9, Note), -ed is generally unvoiced to -te, and -d to -t. The most important of these verbs are as follows:

bring-an, brôh-te, gebrôh-t, *to bring*. byc-gan, boh-te, geboh-t, *to buy*. sêc-an, sôh-te, gesôh-t, *to seek*. sell-an, seal-de, geseal-d, *to give, sell* [hand-sel]. tæ:c-an, tæ:h-te, getæ:h-t, *to teach*. tell-an, teal-de, geteal-d, *to count* [tell]. ðenc-an, ðôh-te, geðôh-t, *to think*. ðync-an, ðûh-te, geðûh-t, *to seem* [methinks]. wyrc-an, worh-te, geworh-t, *to work*.

NOTE.--Such of these verbs as have stems in c or g are frequently written with an inserted e: #bycgean#, #sêcean#, #tæ:cean#, etc. This e indicates that c and g have palatal value; that is, are to be followed with a vanishing y-sound. In such cases, O.E. c usually passes into Mn.E. *ch*: #tæ:c(e)an# > *to teach*; #ræ:c(e)an# > *to reach*; #strecc(e)an# > *to stretch*. #Sêc(e)an# gives *beseech* as well as *seek*. See § 8.

#Conjugation of Class I.#

129. Paradigms of #nerian#, *to save*; #fremman#, *to perform*; #dæ:lan#, *to divide*:

#Indicative.#

PRESENT.

Sing. 1. Ic nerie fremme dæ:le 2. ðû nerest fremest dæ:lst 3. hê nereð fremeð dæ:lð

Plur. 1. wê } 2. gê } neriað fremmað dæ:lað 3. hîe }

PRETERIT.

Sing. 1. Ic nerede fremede dæ:lde 2. ðû neredest fremedest dæ:ldest 3. hê nerede fremede dæ:lde

Plur. 1. wê } 2. gê } neredon fremedon dæ:ldon 3. hîe }

#Subjunctive.#

PRESENT.

Sing. 1. Ic } 2. ðû } nerie fremme dæ:le 3. hê }

Plur. 1. wê } 2. gê } nerien fremmen dæ:len 3. hîe }

PRETERIT.

Sing. 1. Ic } 2. ðû } nerede fremede dæ:lde 3. hê }

Plur. 1. wê } 2. gê } nereden fremeden dæ:lden 3. hîe }

#Imperative.#

Sing. 2. nere freme dæ:l

Plur. 1. nerian fremman dæ:lan 2. neriað fremmað dæ:lað

#Infinitive.#

nerian fremman dæ:lan

#Gerund.#

tô nerianne (-enne) tô fremmanne (-enne) tô dæ:lanne (-enne)

#Present Participle.#

neriende fremmende dæ:lende

#Past Participle.#

genered gefremed gedæ:led

NOTE.--The endings of the preterit present no difficulties; in the 2d and 3d singular present, however, the student will observe (a) that double consonants in the stem are made single: #fremest#, #fremeð# (not #*freemmest#, #*freemmeð#); #ðenest#, #ðeneð#; #setest# (#setst#), #seeteð# (#sett#); #fylst#, #fylð#, from #fyllan#, to fill; (b) that syncope is the rule in stems long by nature: #dæ:lst# (< #dæ:lest#), #dæ:lð# (< #dæ:leð#); #dêmst# (< #dêmest#), #dêmð# (< #dêmeð#); #hîerst# (< #hîerest#), #hîerð# (< #hîereð#). Double consonants are also made single in the imperative 2d singular and in the past participle. Stems long by nature take no final -e in the imperative: #dæ:l#, #hîer#, #dêm#.

#Class II.#

130. The infinitive of verbs belonging to this class ends in -ian (not #-r-ian#), the preterit singular in -ode, the past participle in -od. The preterit plural usually has #-edon#, however, instead of #-odon#:

eard-ian, eard-ode, geeard-od, to dwell [eorðe]. luf-ian, luf-ode, geluf-od, to love [lufu]. rîcs-ian, rîcs-ode, gerîcs-od, to rule [rîce]. sealf-ian, sealf-ode, gesealf-od, to anoint [salve]. segl-ian, segl-ode, gesegl-od, to sail [segel].

NOTE.--These verbs have no trace of original umlaut, since their -ian was once #-ôjan#. Hence, the vowel of the stem was shielded from the influence of the j (= i) by the interposition of ô.

#Conjugation of Class II.#

131. Paradigm of #lufian#, *to love*:

#Indicative.# #Subjunctive.#

PRESENT. PRESENT.

Sing. 1. Ic lufie *Sing.* 1. Ic } 2. ðu lufast 2. ðû } lufie 3. hê lufað 3. hê }

Plur. 1. wê } *Plur.* 1. wê } 2. gê } lufiað 2. gê } lufien 3. hîe } 3. hîe }

PRETERIT. PRETERIT.

Sing. 1. Ic lufode *Sing.* 1. Ic } 2. ðû lufodest 2. ðû } lufode 3. hê lufode 3. hê }

Plur. 1. wê } *Plur.* 1. wê } 2. gê } lufedon (-odon) 2. gê } lufeden (-oden) 3. hîe } 3. hîe }

#Imperative.# #Infinitive.# #Present Participle.#

Sing. 2. lufa lufian lufiende *Plur.* 1. lufian 2. lufiað

#Gerund.# #Past Participle.#

tô lufianne (-enne) gelufod

NOTE 1.--The -ie (-ien) occurring in the present must be pronounced as a dissyllable. The y-sound thus interposed between the i and e is frequently indicated by the letter g: #lufie#, or #lufige#; #lufien#, or #lufigen#. So also for ia: #lufiað#, or #lufigað#; #lufian#, or #lufig(e)an#.

NOTE 2.--In the preterit singular, -ade, -ude, and -ede are not infrequent for -ode.

#Class III.#

132. The few verbs belonging here show a blending of Classes I and II. Like certain verbs of Class I (§ 128), the preterit and past participle are formed by adding -de and -d; like Class II, the 2d and 3d present indicative singular end in -ast and -að, the imperative 2d singular in -a:

habb-an, hæf-de, gehæf-d, *to have*. libb-an, lif-de, gelif-d, *to live*. secg-an, sæ:d-e (sæg-de), gesæ:d (gesæg-d), *to say*.

#Conjugation of Class III.#

133. Paradigms of #habban#, *to have*; #libban#, *to live*; #secgan#, *to say*.

#Indicative.#

PRESENT.

Sing. 1. Ic hæbbe libbe secge 2. ðû hæfst (hafast) lifast sægst (sagast) 3. hê hæfð (hafað) lifað sægð (sagað)

Plur. 1. wê } 2. gê } habbað libbað secgað 3. hîe }

PRETERIT.

Sing. 1. Ic hæfde lifde sæ:de 2. ðû hæfdest lifdest sæ:dest 3. hê hæfde lifde sæ:de

Plur. 1. wê } 2. gê } hæfdon lifdon sæ:don 3. hîe }

#Subjunctive.#

PRESENT.

Sing. 1. Ic } 2. ðû } hæbbe libbe secge 3. hê }

Plur. 1. wê } 2. gê } hæbben libben secgen 3. hîe }

PRETERIT.

Sing. 1. Ic } 2. ðû } hæfde lifde sæ:de 3. hê }

Plur. 1. wê } 2. gê } hæfden lifden sæ:den 3. hîe }

#Imperative.#

Sing. 2. hafa lifa saga *Plur.* 1. habban libban secgan 2. habbað libbað secgað

#Infinitive.#

habban libban secgan

#Gerund.#

tô habbanne (-enne) tô libbanne (-enne) tô secganne (-enne)

#Present Participle.#

hæbbende libbende secgende

#Past Participle.#

gehæfd gelifd gesæ:d

CHAPTER XXII.

REMAINING VERBS; VERB-PHRASES WITH #habban#, #bêon#, AND #weorðan#.

#Anomalous Verbs.# (See § 19.)

134. These are:

bêon (wesan), wæs, wæ:ron, ----, *to be.* willan, wolde, woldon, ----, *to will, intend.* dôn, dyde, dydon, gedôn, *to do, cause.* gân, êode, êodon, gegân, *to go.*

NOTE.--In the original Indo-Germanic language, the first person of the present indicative singular ended in (1) ô or (2) mi. *Cf.* Gk. +lu-ô+, +ei-mi+, Lat. *am-ô, su-m.* The Strong and Weak Conjugations of O.E. are survivals of the ô-class. The four Anomalous Verbs mentioned above are the sole remains in O.E. of the mi-class. Note the surviving m in #eom# *I am*, and #dôm# *I do* (Northumbrian form). These mi-verbs are sometimes called non-Thematic to distinguish them from the Thematic or ô-verbs.

#Conjugation of Anomalous Verbs.#

135. Only the present indicative and subjunctive are at all irregular:

#Indicative.#

PRESENT.

Sing. 1. Ic eom (bêom) wille dô gâ 2. ðû eart (bist) wilt dêst gæ:st 3. hê is (bið) wille dêð gæ:ð

Plur. 1. wê } 2. gê } sind(on) willað dôð gâð 3. hîe }

#Subjunctive.#

PRESENT.

Sing. 1. Ic } 2. ðû } sîe wille dô gâ 3. hê }

Plur. 1. wê } 2. gê } sîen willen dôn gân 3. hîe }

NOTE.--The preterit subjunctive of #bêon# is formed, of course, not from #wæs#, but from #wæ:ron#. See § 103, (3).

#Preterit-Present Verbs.# (See § 19.)

136. These verbs are called Preterit-Present because the present tense (indicative and subjunctive) of each of them is, in form, a strong preterit, the old present having been displaced by the new. They all have weak preterits. Most of the Mn.E. Auxiliary Verbs belong to this class.

witan, { wiste, } wiston, gewiten, *to know* { wisse, } [to wit, wot]. âgan, âhte, âhton, âgen (adj.), *to possess* [owe]. cunnan, cûðe, cûðon, { gecunnen, } *to know, can* { cûð (adj.), } [uncouth, cunning]. durran, dorste, dorston, ---- *to dare*. sculan, sceolde, sceoldon, ---- *shall*. magan, { meahte, meahton, } ---- *to be able, may*. { mihte, mihton, } môtan, môste, môston, ---- *may, must*.

NOTE.--The change in meaning from preterit to present, with retention of the preterit form, is not uncommon in other languages. Several examples are found in Latin and Greek (cf. *nôvi* and +oida+, *I know*). Mn.E. has gone further still: #âhte# and #môste#, which had already suttered the loss of their old preterits (#âh#, #môt#), have been forced back again into the present (*ought, must*). Having exhausted, therefore, the only means of preterit formation known to Germanic, the strong and the weak, it is not likely that either *ought* or *must* will ever develop distinct preterit forms.

#Conjugation of Preterit-Present Verbs.#

137. The irregularities occur in the present indicative and subjunctive:

#Indicative.#

PRESENT.

Sing. 1. Ic wât âh con (can) 2. ðû wâst âhst const (canst) 3. hê wât âh con (can)

Plur. 1. wê } 2. gê } witon âgon cunnon 3. hîe }

Sing. 1. Ic dear sceal mæg môt 2. ðû dearst scealt meaht môst 3. hê dear sceal mæg môt

Plur. 1. wê 2. gê durron sculon magon môton 3. hîe

#Subjunctive.#

PRESENT.

Sing. 1. Ic } 2. ðû } wite âge cunne 3. hê }

Plur. 1. wê } 2. gê } witen âgen cunnen 3. hîe }

Sing. 1. Ic } 2. ðû } durre scule (scyle) mæge môte 3. hê }

Plur. 1. wê } 2. gê } durren sculen (scylen) mægen môten 3. hîe }

NOTE 1.--#Willan# and #sculan# do not often connote simple futurity in Early West Saxon, yet they were fast drifting that way. The Mn.E. use of *shall* only with the 1st person and *will* only with the 2d and 3d, to express simple futurity, was wholly unknown even in Shakespeare's day. The elaborate distinctions drawn between these words by modern grammarians are not only cumbersome and foreign to the genius of English, but equally lacking in psychological basis.

NOTE 2.--#Sculan# originally implied the idea of (1) *duty*, or *compulsion* (= *ought to*, or *must*), and this conception lurks with more or less prominence in almost every function of #sculan# in O.E.: #Dryhten bebêad Moyse hû hê sceolde beran ðâ earce#, *The Lord instructed Moses how he ought to bear the ark*; #Æ:lc mann sceal be his andgietes mæ:ðe ... sprecan ðæt he spricð, and dôn ðæt ðæt hê dêð#, *Every man must, according to the measure of his intelligence, speak what he speaks, and do what he does*. Its next most frequent use is to express (2) *custom*, the transition from the obligatory to the customary being an easy one: #Sê byrdesta sceall gyldan fîfty:ne mearðes fell#, *The man of highest rank pays fifteen marten skins.*

NOTE 3.--#Willan# expressed originally (1) *pure volition*, and this is its most frequent use in O.E. It may occur without the infinitive: #Nylle ic ðæs synfullan dêað, ac ic wille ðæt hê gecyrre and lybbe#, *I do not desire the sinner's death, but I desire that he return and live.* The wish being father to the intention, #willan# soon came to express (2) *purpose*: #Hê sæ:de ðæt hê at sumum cirre wolde fandian hû longe ðæt land norðryhte læ:ge#, *He said that he intended, at some time, to investigate how far that land extended northward.*

#Verb-Phrases with *habban*, *bêon* (*wesan*), and *weorðan*.#

Verb-Phrases in the Active Voice.

138. The present and preterit of #habban#, combined with a past participle, are used in O.E., as in Mn.E., to form the present perfect and past perfect tenses:

PRESENT PERFECT. PAST PERFECT.

Sing. 1. Ic hæbbe gedrifen *Sing.* 1. Ic hæfde gedrifen 2. ðû hæfst gedrifen 2. ðû hæfdest gedrifen 3. hê hæfð gedrifen 3. hê hæfde gedrifen

PRESENT PERFECT. PAST PERFECT.

Plur. 1. wê } *Plur.* 1. wê } 2. gê } habbað gedrifen 2. gê } hæfdon gedrifen 3. hîe } 3. hîe }

The past participle is not usually inflected to agree with the direct object: #Norðymbre ond Êastengle hæfdon Ælfrede cyninge âðas geseald# (not #gesealde#, § 82), *The Northumbrians and East Anglians had given king Alfred oaths*; #ond hæfdon miclne dæ:l ðâra horsa freten# (not #fretenne#), *and (they) had devoured a large part of the horses.*

NOTE.--Many sentences might be quoted in which the participle does agree with the direct object, but there seems to be no clear line of demarcation between them and the sentences just cited. Originally, the participle expressed a *resultant state*, and belonged in sense more to the object than to #habban#; but in Early West Saxon #habban# had already, in the majority of cases, become a pure auxiliary when used with the past participle. This is conclusively proved by the use of #habban# with intransitive verbs. In such a clause, therefore, as #oð ðæt hîe hine ofslægenne hæfdon#, there is no occasion to translate *until they had him slain* (= *resultant state*); the agreement here is more probably due to the proximity of #ofslægenne# to #hine#. So also #ac hî hæfdon þâ hiera stemn gesetenne#, *but they had already served out* (*sat out*) *their military term.*

139. If the verb is intransitive, and denotes *a change of condition, a departure or arrival*, #bêon# (#wesan#) usually replaces #habban#. The past participle, in such cases, partakes of the nature of an adjective, and generally agrees with the subject: #Mîne welan þe ic îo hæfde syndon ealle gewitene ond gedrorene#, *My possessions which I once had are all departed and fallen away*; #wæ:ron þâ men uppe on londe of âgâne#, *the men had gone up ashore*; #ond þâ ôþre wæ:ron hungre âcwolen#, *and the others had perished of hunger*; #ond êac sê micla here wæs þâ þæ:r tô cumen#, *and also the large army had then arrived there.*

140. A progressive present and preterit (not always, however, with distinctively progressive meanings) are formed by combining a present participle with the present and preterit of #bêon# (#wesan#). The participle remains uninflected: #ond hîe alle on ðone cyning wæ:run feohtende#, *and they all were fighting against the king*; #Symle hê bið lôciende, nê slæ:pð hê næ:fre#, *He is always looking, nor does He ever sleep.*

NOTE.--In most sentences of this sort, the subject is masculine (singular or plural); hence no inference can be made as to agreement, since -e is the participial ending for both numbers of the nominative masculine (§ 82). By analogy, therefore, the other genders usually conform in inflection to the masculine: #wæ:ron þâ ealle þâ dêoflu clypigende ânre stefne#, *then were all the devils crying with one voice.*

Verb-Phrases in the Passive Voice.

141. Passive constructions are formed by combining #bêon# (#wesan#) or #weorðan# with a past participle. The participle agrees regularly with the subject: #hîe wæ:ron benumene æ:gðer ge þæs cêapes ge þæs cornes#, *they were deprived both of the cattle and the corn*; #hî bêoð âblende mid ðæ:m þîostrum heora scylda#, *they are blinded with the darkness of their sins*; #and sê wælhrêowa Domiciânus on ðâm ylcan gêare wearð âcweald#, *and the murderous Domitian was killed in the same year*; #ond Æþelwulf aldormon wearð ofslægen#, *and Æthelwulf, alderman, was slain*.

NOTE 1.--To express agency, Mn.E. employs *by*, rarely *of*; M.E. *of*, rarely *by*; O.E. #from# (#fram#), rarely #of#: #Sê ðe Godes bebodu ne gecnæ:wð, ne bið hê oncnâwen from Gode#, *He who does not recognise God's commands, will not be recognized by God*; #Betwux þæ:m wearð ofslagen Êadwine ... fram Brytta cyninge#, *Meanwhile, Edwin was slain by the king of the Britons*.

NOTE 2.--O.E. had no progressive forms for the passive, and could not, therefore, distinguish between *He is being wounded* and *He is wounded*. It was not until more than a hundred years after Shakespeare's death that *being* assumed this function. #Weorðan#, which originally denoted *a passage from one state to another*, was ultimately driven out by #bêon# (#wesan#), and survives now only in *Woe worth* (= *be to*).

142. VOCABULARY.

ðâ Beormas, *Permians*. ðâ Deeniscan, *the Danish (men), Danes*. ðâ Finnas, *Fins*. ðæt gewald, *control* [#wealdan#]. sêo sæ:, *sea*. sêo scîr, *shire, district*. sêo wælstôw, *battle-field*. âgan wælstôwe gewald, *to maintain possession of the battle-field*. sê wealdend, *ruler, wielder*.

geflîeman, geflîemde, geflîemed, *to put to flight*. gestaðelian, gestaðelode, gestaðelod, *to establish, restore*. gewissian, gewissode, gewissod, *to guide, direct*. wîcian, wîcode, gewîcod, *to dwell* [wîc = village].

143. EXERCISES.

I. 1. Ond ðær wæs micel wæl geslægen on gehwæþre hond, ond Æþelwulf ealdormon wearþ ofslægen; ond þâ Deniscan âhton wælstôwe gewald. 2. Ond þæs ymb ânne mônaþ gefeaht Ælfred cyning wiþ ealne þone here ond hine geflîemde. 3. Hê sæ:de þêah þæt þæt land sîe swîþe lang norþ þonan. 4. Þâ Beormas hæfdon swîþe wel gebûd (§ 126, Note 2) hiera land. 5. Ohthere sæ:de þæt sêo scîr hâtte (§ 117, Note 2) Hâlgoland, þe hê on (§ 94, (5)) bûde. 6. Þâ Finnas wîcedon be þæ:re sæ:. 7. Dryhten, ælmihtiga (§ 78, Note) God, Wyrhta and Wealdend ealra gesceafta, ic bidde ðê for ðînre miclan mildheortnesse ðæt ðû mê gewissie tô ðînum willan; and gestaðela mîn môd tô ðînum willan and tô mînre sâwle ðearfe. 8. Þâ sceolde hê ðæ:r bîdan ryhtnorþanwindes, for ðæ:m þæt land bêag þæ:r sûðryhte, oþþe sêo sæ: in on ðæt land, hê nysse hwæðer. 9. For ðy:, mê ðyncð betre, gif êow swâ ðyncð, ðæt wê êac ðâs bêc on ðæt geðêode wenden ðe wê ealle gecnâwan mægen.

II. 1. When the king heard that, he went (= then went he) westward with his army to Ashdown. 2. Lovest thou me more than these? 3. The men said that the shire which they lived in was called Halgoland. 4. All things were made (#wyrcan#) by God. 5. They were fighting for two days with (= against) the Danes. 6. King Alfred fought with the Danes, and gained the victory; but the Danes retained possession of the battle-field. 7. These men dwelt in England before they came hither. 8. I have not seen the book of (#ymbe#) which you speak (#sprecan#).

PART III.

SELECTIONS FOR READING.

PROSE.

INTRODUCTORY.

I. #The Anglo-Saxon Chronicle.#

This famous work, a series of progressive annals by unknown hands, embraces a period extending from Cæsar's invasion of England to

1154. It is not known when or where these annals began to be recorded in English.

"The annals from the year 866--that of Ethelred's ascent of the throne--to the year 887 seem to be the work of one mind. Not a single year is passed over, and to several is granted considerable space, especially to the years 871, 878, and 885. The whole has gained a certain roundness and fulness, because the events--nearly all of them episodes in the ever-recurring conflict with the Danes--are taken in their connection, and the thread dropped in one year is resumed in the next. Not only is the style in itself concise; it has a sort of nervous severity and pithy rigor. The construction is often antiquated, and suggests at times the freedom of poetry; though this purely historical prose is far removed from poetry in profusion of language." (Ten Brink, *Early Eng. Lit.*, I.)

II. #The Translations of Alfred.#

Alfred's reign (871-901) may be divided into four periods. The *first*, the period of Danish invasion, extends from 871 to 881; the *second*, the period of comparative quiet, from 881 to 893; the *third*, the period of renewed strife (beginning with the incursions of Hasting), from 893 to 897; the *fourth*, the period of peace, from 897 to 901. His literary work probably falls in the second period.[A]

The works translated by Alfred from Latin into the vernacular were (1) *Consolation of Philosophy* (*De Consolatione Philosophiae*) by Boëthius (475-525), (2) *Compendious History of the World* (*Historiarum Libri VII*) by Orosius (c. 418), (3) *Ecclesiastical History of the English* (*Historia Ecclesiastica Gentis Anglorum*) by Bede (672-735), and (4) *Pastoral Care* (*De Cura Pastorali*) by Pope Gregory the Great (540-604).

The chronological sequence of these works is wholly unknown. That given is supported by Turner, Arend, Morley, Grein, and Pauli. Wülker argues for an exact reversal of this order. According to Ten Brink, the order was more probably (1) *Orosius*, (2) *Bede*, (3) *Boëthius*, and (4) *Pastoral Care*. The most recent contribution to the subject is from Wülfing, who contends for (1) *Bede*, (2) *Orosius*, (3) *Pastoral Care*, and (4) *Boëthius.*

[Footnote A: There is something inexpressibly touching in this clause from the great king's pen: gif wê ðâ stilnesse habbað. He is speaking of how much he hopes to do, by his translations, for the enlightenment of his people.]

I. THE BATTLE OF ASHDOWN.

[From the *Chronicle*, Parker MS. The event and date are significant. The Danes had for the first time invaded Wessex. Alfred's older brother, Ethelred, was king; but to Alfred belongs the glory of the victory at Ashdown (Berkshire). Asser (*Life of Alfred*) tells us that for a long time Ethelred remained praying in his tent, while Alfred and his followers went forth "like a wild boar against the hounds."]

[[page 99]]

1 871. Hêr cuôm[1] sê here tô Rêadingum on Westseaxe, 2 ond þæs ymb iii niht ridon ii eorlas ûp. Þa gemêtte hîe

[[page 100]]

1 Æþelwulf aldorman[2] on Englafelda, ond him þæ:r wiþ gefeaht, 2 ond sige nam. Þæs ymb iiii niht Æþered cyning 3 ond Ælfred his brôþur[3] þæ:r micle fierd tô Rêadingum 4 gelæ:ddon, ond wiþ þone here gefuhton; ond þæ:r wæs 5 micel wæl geslægen on gehwæþre hond, ond Æþelwulf 6 aldormon wearþ ofslægen; ond þa Deniscan âhton wælstôwe 7 gewald.

8 Ond þæs ymb iiii niht gefeaht Æþered cyning ond 9 Ælfred his brôþur wiþ alne[4] þone here on Æscesdûne. 10 Ond hîe wæ:run[5] on twæ:m gefylcum: on ôþrum wæs 11 Bâchsecg ond Halfdene þâ hæ:þnan cyningas, ond on 12 ôþrum wæ:ron þâ eorlas. Ond þâ gefeaht sê cyning 13 Æþered wiþ þâra cyninga getruman, ond þæ:r wearþ sê 14 cyning Bâgsecg ofslægen; ond Ælfred his brôþur wiþ 15 þâra eorla getruman, ond þæ:r wearþ Sidroc eorl ofslægen 16 sê alda,[6] ond Sidroc eorl sê gioncga,[7] ond Ôsbearn eorl, 17 ond Fræ:na eorl, ond Hareld eorl; ond þâ hergas[8] bêgen 18 geflîemde,

ond fela þûsenda ofslægenra, ond onfeohtende 19 wæ:ron oþ niht.

20 Ond þæs ymb xiiii niht gefeaht Æþered cyning ond 21 Ælfred his brôður wiþ þone here æt Basengum, ond þæ:r 22 þa Deniscan sige nâmon.

23 Ond þæs ymb ii mônaþ gefeaht Æþered cyning ond 24 Ælfred his brôþur wiþ þone here æt Meretûne, ond hîe 25 wæ:run on tuæ:m[9] gefylcium, ond hîe bûtû geflîemdon, ond 26 longe on dæg sige âhton; ond þæ:r wearþ micel wælsliht 27 on gehwæþere hond; ond þâ Deniscan âhton wælstôwe

[[page 101]]

1 gewald; ond þær wearþ Hêahmund bisceop ofslægen, 2 ond fela gôdra monna. Ond æfter þissum gefeohte cuôm[1] 3 micel sumorlida.

4 Ond þæs ofer Êastron gefôr Æþered cyning; ond hê 5 rîcsode v gêar; ond his lîc lîþ æt Wînburnan.

6 Þâ fêng Ælfred Æþelwulfing his brôþur tô Wesseaxna 7 rîce. Ond þæs ymb ânne mônaþ gefeaht Ælfred cyning 8 wiþ alne[4] þone here ly:tle werede[10] æt Wiltûne, ond hine 9 longe on dæg geflîemde, ond þâ Deniscan âhton wælstôwe 10 gewald.

11 Ond þæs gêares wurdon viiii folcgefeoht gefohten wiþ 12 þone here on þy: cynerîce be sûþan Temese, bûtan þâm þe 13 him Ælfred þæs cyninges brôþur ond ânlîpig aldormon[2] ond 14 cyninges þegnas oft râde onridon þe mon nâ ne rîmde; 15 ond þæs gêares wæ:run[5] ofslægene viiii eorlas ond ân cyning. 16 Ond þy: gêare nâmon Westseaxe friþ wiþ þone here.

CONSULT GLOSSARY AND PARADIGMS UNDER FORMS GIVEN BELOW.

No note is made of such variants as y (y:) or i (î) for ie (îe). See Glossary under ie (îe); occurrences, also, of #and# for #ond#, #land# for #lond#, are found on almost every page of Early West Saxon. Such words should be sought for under the more common forms, #ond#,

#lond#.

[1] = cwôm. [2] = ealdormon. [3] = brôþor. [4] = ealne. [5] = wæ:ron. [6] = ealda. [7] = geonga. [8] = heras. [9] = twæ:m. [10] = werode.

[Linenotes:

100.8. #gefeaht#. Notice that the singular is used. This is the more common construction in O.E. when a compound subject, composed of singular members, follows its predicate. Cf. *For thine is the kingdom, and the power, and the glory.* See also p. 107, note on #wæs#.]
[[Linenote 107.14-15]]

100.18. #ond fela þûsenda ofslægenra#, *and there were many thousands of slain* (§ 91).

101.12: #bûtan þâm þe#, etc., *besides which, Alfred ... made raids against them* (#him#), *which were not counted.* See § 70, Note.]

II. A PRAYER OF KING ALFRED.

[With this characteristic prayer, Alfred concludes his translation of Boëthius's *Consolation of Philosophy.* Unfortunately, the only extant MS. (Bodleian 180) is Late West Saxon. I follow, therefore, Prof. A. S. Cook's normalization on an Early West Saxon basis. See Cook's *First Book in Old English,* p. 163.]

[[page 102]]

1 Dryhten, ælmihtiga God, Wyrhta and Wealdend ealra 2 gesceafta, ic bidde ðê for ðînre miclan mildheortnesse, 3 and for ðæ:re hâlgan rôde tâcne, and for Sanctæ Marian 4 mægðhâde, and for Sancti Michaeles gehîersumnesse, and 5 for ealra ðînra hâlgena lufan and hîera earnungum, ðæt 6 ðû mê gewissie bet ðonne ic âworhte tô ðê; and gewissa 7 mê tô ðînum willan, and tô mînre sâwle ðearfe, bet ðonne 8 ic self cunne; and gestaðela mîn môd tô ðinum willan and 9 tô mînre sâwle ðearfe; and gestranga mê wið ðæs dêofles 10 costnungum; and âfierr fram mê ðâ fûlan gâlnesse and 11 æ:lce unrihtwîsnesse; and gescield mê wið mînum wiðerwinnum, 12 gesewenlîcum and

ungesewenlîcum; and tæ:c mê 13 ðînne willan tô wyrceanne; ðæt ic
mæge ðê inweardlîce 14 lufian tôforan eallum ðingum, mid clæ:num
geðance and 15 mid clæ:num lîchaman. For ðon ðe ðû eart mîn
Scieppend, 16 and mîn Alîesend, mîn Fultum, mîn Frôfor, mîn
Trêownes, 17 and mîn Tôhopa. Sîe ðê lof and wuldor nû and 18 â â â,
tô worulde bûtan æ:ghwilcum ende. Amen.

[Linenotes:

3-4: #Marian ... Michaeles#. O.E. is inconsistent in the treatment of
foreign names. They are sometimes naturalized, and sometimes retain
in part their original inflections. #Marian#, an original accusative, is
here used as a genitive; while #Michaeles# has the O.E. genitive
ending.

17: #Sîe ðê lof#. See § 105, 1.]

III. THE VOYAGES OF OHTHERE AND WULFSTAN.

[Lauderdale and Cottonian MSS. These voyages are an original
insertion by Alfred into his translation of Orosius's *Compendious
History of the World.*

"They consist," says Ten Brink, "of a complete description of all the
countries in which the Teutonic tongue prevailed at Alfred's time, and a
full narrative of the travels of two voyagers, which the king wrote down
from their own lips. One of these, a Norwegian named Ohthere, had
quite circumnavigated the coast of Scandinavia in his travels, and had
even penetrated to the White Sea; the other, named Wulfstan, had
sailed from Schleswig to Frische Haff. The geographical and
ethnographical details of both accounts are exceedingly interesting,
and their style is attractive, clear, and concrete."

Ohthere made two voyages. Sailing first northward along the western
coast of Norway, he rounded the North Cape, passed into the White
Sea, and entered the Dwina River (#ân micel êa#). On his second
voyage he sailed southward along the western coast of Norway,
entered the Skager Rack (#wîdsæ:#), passed through the Cattegat,
and anchored at the Danish port of Haddeby (#æt Hæ:þum#), modern

Schleswig.

Wulfstan sailed only in the Baltic Sea. His voyage of seven days from Schleswig brought him to Drausen (#Trûsô#) on the shore of the Drausensea.]

[[page 103]]

#Ohthere's First Voyage.#

1 Ôthere sæ:de his hlâforde, Ælfrede cyninge, þæt hê 2 ealra Norðmonna norþmest bûde. Hê cwæð þæt hê bûde 3 on þæ:m lande norþweardum wiþ þâ Westsæ. Hê sæ:de 4 þêah þæt þæt land sîe swîþe lang norþ þonan; ac hit is 5 eal wêste, bûton on fêawum stôwum styccemælum wîciað 6 Finnas, on huntoðe on wintra, ond on sumera on fiscaþe 7 be þæ:re sæ:. Hê sæ:de þæt hê æt sumum cirre wolde 8 fandian hû longe þæt land norþryhte læ:ge, oþþe hwæðer 9 æ:nig mon be norðan þæ:m wêstenne bûde. Þâ fôr hê 10 norþryhte be þæ:m lande: lêt him ealne weg þæt wêste 11 land on ðæt stêorbord, ond þâ wîdsæ: on ðæt bæcbord þrîe 12 dagas. Þâ wæs hê swâ feor norþ swâ þâ hwælhuntan 13 firrest faraþ. Þâ fôr hê þâ gîet norþryhte swâ feor swâ 14 hê meahte on þæ:m ôþrum þrîm dagum gesiglan. Þâ bêag 15 þæt land þæ:r êastryhte, oþþe sêo sæ: in on ðæt lond, hê 16 nysse hwæðer, bûton hê wisse ðæt hê ðæ:r bâd westanwindes 17 ond hwôn norþan, ond siglde ðâ êast be lande 18 swâ swâ hê meahte on fêower dagum gesiglan. Þâ 19 sceolde hê ðæ:r bîdan ryhtnorþanwindes, for ðæ:m þæt 20 land bêag þæ:r sûþryhte, oþþe sêo sæ: in on ðæt land, hê 21 nysse hwæþer. Þâ siglde hê þonan sûðryhte be lande

[[page 104]]

1 swâ swâ hê mehte[1] on fîf dagum gesiglan. Ðâ læg þæ:r 2 ân micel êa ûp in on þæt land. Þâ cirdon hîe ûp in on 3 ðâ êa, for þæ:m hîe ne dorston forþ bî þæ:re êa siglan for 4 unfriþe; for þæ:m ðæt land wæs eall gebûn on ôþre healfe 5 þæ:re êas. Ne mêtte hê æ:r nân gebûn land, siþþan hê 6 from his âgnum hâm fôr; ac him wæs ealne weg wêste 7 land on þæt stêorbord, bûtan fiscerum ond fugelerum ônd 8 huntum, ond þæt wæ:ron eall Finnas; ond him wæs â 9 wîdsæ: on ðæt bæcbord. Þâ Beormas hæfdon swîþe wel 10 gebûd hira land: ac hîe

ne dorston þæ:r on cuman. Ac 11 þâra Terfinna land wæs eal wêste, bûton ðæ:r huntan 12 gewîcodon, oþþe fisceras, oþþe fugeleras.

[1] = meahte, mihte.

[Linenotes:

104.6: #from his âgnum hâm#. An adverbial dative singular without an inflectional ending is found with #hâm#, #dæg#, #morgen#, and #æ:fen#.

104.8: #ond þæt wæ:ron#. See § 40, Note 3.]

13 Fela spella him sæ:don þâ Beormas æ:gþer ge of hiera 14 âgnum lande ge of þæ:m landum þe ymb hîe ûtan wæ:ron; 15 ac hê nyste hwæt þæs sôþes wæs, for þæ:m hê hit self ne 16 geseah. Þâ Finnas, him þûhte, ond þâ Beormas spræ:con 17 nêah ân geþêode. Swîþost hê fôr ðider, tô êacan þæs 18 landes scêawunge, for þæ:m horshwælum, for ðæ:m hîe 19 habbað swîþe æþele bân on hiora[2] tôþum--þâ têð hîe brôhton 20 sume þæ:m cyninge--ond hiora hy:d bið swîðe gôd tô 21 sciprâpum. Sê hwæl bið micle læ:ssa þonne ôðre hwalas: 22 ne bið hê lengra ðonne syfan[3] elna lang; ac on his âgnum 23 lande is sê betsta hwælhuntað: þâ bêoð eahta and fêowertiges 24 elna lange, and þâ mæ:stan fîftiges elna lange; 25 þâra hê sæ:de þæt hê syxa sum ofslôge syxtig on twâm 26 dagum.

[2] = hiera. [3] = seofon.

[Linenotes:

104.15: #hwæt þæs sôþes wæs#. Sweet errs in explaining #sôþes# as attracted into the genitive by #þæs#. It is not a predicate adjective, but a partitive genitive after #hwæt#.

104.25: #syxa sum#. See § 91, Note 2.]

[[page 105]]

1 Hê wæs swy:ðe spêdig man on þæ:m æ:htum þe heora[2] 2 spêda on bêoð, þæt is, on wildrum. Hê hæfde þâ gy:t, ðâ 3 hê þone cyningc[5] sôhte, tamra dêora unbebohtra syx hund. 4 Þâ dêor hî hâtað 'hrânas'; þâra wæ:ron syx stælhrânas; 5 ðâ bêoð swy:ðe dy:re mid Finnum, for ðæ:m hy: fôð þâ 6 wildan hrânas mid. Hê wæs mid þæ:m fyrstum mannum 7 on þæ:m lande: næfde hê þêah mâ ðonne twêntig hry:ðera, 8 and twêntig scêapa, and twêntig swy:na; and þæt ly:tle 9 þæt hê erede, hê erede mid horsan.[4] Ac hyra âr is mæ:st 10 on þæ:m gafole þe ðâ Finnas him gyldað. Þæt gafol bið 11 on dêora fellum, and on fugela feðerum, and hwales bâne, 12 and on þæ:m sciprâpum þe bêoð of hwæles hy:de geworht 13 and of sêoles. Æ:ghwilc gylt be hys gebyrdum. Sê byrdesta 14 sceall gyldan fîfty:ne mearðes fell, and fîf hrânes, 15 and ân beren fel, and ty:n ambra feðra, and berenne kyrtel 16 oððe yterenne, and twêgen sciprâpas; æ:gþer sy: syxtig 17 elna lang, ôþer sy: of hwæles hy:de geworht, ôþer of sîoles.[6]

[2] = hiera. [4] = horsum. [5] = cyning. [6] = sêoles.

[Linenote:

105.2: #on bêoð#. See § 94, (5).]

18 Hê sæ:de ðæt Norðmanna land wæ:re swy:þe lang and 19 swy:ðe smæl. Eal þæt his man âðer oððe ettan oððe erian 20 mæg, þæt lîð wið ðâ sæ:; and þæt is þêah on sumum 21 stôwum swy:ðe clûdig; and licgað wilde môras wið êastan 22 and wið ûpp on emnlange þæ:m by:num lande. On þæ:m 23 môrum eardiað Finnas. And þæt by:ne land is êasteweard 24 brâdost, and symle swâ norðor swâ smælre. Êastewerd[7] 25 hit mæg bîon[8] syxtig mîla brâd, oþþe hwêne bræ:dre; 26 and middeweard þrîtig oððe brâdre; and norðeweard hê 27 cwæð, þæ:r hit smalost wæ:re, þæt hit mihte bêon þrêora 28 mîla brâd tô þæ:m môre; and sê môr syðþan,[9] on sumum

[[page 106]]

1 stôwum, swâ brâd swâ man mæg on twâm wucum oferfêran; 2 and on sumum stôwum swâ brâd swâ man mæg 3 on syx dagum oferfêran.

[7] = -weard. [8] = bêon. [9] = siðð̃an.

[Linenote:

105.19: #Eal þæt his man#. Pronominal genitives are not always possessive in O.E.; #his# is here the partitive genitive of #hit#, the succeeding relative pronoun being omitted: *All that (portion) of it that may, either-of-the-two, either be grazed or plowed*, etc. (§ 70, Note).]

4 Ðonne is tôemnes þæ:m lande sûðeweardum, on ôðre 5 healfe þæs môres, Swêoland, oþ þæt land norðeweard; 6 and tôemnes þæ:m lande norðeweardum, Cwêna land. Þâ 7 Cwênas hergiað hwîlum on ðâ Norðmen ofer ðone môr, 8 hwîlum þâ Norðmen on hy:. And þæ:r sint swîðe micle 9 meras fersce geond þâ môras; and berað þâ Cwênas hyra 10 scypu ofer land on ðâ meras, and þanon hergiað on ðâ 11 Norðmen; hy: habbað swy:ðe ly:tle scypa and swy:ðe 12 leohte.

[Linenote:

106.11-12: #scypa ... leohte#. These words exhibit inflections more frequent in Late than in Early West Saxon. The normal forms would be #scypu#, #leoht#; but in Late West Saxon the -u of short-stemmed neuters is generally replaced by -a; and the nominative accusative plural neuter of adjectives takes, by analogy, the masculine endings; #hwate#, #gôde#, #hâlge#, instead of #hwatu#, #gôd#, #hâlgu#.]

#Ohthere's Second Voyage.#

13 Ôhthere sæ:de þæt sîo[1] scîr hâtte Hâlgoland, þe hê on 14 bûde. Hê cwæð þæt nân man ne bûde be norðan him. 15 Ponne is ân port on sûðeweardum þæ:m lande, þone man 16 hæ:t Sciringeshêal. Þyder hê cwæð þæt man ne mihte 17 geseglian on ânum mônðe, gyf man on niht wîcode, and 18 æ:lce dæge hæfde ambyrne wind; and ealle ðâ hwîle hê 19 sceal seglian be lande. And on þæt stêorbord him bið 20 æ:rest Îraland, and þonne ðâ îgland þe synd betux Îralande 21 and þissum lande. Þonne is þis land, oð hê cymð 22 tô Scirincgeshêale, and ealne weg on þæt bæcbord Norðweg.

[[page 107]]

1 Wið sûðan þone Sciringeshêal fylð swy:ðe mycel 2 sæ: ûp in on ðæt land; sêo is brâdre þonne æ:nig man ofer 3 sêon mæge. And is Gotland on ôðre healfe ongêan, and 4 siððan Sillende. Sêo sæ: lîð mænig[2] hund mîla ûp in on 5 þæt land.

[1] = sêo. [2] = monig.

6 And of Sciringeshêale hê cwæð ðæt hê seglode on fîf 7 dagan[3] tô þæ:m porte þe mon hæ:t æt Hæ:þum; sê stent 8 betuh Winedum, and Seaxum, and Angle, and hy:rð in 9 on Dene. Ðâ hê þiderweard seglode fram Sciringeshêale, 10 þâ wæs him on þæt bæcbord Denamearc and on 11 þæt stêorbord wîdsæ: þry: dagas; and þâ, twêgen dagas æ:r 12 hê tô Hæ:þum côme, him wæs on þæt stêorbord Gotland, 13 and Sillende, and îglanda fela. On þæ:m landum eardodon 14 Engle, æ:r hî hider on land côman.[4] And hym wæs 15 ðâ twêgen dagas on ðæt bæcbord þâ îgland þe in on 16 Denemearce hy:rað.

[3] = dagum. [4] = cômen.

[Linenotes:

107.7: #æt Hæ:þum#. "This pleonastic use of *æt* with names of places occurs elsewhere in the older writings, as in the Chronicle (552), 'in þæ:re stôwe þe is genemned æt Searobyrg,' where the *æt* has been erased by some later hand, showing that the idiom had become obsolete. *Cp.* the German 'Gasthaus zur Krone,' Stamboul = *es tân pólin*." (Sweet.) See, also, *Atterbury*, § 28, Note 3.

107.14-15: #wæs ... þâ îgland#. The singular predicate is due again to inversion (p. 100, note on #gefeaht# [[linenote 100.8]]). The construction is comparatively rare in O.E., but frequent in Shakespeare and in the popular speech of to-day. Cf. *There is*, *Here is*, *There has been*, etc., with a (single) plural subject following.]

#Wulfstan's Voyage.#

17 Wulfstân sæ:de þæt hê gefôre of Hæ:ðum, þæt hê wæ:re 18 on Trûsô on syfan dagum and nihtum, þæt þæt scip wæs 19 ealne weg yrnende under segle. Weonoðland him wæs

[[page 108]]

1 on stêorbord, and on bæcbord him wæs Langaland, and 2 Læ:land, and Falster, and Scônêg; and þâs land eall 3 hy:rað tô Denemearcan. And þonne Burgenda land wæs 4 ûs on bæcbord, and þâ habbað him sylfe[1] cyning. Þonne 5 æfter Burgenda lande wæ:ron ûs þâs land, þâ synd hâtene 6 æ:rest Blêcinga-êg, and Mêore, and Êowland, and Gotland 7 on bæcbord; and þâs land hy:rað tô Swêom. And Weonodland 8 wæs ûs ealne weg on stêorbord oð Wîslemûðan. 9 Sêo Wîsle is swy:ðe mycel êa, and hîo[2] tôlîð Wîtland and 10 Weonodland; and þæt Wîtland belimpeð tô Estum; and 11 sêo Wîsle lîð ût of Weonodlande, and lîð in Estmere; 12 and sê Estmere is hûru fîftêne[3] mîla brâd. Þonne cymeð 13 Ilfing êastan in Estmere of ðâm mere, ðe Trûsô standeð 14 in stæðe; and cumað ût samod in Estmere, Ilfing êastan 15 of Estlande, and Wîsle sûðan of Winodlande. And 16 þonne benimð Wîsle Ilfing hire naman, and ligeð of þæ:m 17 mere west and norð on sæ:; for ðy: hit man hæ:t 18 Wîslemûða.

[1] = selfe. [2] = hêo. [3] = fîftîene.

[Linenote:

108.1-4: #him ... ûs#. Note the characteristic change of person, the transition from *indirect* to *direct discourse.*]

19 Þæt Estland is swy:ðe mycel, and þæ:r bið swy:ðe manig 20 burh, and on æ:lcere byrig bið cyning. And þæ:r bið 21 swy:ðe mycel hunig, and fiscnað; and sê cyning and þâ 22 rîcostan men drincað my:ran meolc, and þâ unspêdigan 23 and þâ þêowan drincað medo.[4] Þæ:r bið swy:ðe mycel 24 gewinn betwêonan him. And ne bið ðæ:r næ:nig calo[5] 25 gebrowen mid Estum, ac þæ:r bið medo genôh. And þæ:r 26 is mid Estum ðêaw, þonne þæ:r bið man dêad, þæt hê lîð 27 inne unforbærned mid his mâgum and frêondum mônað, 28 ge hwîlum twêgen; and þâ cyningas, and þâ ôðre hêahðungene 29 men, swâ micle lencg[6] swâ hî mâran spêda 30 habbað, hwîlum healf gêar þæt hî bêoð unforbærned, and

[[page 109]]

1 licgað bufan eorðan on hyra hûsum. And ealle þâ hwîle 2 þe þæt lîc
bið inne, þæ:r sceal bêon gedrync and plega, 3 oð ðone dæg þe hî
hine forbærnað. Þonne þy: ylcan dæge 4 þe hî hine tô pæ:m âde
beran wyllað, þonne tôdæ:lað hî 5 his feoh, þæt þæ:r tô lâfe bið æfter
þæ:m gedrynce and þæ:m 6 plegan, on fîf oððe syx, hwy:lum on mâ,
swâ swâ þæs fêos 7 andêfn bið. Âlecgað hit ðonne forhwæga on ânre
mîle 8 þone mæ:stan dæ:l fram þæ:m tûne, þonne ôðerne, ðonne 9
þone þriddan, oþ þe hyt eall âlêd bið on þæ:re ânre mîle; 10 and sceall
bêon sê læ:sta dæ:l ny:hst þæ:m tûne ðe sê dêada 11 man on lið.
Ðonne sceolon[7] bêon gesamnode ealle ðâ 12 menn ðe swyftoste
hors habbað on þæ:m lande, forhwæga 13 on fîf mîlum oððe on syx
mîlum fram þæ:m fêo. Þonne 14 ærnað hy: ealle tôweard þæ:m fêo:
ðonne cymeð sê man 15 sê þæt swiftoste hors hafað tô þæ:m
æ:restan dæ:le and tô 16 þæ:m mæ:stan, and swâ æ:lc æfter ôðrum,
oþ hit bið eall 17 genumen; and sê nimð þone læ:stan dæ:l sê ny:hst
þæ:m 18 tûne þæt feoh geærneð. And þonne rîdeð æ:lc hys weges 19
mid ðæ:m fêo, and hyt môtan[8] habban eall; and for ðy: 20 þæ:r bêoð
þâ swiftan hors ungefôge dy:re. And þonne his 21 gestrêon bêoð þus
eall âspended, þonne byrð man hine ût, 22 and forbærneð mid his
wæ:pnum and hrægle; and swîðost

[[page 110]]

1 ealle hys spêda hy: forspendað mid þæ:m langan legere 2 þæs
dêadan mannes inne, and þæs þe hy: be þæ:m wegum 3 âlecgað, þe
ðâ fremdan tô ærnað, and nimað. And þæt 4 is mid Estum þêaw þæt
þæ:r sceal æ:lces geðêodes man 5 bêon forbærned; and gyf þâr[9]
man ân bân findeð unforbærned, 6 hî hit sceolan[7] miclum gebêtan.
And þæ:r is mid 7 Estum ân mæ:gð þæt hî magon cyle gewyrcan; and
þy: 8 þæ:r licgað þâ dêadan men swâ lange, and ne fûliað, þæt 9 hy:
wyrcað þone cyle him on. And þêah man âsette 10 twêgen fæ:tels full
ealað oððe wæteres, hy: gedôð þæt 11 æ:gþer bið oferfroren, sam hit
sy: sumor sam winter.

[4] = medu. [5] = ealu. [6] = leng. [7] = sculon. [8] = môton. [9] = ðæ:r.

[Linenotes:

109.2: #sceal#. See § 137, Note 2 (2).

109.7: #Âlecgað hit#. Bosworth illustrates thus:

vi v iv iii ii i 1 2 3 4 5 6 | | | | | | X | | | | | | XX X X | | | | | | XXX XX XX X X
----------------------------- XXXX XXX XXX XX XX X *e d c b a* Where the horsemen The six parts of the property assemble. placed within one mile.

"The horsemen assemble five or six miles from the property, at *d* or *e*, and run towards *c*; the man who has the swiftest horse, coming first to 1 or *c*, takes the first and largest part. The man who has the horse coming second takes part 2 or *b*, and so, in succession, till the least part, 6 or *a*, is taken."

110.5-6: #man ... hî#. Here the plural #hî# refers to the singular #man#. *Cf.* p. 109, ll. 18-19, #æ:lc ... môtan#. In *Exodus* xxxii, 24, we find "*Whosoever* hath any gold, let *them* break it off"; and Addison writes, "I do not mean that I think *anyone* to blame for taking due care of *their* health." The construction, though outlawed now, has been common in all periods of our language. Paul remarks (*Prinzipien der Sprachgeschichte*, 3d ed., § 186) that "When a word is used as an indefinite [one, man, somebody, etc.] it is, strictly speaking, incapable of any distinction of number. Since, however, in respect of the external form, a particular number has to be chosen, it is a matter of indifference which this is.... Hence a change of numbers is common in the different languages." Paul fails to observe that the change is always from singular to plural, not from plural to singular. See *Note on the Concord of Collectives and Indefinites* (Anglia XI, 1901). See p. 119, note on ll. 19-21.]

IV. THE STORY OF CÆDMON.

[From the so-called Alfredian version of Bede's *Ecclesiastical History*. The text generally followed is that of MS. Bodley, Tanner 10. Miller (*Early English Text Society*, No. 95, *Introd.*) argues, chiefly from the use of the prepositions, that the original O.E. MS. was Mercian, composed possibly in Lichfield (Staffordshire). At any rate, O.E. idiom is frequently sacrificed to the Latin original.

"Cædmon, as he is called, is the first Englishman whose name we know who wrote poetry in our island of England; and the first to embody in verse the new passions and ideas which Christianity had brought into England.... Undisturbed by any previous making of lighter poetry, he came fresh to the work of Christianising English song. It was a great step to make. He built the chariot in which all the new religious emotions of England could now drive along." (Brooke, *The History of Early English Literature*, cap. XV.) There is no reason to doubt the historical existence of Cædmon; for Bede, who relates the story, lived near Whitby, and was seven years old when Cædmon died (A.D. 680)].

[[page 111]]

1 In ðysse abbudissan mynstre wæs sum brôðor syndriglîce 2 mid godcundre gife gemæ:red ond geweorðad, for þon 3 he gewunade gerisenlîce lêoð wyrcan, þâ ðe tô æ:festnisse[1] 4 ond tô ârfæstnisse belumpon; swâ ðætte swâ hwæt swâ 5 hê of godcundum stafum þurh bôceras geleornode, þæt hê 6 æfter medmiclum fæce in scopgereorde mid þâ mæ:stan 7 swêtnisse ond inbryrdnisse geglengde, ond in Engliscgereorde 8 wel geworht forþ brôhte. Ond for his lêoþsongum

[[page 112]]

1 monigra monna môd oft to worulde forhogdnisse ond tô 2 geþêodnisse þæs heofonlîcan lîfes onbærnde wæ:ron. Ond 3 êac swelce[2] monige ôðre æfter him in Ongelþêode ongunnon 4 æ:feste lêoð wyrcan, ac næ:nig hwæðre him þæt gelîce 5 dôn ne meahte; for þon hê nâlæs from monnum nê ðurh 6 mon gelæ:red wæs þæt hê ðone lêoðcræft leornade, ac hê 7 wæs godcundlîce gefultumod, ond þurh Godes gife þone 8 songcræft onfêng; ond hê for ðon næ:fre nôht lêasunge, 9 nê îdles lêoþes wyrcan ne meahte, ac efne þâ ân ðâ ðê tô 10 æ:festnisse[1] belumpon ond his þâ æ:festan tungan gedafenode 11 singan.

[1] = æ:fæstnesse. [2] = swilce.

[Linenotes:

111.1: #ðysse abbudissan.# The abbess referred to is the famous Hild, or Hilda, then living in the monastery at Streones-halh, which, according to Bede, means "Bay of the Beacon." The Danes afterward gave it the name Whitby, or "White Town." The surroundings were eminently fitted to nurture England's first poet. "The natural scenery which surrounded him, the valley of the Esk, on whose sides he probably lived, the great cliffs, the billowy sea, the vast sky seen from the heights over the ocean, played incessantly upon him." (Brooke.)

Note, also, in this connection, the numerous Latin words that the introduction of Christianity (A.D. 597) brought into the vocabulary of O.E.: #abbudisse#, #mynster#, #bisceop#, #Læ:den#, #prêost#, #æstel#, #mancus#.

112.4-5: The more usual order of words would be #ac næ:nig, hwæðre, ne meahte ðæt dôn gelîce him#.

112.10-11: #ond his ... singan#, *and which it became his (the) pious tongue to sing.*]

12 Wæs hê, sê mon, in weoruldhâde[3] geseted oð þâ tîde þe 13 hê wæs gely:fdre ylde, ond næ:fre næ:nig lêoð geleornade. 14 Ond hê for þon oft in gebêorscipe, þonne þæ:r wæs blisse 15 intinga gedêmed, þæt hêo[4] ealle sceolden þurh endebyrdnesse 16 be hearpan singan, þonne hê geseah þâ hearpan him 17 nêalêcan, þonne ârâs hê for scome from þæ:m symble, 18 ond hâm êode tô his hûse. Þâ hê þæt þâ sumre tîde 19 dyde, þæt hê forlêt þæt hûs þæs gebêorscipes, ond ût wæs

[[page 113]]

1 gongende tô nêata scipene, þâra heord him wæs þæ:re 2 nihte beboden; þâ hê ðâ þæ:r on gelimplîcre tîde his 3 leomu[5] on reste gesette ond onslêpte, þa stôd him sum 4 mon æt þurh swefn, ond hine hâlette ond grêtte, ond hine 5 be his noman nemnde: "Cædmon, sing mê hwæthwugu." 6 Þâ ondswarede hê, ond cwæð: "Ne con ic nôht singan; 7 ond ic for þon of þyssum gebêorscipe ût êode ond hider 8 gewât, for þon ic nâht singan ne cûðe." Eft hê cwæð sê ðe 9 wið hine sprecende wæs: "Hwæðre þû meaht mê singan." 10 Þâ cwæð hê:

"Hwæt sceal ic singan?" Cwæð hê: "Sing 11 mê frumsceaft." Þâ hê ðâ
þâs andsware onfêng, þâ 12 ongon hê sôna singan, in herenesse
Godes Scyppendes, 13 þâ fers ond þâ word þe hê næ:fre ne gehy:rde,
þâra endebyrdnes 14 þis is:

[3] = woruldhâde. [4] = hîe. [5] = limu.

[Linenotes:

112.14-15: #blisse intinga#, *for the sake of joy*; but the translator has
confused *laetitiae causâ* (ablative) and *laetitiae causa* (nominative).
The proper form would be #for blisse# with omission of #intingan#, just
as *for my sake* is usually #for mê#; *for his (or their) sake*, #for him#. *Cf.
Mark* vi, 26: "Yet *for his oath's sake, and for their sakes which sat with
him*, he would not reject her," #for ðæ:m âðe, ond for ðæ:m þe him mid
sæ:ton#. *For his sake* is frequently #for his ðingon# (#ðingum#), rarely
#for his intingan#. #Þingon# is regularly used when the preceding
genitive is a noun denoting a person: *for my wife's sake*, #for mînes
wîfes ðingon# (*Genesis* xx, 11), etc.

112.18-19: #þæt ... þæt hê forlêt#. The substantival clause introduced
by the second #þæt# amplifies by apposition the first #þæt#: *When he
then, at a certain time* (instrumental case, § 98, (2)), *did that, namely,
when he left the house.* The better Mn.E. would be *this ... that*: "Added
yet *this* above all, *that* he shut up John in prison" (*Luke* iv, 20).

113.1-2: #þâra ... beboden#. This does not mean that Cædmon was a
herdsman, but that he served in turn as did the other secular
attendants at the monastery.

113.13-14: #þâra endebyrdnes þis is#. Bede writes *Hic est sensus,
non autem ordo ipse verborum*, and gives in Latin prose a translation
of the hymn from the Northumbrian dialect, in which Cædmon wrote.
The O.E. version given above is, of course, not the Northumbrian
original (which, however, with some variations is preserved in several
of the Latin MSS. of Bede's *History*), but a West Saxon version made
also from the Northumbrian, not from the Latin.]

15 Nû sculon herigean[6] heofonrîces Weard, 16 Metodes meahte ond his môdgeþanc, 17 weorc Wuldorfæder, swâ hê wundra gehwæs, 18 êce Drihten ôr onstealde.

[[page 114]]

1 Hê æ:rest scêop eorðan bearnum 2 heofon tô hrôfe, hâlig Scyppend; 3 þâ middangeard monncynnes Weard, 4 êce Drihten, æfter têode 5 fîrum foldan, Frêa ælmihtig.

[6] = herian.

[Linenotes:

113.15: #Nû sculon herigean#, *Now ought we to praise*. The subject #wê# is omitted in the best MSS. Note the characteristic use of synonyms, or epithets, in this bit of O.E. poetry. Observe that it is not the *thought* that is repeated, but rather the *idea*, the *concept*, God. See p. 124. [[Poetry: Structure]]

113.17: #wundra gehwæs#. See p. 140, note on #cênra gehwylcum# [[*Beowulf* 769]].]

6 Þâ ârâs hê from þæ:m slæ:pe, ond eal þâ þe hê slæ:pende 7 song fæste in gemynde hæfde; ond þæ:m wordum sôna 8 monig word in þæt ilce gemet Gode wyrðes songcs 9 tôgeþêudde. Þâ côm hê on morgenne tô þæ:m tûngerêfan, 10 sê þe his ealdormon wæs: sægde him hwylce gife hê 11 onfêng; ond hê hine sôna tô þæ:re abbudissan gelæ:dde, 12 ond hire þæt cy:ðde ond sægde. Þâ heht hêo gesomnian 13 ealle þâ gelæ:redestan men ond þâ leorneras, ond him 14 ondwcardum hêt secyan þæt swefn, ond þæt lêoð singan, 15 þæt ealra heora[7] dôme gecoren wæ:re, hwæt oððe hwonan 16 þæt cumen wæ:re. Þâ wæs him eallum gesewen, swâ swâ 17 hit wæs, þæt him wæ:re from Drihtne sylfum heofonlîc

[[page 115]]

1 gifu forgifen. Þâ rehton heo[4] him ond sægdon sum hâlig 2 spell ond godcundre lâre word: bebudon him þâ, gif hê 3 meahte, þæt hê in

swînsunge lêoþsonges þæt gehwyrfde. 4 Þâ hê ðâ hæfde þâ wîsan onfongne, þâ êode hê hâm tô 5 his hûse, ond cwôm eft on morgenne, ond þy: betstan 6 lêoðe geglenged him âsong ond âgeaf þæt him beboden 7 wæs.

[4] = hîe. [7] = hiera.

[Linenotes:

114.7-9: #ond þæ:m wordum ... tôgeþêodde#, *and to those words he soon joined, in the same meter, many (other) words of song worthy of God.* But the translator has not only blundered over Bede's Latin (*eis mox plura in eundem modum verba Deo digna carminis adjunxit*), but sacrificed still more the idiom of O.E. The predicate should not come at the end; #in# should be followed by the dative; and for #Gode wyrðes songes# the better O.E. would be #songes Godes wyrðes#. When used with the dative #wyrð# (#weorð#) usually means *dear* (= *of worth*) *to*.

114.16: #þâ ... gesewen#. We should expect #from him eallum#; but the translator has again closely followed the Latin (*visumque est omnibus*), as later (in the *Conversion of Edwin*) he renders *Talis mihi videtur* by #þyslîc mê is gesewen#. *Talis* (#þyslîc#) agreeing with a following *vita* (#lîf#). Ælfric, however, with no Latin before him, writes that John #wearð ðâ him# [= #from Drihtene#] #inweardlîce gelufod#. It would seem that in proportion as a past participle has the force of an adjective, the *to* relation may supplant the *by* relation; just as we say *unknown to* instead of *unknown by*, *unknown* being more adjectival than participial. #Gesewen#, therefore, may here be translated *visible, evident, patent* (= #gesynelîc#, #sweotol#); and #gelufod#, *dear* (= #weorð#, #lêof#).

A survival of adjectival #gesewen# is found in Wycliffe's *New Testament* (1 *Cor.* xv, 5-8): "He was *seyn to* Cephas, and aftir these thingis *to* enleuene; aftirward he was *seyn to* mo than fyue hundrid britheren togidere ... aftirward he was *seyn to* James, and aftirward *to* alle the apostlis. And last of alle he was *seyn to* me, as *to* a deed borun child." The construction is frequent in Chaucer.]

8 Ðâ ongan sêo abbudisse clyppan ond lufigean[8] þâ Godes 9 gife in þæ:m men, ond hêo hine þâ monade ond læ:rde 10 þæt hê woruldhâd forlête ond munuchâd onfênge: ond 11 hê þæt wel þafode. Ond hêo hine in þæt mynster onfêng 12 mid his gôdum, ond hine geþêodde tô gesomnunge þâra 13 Godes þêowa, ond heht hine læ:ran þæt getæl þæs hâlgan 14 stæ:res ond spelles. Ond hê eal þâ hê in gehy:rnesse 15 geleornian meahte, mid hine gemyndgade, ond swâ swâ 16 clæ:ne nêten[9] eodorcende in þæt swêteste lêoð gehwyrfde. 17 Ond his song ond his lêoð wæ:ron swâ wynsumu tô gehy:ranne, 18 þætte þâ seolfan[10] his lârêowas æt his mûðe writon 19 ond leornodon. Song hê æ:rest be middangeardes gesceape, 20 ond bî fruman moncynnes, ond eal þæt stæ:r Genesis (þæt 21 is sêo æ:reste Moyses bôc); ond eft bî ûtgonge Israhêla 22 folces of Æ:gypta londe, ond bî ingonge þæs gehâtlandes; 23 ond bî ôðrum monegum spellum þæs hâlgan gewrites

[[page 116]]

1 canônes bôca; ond bî Crîstes menniscnesse, ond bî his 2 þrôwunge, ond bî his ûpâstîgnesse in heofonas; ond bî 3 þæs Hâlgan Gâstes cyme, ond þâra apostola lâre; ond eft 4 bî þæ:m dæge þæs tôweardan dômes, ond bî fyrhtu þæs 5 tintreglîcan wîtes, ond bî swêtnesse þæs heofonlîcan rîces, 6 hê monig lêoð geworhte; ond swelce[2] êac ôðer monig be 7 þæ:m godcundan fremsumnessum ond dômum hê geworhte. 8 In eallum þæ:m hê geornlîce gêmde[11] þæt hê men âtuge 9 from synna lufan ond mândæ:da, ond tô lufan ond tô 10 geornfulnesse âwehte gôdra dæ:da, for þon hê wæs, sê 11 mon, swîþe æ:fest ond regollîcum þêodscipum êaðmôdlîce 12 underþêoded; ond wið þæ:m þâ ðe in ôðre wîsan dôn woldon, 13 hê wæs mid welme[12] micelre ellenwôdnisse onbærned. 14 Ond hê for ðon fægre ende his lîf bety:nde ond geendade.

[2] = swilce. [8] = lufian. [9] = nîeten. [10] = selfan. [11] = gîemde. [12] = wielme.

[Linenotes:

115.9-10: #ond hêo hine þâ monade ... munuchâd onfênge#. Hild's advice has in it the suggestion of a personal experience, for she herself had lived half of her life (thirty-three years) "before," says Bede, "she dedicated the remaining half to our Lord in a monastic life."

116.6: #hê monig lêoð geworhte#. The opinion is now gaining ground that of these "many poems" only the short hymn, already given, has come down to us. Of other poems claimed for Cædmon, the strongest arguments are advanced in favor of a part of the fragmentary poetical paraphrase of *Genesis*.]

V. ALFRED'S PREFACE TO THE PASTORAL CARE.

[Based on the Hatton MS. Of the year 597, the *Chronicle* says: "In this year, Gregory the Pope sent into Britain Augustine with very many monks, who gospelled [preached] God's word to the English folk." Gregory I, surnamed "The Great," has ever since been considered the apostle of English Christianity, and his *Pastoral Care*, which contains instruction in conduct and doctrine for all bishops, was a work that Alfred could not afford to leave untranslated. For this translation Alfred wrote a *Preface*, the historical value of which it would be hard to overrate. In it he describes vividly the intellectual ruin that the Danes had wrought, and develops at the same time his plan for repairing that ruin.

This *Preface* and the *Battle of Ashdown* (p. 99) show the great king in his twofold character of warrior and statesman, and justify the inscription on the base of the statue erected to him in 1877, at Wantage (Berkshire), his birth-place: "Ælfred found Learning dead, and he restored it; Education neglected, and he revived it; the laws powerless, and he gave them force; the Church debased, and he raised it; the Land ravaged by a fearful Enemy, from which he delivered it. Ælfred's name will live as long as mankind shall respect the Past."]

[[page 117]]

1 Ælfred kyning hâteð grêtan Wærferð biscep[1] his wordum 2 luflîce ond frêondlîce; ond ðê cy:ðan hâte ðæt mê côm 3 swîðe oft on gemynd, hwelce[2] witan îu[3] wæ:ron giond[4] 4 Angelcynn, æ:gðer ge godcundra hâda ge woruldcundra; 5 ond hû gesæ:liglîca tîda ðâ

wæ:ron giond Angelcynn; ond 6 hû ðâ kyningas ðe ðone onwald
hæfdon ðæs folces on 7 ðâm dagum Gode ond his æ:rendwrecum
hêrsumedon[5]; 8 ond hû hîe æ:gðer ge hiora sibbe ge hiora siodo[6]
ge hiora 9 onweald innanbordes gehîoldon,[4] ond êac ût hiora êðel 10
gery:mdon; ond hû him ðâ spêow æ:gðer ge mid wîge ge 11 mid
wîsdôme; ond êac ða godcundan hâdas hû giorne 12 hîe wæ:ron
æ:gðer ge ymb lâre ge ymb liornunga, ge ymb 13 ealle ðâ
ðîowotdômas ðe hîe Gode dôn scoldon; ond hû 14 man ûtanbordes
wîsdôm ond lâre hieder on lond sôhte, 15 ond hû wê hîe nû sceoldon
ûte begietan, gif wê hîe habban 16 sceoldon. Swæ:[7] clæ:ne hîo wæs
oðfeallenu on Angelcynne 17 ðæt swîðe fêawa wæ:ron behionan
Humbre ðe hiora ðêninga 18 cûðen understondan on Englisc oððe
furðum ân æ:rendgewrit 19 of Læ:dene on Englisc âreccean; ond ic
wêne ðætte 20 nôht monige begiondan Humbre næ:ren. Swæ:[7]
fêawa 21 hiora wæ:ron ðæt ic furðum ânne ânlêpne[8] ne mæg
geðencean

[[page 118]]

1 be sûðan Temese, ðâ ðâ ic tô rîce fêng. Gode ælmihtegum 2 sîe
ðonc ðætte wê nû æ:nigne onstâl habbað 3 lârêowa. Ond for ðon ic ðê
bebîode ðæt ðû dô swæ:[7] ic 4 gelîefe ðæt ðû wille, ðæt ðû ðê ðissa
woruldðinga tô ðæ:m 5 geæ:metige, swæ: ðû oftost mæge, ðæt ðû
ðone wîsdôm ðe 6 ðê God sealde ðæ:r ðæ:r ðû hiene befæstan
mæge, befæste. 7 Geðenc hwelc[9] wîtu ûs ðâ becômon for ðisse
worulde, ðâ 8 ðâ wê hit nôhwæðer nê selfe ne lufodon, nê êac ôðrum
9 monnum ne lêfdon[10]: ðone naman ânne wê lufodon ðætte 10 wê
Crîstne wæ:ren, ond swîðe fêawe ðâ ðêawas.

[1] = bisceop. [2] = hwilce. [3] = gîu. [4] = For all words with *io* (*îo*),
consult Glossary under *eo* (*êo*). [5] = hîersumedon. [6] = sidu (siodu).
[7] = swâ. [8] = ânlîpigne. [9] = hwilc. [10] = lîefdon.

[Linenotes:

117.1-2: #Ælfred kyning hâteð ... hâte#. Note the change from the
formal and official third person (#hâteð#) to the more familiar first
person (#hâte#). So Ælfric, in his *Preface to Genesis*, writes #Ælfric
munuc grêt Æðelwærd ealdormann êadmôdlîce. Þû bæ:de mê, lêof,

þæt ic#, etc.: *Ælfric, monk, greets Æthelweard, alderman, humbly. Thou, beloved, didst bid me that I,* etc.

118.5: Notice that #mæge# (l. 5) and #mæge# (l. 6) are not in the subjunctive because the sense requires it, but because they have been attracted by #gæ:metige# and #befæste#. #Sîen# (p. 119, l. 15) and #hæbben# (p. 119, l. 20) illustrate the same construction.

118.9-10: *We liked only the reputation of being Christians, very few (of us) the Christian virtues.*]

11 Ðâ ic ðâ ðis eall gemunde, ðâ gemunde ic êac hû ic 12 geseah, æ:r ðæ:m ðe hit eall forhergod wæ:re ond forbærned, 13 hû ðâ ciricean giond eall Angelcynn stôdon 14 mâðma ond bôca gefylda, ond êac micel menigeo[11] Godes 15 ðîowa; ond ðâ swîðe ly:tle fiorme ðâra bôca wiston, for 16 ðæ:m ðe hîe hiora nânwuht[12] ongietan ne meahton, for 17 ðæ:m ðe hîe næ:ron on hiora âgen geðîode awritene. 18 Swelce[13] hîe cwæ:den: "Ure ieldran, ðâ ðe ðâs stôwa æ:r 19 hîoldon, hîe lufodon wîsdôm, ond ðurh ðone hîe begêaton 20 welan, ond ûs læ:fdon. Hêr mon mæg gîet gesîon hiora 21 swæð, ac wê him ne cunnon æfter spyrigean,[14] ond for 22 ðæ:m wê habbað nû æ:gðer forlæ:ten ge ðone welan ge ðone 23 wîsdôm, for ðæ:m ðe wê noldon tô ðæ:m spore mid ûre 24 môde onlûtan."

[11] = menigu. [12] = nânwiht. [13] = swilce. [14] = spyrian.

25 Ðâ ic ðâ ðis eall gemunde, ðâ wundrade ic swîðe swîðe 26 ðâra gôdena wiotona[15] ðe gîu wæ:ron giond Angelcynn, ond 27 ðâ bêc ealla be fullan geliornod hæfdon, ðæt hîe hiora ðâ

[[page 119]]

1 næ:nne dæ:l noldon on hiora âgen geðîode wendan. Ac 2 ic ðâ sôna eft mê selfum andwyrde, ond cwæð: "Hîe ne 3 wêndon þætte æ:fre menn sceolden swæ:[7] reccelêase weorðan, 4 ond sîo lâr swæ: oðfeallan; for ðæ:re wilnunga hîe 5 hit forlêton, ond woldon ðæt hêr ðy: mâra wîsdôm on 6 londe wæ:re ðy: wê mâ geðêoda cûðon."

[7] = swâ. [15] = witena.

7 Ðâ gemunde ic hû sîo æ: wæs æ:rest on Ebrêisc geðîode 8 funden, ond eft, ðâ hîe Crêacas geliornodon, ðâ wendon 9 hîe hîe on hiora âgen geðîode ealle, ond êac ealle ôðre 10 bêc. Ond eft Læ:denware swæ: same, siððan hîe hîe geliornodon, 11 hîe hîe wendon ealla ðurh wîse wealhstôdas 12 on hiora âgen geðîode. Ond êac ealla ôðra Crîstena 13 ðîoda sumne dæ:l hiora on hiora âgen geðîode wendon. 14 For ðy: mê ðyncð betre, gif îow swæ: ðyncð, ðæt wê êac 15 suma bêc, ðâ ðe nîedbeðearfosta sîen eallum monnum 16 tô wiotonne,[16] ðæt wê ðâ on ðæt geðîode wenden ðe wê 17 ealle gecnâwan mægen, ond gedôn swæ: wê swîðe êaðe 18 magon mid Godes fultume, gif wê ðâ stilnesse habbað, 19 ðætte eall sîo gioguð ðe nû is on Angelcynne friora 20 monna, ðâra ðe ðâ spêda hæbben ðæt hîe ðæ:m befêolan 21 mægen, sîen tô liornunga oðfæste, ðâ hwîle ðe hîe tô

[[page 120]]

1 nânre ôðerre note ne mægen, oð ðone first ðe hîe wel 2 cunnen Englisc gewrit âræ:dan: læ:re mon siððan furður 3 on Læ:dengeðîode ðâ ðe mon furðor læ:ran wille, ond tô 4 hîerran hâde dôn wille. Ðâ ic ðâ gemunde hû sîo lâr 5 Læ:dengeðîodes æ:r ðissum âfeallen wæs giond Angelcynn, 6 ond ðeah monige cûðon Englisc gewrit âræ:dan, ðâ 7 ongan ic ongemang oðrum mislîcum ond manigfealdum 8 bisgum ðisses kynerîces ðâ bôc wendan on Englisc ðe is 9 genemned on Læ:den "Pastoralis," ond on Englisc "Hierdebôc," 10 hwîlum word be worde, hwîlum andgit of andgiete, 11 swæ: swæ: ic hîe geliornode æt Plegmunde mînum 12 ærcebiscepe, ond æt Assere mînum biscepe, ond æt Grimbolde 13 mînum mæsseprîoste, ond æt Iôhanne mînum mæsseprêoste. 14 Siððan ic hîe ðâ geliornod hæfde, swæ: swæ: 15 ic hîe forstôd, ond swæ: ic hîe andgitfullîcost âreccean 16 meahte, ic hîe on Englisc âwende; ond tô æ:lcum biscepstôle 17 on mînum rîce wille âne onsendan; ond on æ:lcre 18 bið ân æstel, sê bið on fîftegum mancessa. Ond ic bebîode 19 on Godes naman ðæt nân mon ðone æstel from 20 ðæ:re bêc ne dô, nê ðâ bôc from ðæ:m mynstre; uncûð hû 21 longe ðæ:r swæ: gelæ:rede biscepas sîen, swæ: swæ: nû, Gode 22 ðonc, wel hwæ:r siendon. For ðy: ic wolde ðætte hîe ealneg

[[page 121]]

1 æt ðæ:re stôwe wæ:ren, bûton sê biscep hîe mid him 2 habban wille, oððe hîo hwæ:r tô læ:ne sîe, oððe hwâ ôðre 3 bî wrîte.

[16] = witanne.

[Linenotes:

119.14: Alfred is here addressing the bishops collectively, and hence uses the plural #îow# (= #êow#), not #þê#.

119.16: #ðæt wê ðâ#. These three words are not necessary to the sense. They constitute the figure known as epanalepsis, in which "the same word or phrase is repeated after one or more intervening words." #Þâ# is the pronominal substitute for #suma bêc#.

119.17: #Gedôn# is the first person plural subjunctive (from infinitive #gedôn#). It and #wenden# are in the same construction. Two things seem "better" to Alfred: (1) *that we translate*, etc., (2) *that we cause*, etc.

119.19-21: #sîo gioguð ... is ... hîe ... sîen#. Notice how the collective noun, #gioguð#, singular at first both in form and function, gradually loses its oneness before the close of the sentence is reached, and becomes plural. The construction is entirely legitimate in Mn.E. Spanish is the only modern language known to me that condemns such an idiom: "Spanish ideas of congruity do not permit a collective noun, though denoting a plurality, to be accompanied by a plural verb or adjective in the same clause" (Ramsey, *Text-Book of Modern Spanish*, § 1452).

120.2: #læ:re mon#. See § 105, 1.

120.11-13: That none of these advisers of the king, except Plegmond, a Mercian, were natives, bears out what Alfred says about the scarcity of learned men in England when he began to reign. Asser, to whose Latin *Life of Alfred*, in spite of its mutilations, we owe almost all of our knowledge of the king, came from St. David's (in Wales), and was made Bishop of Sherborne.

121.1: Translate #æ:t ðæ:re stôwe# by *each in its place*. The change from plural #hîe# (in #hîe ... wæ:ren#) to singular #hîe# (in the clauses that follow) will thus be prepared for.

121.2-3: #oððe hwâ ôðre bî wrîte#, *or unless some one wish to copy a new one (write thereby another)*.]

POETRY.

INTRODUCTORY.

[Transcriber's Note:

In Section II., Structure, the stress markers ´ and ` are intended to display above the macron (ˉ) or breve (u or [)]). In this simplified Latin-1 text, they are shown before (to the left of) the macron:

´ˉ × `ˉ

"Resolved stress" (two short syllables acting as one long) is shown with braces:

{´u ×}

Where there is no risk of ambiguity, the breve is shown as the letter u; elsewhere it is shown in brackets as [)].]

I. HISTORY.

(a) #Old English Poetry as a Whole.#

Northumbria was the home of Old English poetry. Beginning with Cædmon and his school A.D. 670, Northumbria maintained her poetical supremacy till A.D. 800, seven years before which date the ravages of the Danes had begun. When Alfred ascended the throne of Wessex (871), the Danes had destroyed the seats of learning throughout the whole of Northumbria. As Whitby had been "the cradle of English poetry," Winchester (Alfred's capital) became now the cradle of English prose; and the older poems that had survived the fire and sword of the Vikings were translated from the original Northumbrian dialect into the West Saxon dialect. It is, therefore, in the West Saxon dialect that these poems[1] have come down to us.

Old English poetry contains in all only about thirty thousand lines; but it includes epic, lyric, didactic, elegiac, and allegorical poems, together with war-ballads, paraphrases, riddles, and charms. Of the five elegiac poems (*Wanderer, Seafarer, Ruin, Wife's Complaint*, and *Husband's Message*), the *Wanderer* is the most artistic, and best portrays the gloomy contrast between past happiness and present grief so characteristic of the Old English lyric.

Old English literature has no love poems. The central themes of its poets are battle and bereavement, with a certain grim resignation on the part of the hero to the issues of either. The movement of the thought is usually abrupt, there being a noticeable poverty of transitional particles, or connectives, "which," says Ten Brink, "are the cement of sentence-structure."

(b) #Beowulf.#

The greatest of all Old English poems is the epic, *Beowulf*.[2] It consists of more than three thousand lines, and probably assumed approximately its present form in Northumbria about A.D. 700. It is a crystallization of continental myths; and, though nothing is said of England, the story is an invaluable index to the social, political, and ethical ideals of our Germanic ancestors before and after they settled along the English coast. It is most poetical, and its testimony is historically most valuable, in the character-portraits that it contains. The fatalism that runs through it, instead of making the characters weak and less human, serves at times rather to dignify and elevate them. "Fate," says Beowulf (l. 572), recounting his battle with the sea-monsters, "often saves an undoomed man *if his courage hold out.*"

"The ethical essence of this poetry," says Ten Brink, "lies principally in the conception of manly virtue, undismayed courage, the stoical encounter with death, silent submission to fate, in the readiness to help others, in the clemency and liberality of the prince toward his thanes, and the self-sacrificing loyalty with which they reward him."

NOTE 1.--Many different interpretations have been put upon the story of *Beowulf* (for argument of story, see texts). Thus Müllenhoff sees in Grendel the giant-god of the storm-tossed equinoctial sea, while Beowulf is the Scandinavian god Freyr, who in the spring drives back the sea and restores the land. Laistner finds the prototype of Grendel in the noxious exhalations that rise from the Frisian coast-marshes during the summer months; Beowulf is the wind-hero, the autumnal storm-god, who dissipates the effluvia.

[Footnote 1: This does not, of course, include the few short poems in the *Chronicle*, or that portion of *Genesis* (*Genesis B*) supposed to have been put directly into West Saxon from an Old Saxon original. There still remain in Northumbrian the version of *Cædmon's Hymn*, fragments of the *Ruthwell Cross*, *Bede's Death-Song*, and the *Leiden Riddle*.]

[Footnote 2: The word *bêowulf*, says Grimm, meant originally *bee-wolf*, or *bee-enemy*, one of the names of the woodpecker. Sweet thinks the bear was meant. But the word is almost certainly a compound of *Bêow* (cf. O.E. #bêow# = grain), a Danish demigod, and *wulf* used as a mere suffix.]

II. STRUCTURE.

(a) #Style.#

In the structure of Old English poetry the most characteristic feature is the constant repetition of the idea (sometimes of the thought) with a corresponding variation of phrase, or epithet. When, for example, the Queen passes into the banquet hall in *Beowulf*, she is designated at first by her name, #Wealhþêow#; she is then described in turn as #cwên Hrôðgâres# (*Hrothgar's queen*), #gold-hroden# (*the gold-adorned*), #frêolîc wîf# (*the noble woman*), #ides Helminga# (*the Helmings' lady*), #bêag-hroden cwên# (*the ring-adorned queen*), #môde geþungen# (*the high-spirited*), and #gold-hroden frêolîcu folc-cwên# (*the gold-adorned, noble folk-queen*).

And whenever the sea enters largely into the poet's verse, not content with simple (uncompounded) words (such as #sæ:#, #lagu#, #holm#, #strêam#, #mere#, etc.), he will use numerous other equivalents (phrases or compounds), such as #waþema gebind# (*the commingling of waves*), #lagu-flôd# (*the sea-flood*), #lagu-stræ:t# (*the sea-street*), #swan-râd# (*the swan-road*), etc. These compounds are usually nouns, or adjectives and participles used in a sense more appositive than attributive.

It is evident, therefore, that this abundant use of compounds, or periphrastic synonyms, grows out of the desire to repeat the idea in varying language. It is to be observed, also, that the Old English poets rarely make any studied attempt to balance phrase against phrase or clause against clause. Theirs is a repetition of idea, rather than a parallelism of structure.

NOTE 1.--It is impossible to tell how many of these synonymous expressions had already become stereotyped, and were used, like many of the epithets in the *Iliad* and *Odyssey*, purely as padding. When, for example, the poet tells us that at the most critical moment Beowulf's sword failed him, adding in the same breath, #îren æ:r-gôd# (*matchless blade*), we conclude that the bard is either nodding or parroting.

(b) #Meter.#

[Re-read § 10, (3).]

Primary Stress.

Old English poetry is composed of certain rhythmically ordered combinations of accented and unaccented syllables. The accented syllable (the arsis) is usually long, and will be indicated by the macron with the acute accent over it (¯´); when short, by the breve with the same accent (´u). The unaccented syllable or syllables (the thesis) may be long or short, and will be indicated by the oblique cross (×).

Secondary Stress.

A secondary accent, or stress, is usually put upon the second member of compound and derivative nouns, adjectives, and adverbs. This will be indicated by the macron with the grave accent, if the secondary stress falls on a long syllable (ˉˋ); by the breve with the same accent, if the secondary stress falls on a short syllable (ˋu).

Nouns:

Hrôðgâres (ˊˉ ˋˉ ×), fêondgrâpum (ˊˉ ˋˉ ×), frêomæ:gum (ˊˉ ˋˉ ×), Êast-Dena (ˊˉ ˋu ×), Helminga (ˊˉ ˋˉ ×), Scyldinga (ˊˉ ˋˉ ×), ânhaga (ˊˉ ˋu ×), Ecgþêowes (ˊˉ ˋˉ ×), sinc-fato (ˊˉ ˋu ×).

Adjectives:[1]

æ:ghwylcne (ˊˉ ˋˉ ×), þrîsthy:dig (ˊˉ ˋˉ ×), gold-hroden (ˊˉ ˋu ×), drêorigne (ˊˉ ˋˉ ×), gyldenne (ˊˉ ˋˉ ×), ôðerne (ˊˉ ˋˉ ×), gæ:stlîcum (ˊˉ ˋˉ ×), wynsume (ˊˉ ˋu ×), æ:nigne (ˊˉ ˋˉ ×).

Adverbs:[2]

unsôfte (ˊˉ ˋˉ ×), heardlîce (ˊˉ ˋˉ ×), semninga (ˊˉ ˋˉ ×).

The Old English poets place also a secondary accent upon the ending of present participles (#-ende#), and upon the penultimate of weak verbs of the second class (§ 130), provided the root-syllable is long.[3]

Present participles:

slœ:pendne (ˊˉ ˋˉ ×), wîs-hycgende (ˊˉ ˊˉ ˋˉ ×), flêotendra (ˊˉ ˋˉ ×), hrêosende (ˊˉ ˋˉ ×).

Weak verbs:

swynsode (ˊˉ ˋu ×), þancode (ˊˉ ˋu ×), wânigean (ˊˉ ˋu ×), scêawian (ˊˉ ˋu ×), scêawige (ˊˉ ˋu ×), hlîfian (ˊˉ ˋu ×).

[Footnote 1: It will be seen that the adjectives are chiefly derivatives in -ig, -en, -er, -lîc, and -sum.]

[Footnote 2: Most of the adverbs belonging here end in #-lîce#, #-unga#, and #-inga#, § 93, (1), (2): such words as #æt-g[ˊæ]dere#, #on-g[ˊê]an#, #on-wég#, #tô-g[ˊê]anes#, #tô-míddes#, etc., are invariably accented as here indicated.]

[Footnote 3: It will save the student some trouble to remember that this means long by nature (#lîcodon#), or long by position (#swynsode#), or long by resolution of stress (#maðelode#),--see next paragraph.]

Resolved Stress.

A short accented syllable followed in the same word by an unaccented syllable (usually short also) is equivalent to one long accented syllable (´u × = ´‾). This is known as a resolved stress, and will be indicated thus, {´u ×};

hæleða ({´u ×}×), guman ({´u ×}), Gode ({´u ×}), sele-ful ({´u ×}×), ides ({´u ×}), fyrena ({´u ×}×), maðelode ({´u ×}´u ×), hogode ({´u ×}×), mægen-ellen ({´u ×}`‾ ×), hige-þihtigne ({´u ×}´‾ `‾ ×), Metudes ({´u ×}×), lagulâde ({´u ×}`‾ ×), unlyfigendes (´‾{´u ×}`‾ ×), biforan (×{´u ×}), forþolian (×{´u ×}×), baðian ({´u ×}×), worolde ({´u ‾} ×).

Resolution of stress may also attend secondary stresses:

sinc-fato (´‾ {`u ×}), dryht-sele (´‾ {`u ×}), ferðloca (´‾ {`u ×}), forðwege (´‾ {`u ×}).

The Normal Line.

Every normal line of Old English poetry has four primary accents, two in the first half-line and two in the second half-line. These half-lines are separated by the cesura and united by alliteration, the alliterative letter being found in the first stressed syllable of the second half-line. This syllable, therefore, gives the cue to the scansion of the whole line. It is also the only alliterating syllable in the second half-line. The first half-line, however, usually has two alliterating syllables, but frequently only one (the ratio being about three to two in the following selections). When the first half-line contains but one alliterating syllable, that syllable marks the first stress, rarely the second. The following lines are given in the order of their frequency:

(1) þæ:r wæs h['æ]leða hléahtor; hl['y]n sw['y]nsode. (2) m['ô]de gebúngen, médo-ful ætb['æ]r. (3) s['ô]na þæt onfúnde f['y]rena h['y]rde.

Any initial vowel or diphthong may alliterate with any other initial vowel or diphthong; but a consonant requires the same consonant, except st, sp, and sc, each of which alliterates only with itself.

Remembering, now, that either half-line (especially the second) may begin with several unaccented syllables (these syllables being known in types A, D, and E as the *anacrusis*), but that neither half-line can end with more than one unaccented syllable, the student may begin at once to read and properly accentuate Old English poetry. It will be found that the alliterative principle does not operate mechanically, but that the poet employs it for the purpose of emphasizing the words that are really most important. Sound is made subservient to sense.

When, from the lack of alliteration, the student is in doubt as to what word to stress, let him first get the exact meaning of the line, and then put the emphasis on the word or words that seem to bear the chief burden of the poet's thought.

NOTE 1.--A few lines, rare or abnormal in their alliteration or lack of alliteration, may here be noted. In the texts to be read, there is one line with no alliteration: *Wanderer* 58; three of the type *a* ⋯ *b* | *a* ⋯ *b*: *Beowulf* 654, 830, 2746; one of the type *a*   *a* | *b*   *a*: *Beowulf* 2711; one of the type *a* ⋯ *a* | *b* ⋯ *c*: *Beowulf* 2718; and one of the type *a* ⋯ *b* | *c* ⋯ *a*: *Beowulf* 2738.

The Five Types.

By an exhaustive comparative study of the metrical unit in Old English verse, the half-line, Professor Eduard Sievers,[4] of the University of Leipzig, has shown that there are only five types, or varieties, employed. These he classifies as follows, the perpendicular line serving to separate the so-called feet, or measures:

1. A ´‾ × | ´‾ ×

2. B × ´͟ | × ´͟

3. C × ´͟ | ´͟ ×

4. D { D^1 ´͟ | ´͟ `͟ × { D^2 ´͟ | ´͟ × `͟

5. E { E^1 ´͟ `͟ × | ´͟ { E^2 ´͟ × `͟ | ´͟

It will be seen (1) that each half-line contains two, and only two, feet; (2) that each foot contains one, and only one, primary stress; (3) that A is trochaic, B iambic; (4) that C is iambic-trochaic; (5) that D and E consist of the same feet but in inverse order.

[Footnote 4: Sievers' two articles appeared in the *Beiträge zur Geschichte der deutschen Sprache und Literatur*, Vols. X (1885) and XII (1887). A brief summary, with slight modifications, is found in the same author's *Altgermanische Metrik*, pp. 120-144 (1893).

Before attempting to employ Sievers' types, the student would do well to read several pages of Old English poetry, taking care to accentuate according to the principles already laid down. In this way his ear will become accustomed to the rhythm of the line, and he will see more clearly that Sievers' work was one primarily of systematization. Sievers himself says: "I had read Old English poetry for years exactly as I now scan it, and long before I had the slightest idea that what I did instinctively could be formulated into a system of set rules." (*Altgermanische Metrik*, Vorwort, p. 10.)]

The Five Types Illustrated.

[[Transcriber's Note: In the printed book, all examples line up vertically at the main |.]]

[All the illustrations, as hitherto, are taken from the texts to be read. The figures prefixed indicate whether first or second half-line is cited. B = *Beowulf*; W = *Wanderer*.]

1. TYPE A, ´͟ × | ´͟ ×

Two or more unaccented syllables (instead of one) may intervene between the two stresses, but only one may follow the last stress. If the thesis in either foot is the second part of a compound it receives, of course, a secondary stress.

(2) ful gesealde, B. 616, ‿̋ × | ‿̋ × (1) wîdre gewindan, B. 764, ‿̋ × × | ‿̋ × (1)[5] Gemunde þâ sê gôda, B. 759 × | ‿̋ × × × | ‿̋ × (1)[5] swylce hê on ealder-dagum, B. 758, × × × × | ‿̋ × | ´u × (1) y:þde swâ þisne eardgeard, W. 85, ‿̋ × × × × | ‿̋ `‿̋ (1) wîs-fæst wordum, B. 627, ‿̋ `̄ | ‿̋ × (1) gryre-lêoð galan, B. 787, {´u ×} `̄ | ´u × (2) somod ætgædre, W. 39, {´u ×} × | ‿̋ × (1) duguðe ond geogoðe, B. 622, {´u ×} × × | {´u ×} × (1) fæ:ger fold-bold, B. 774, ‿̋ × | ‿̋ `‿̋ (1) atelîc egesa, B. 785, {´u ×} `̄ | {´u ×} × (2) goldwine mînne, W. 22, ‿̋ {´u ×} | ‿̋ × (1) egesan þêon [> *þîhan: § 118], B. 2737, {´u ×} × | ‿̋ ×

NOTE.--Rare forms of A are ‿̋ `‿̋ × | ‿̋ × (does not occur in texts), ‿̋ `̄ × | ‿̋ `‿̋ (occurs once, B. 781 (1)), and ‿̋ × `̄ | ‿̋ × (once, B. 2743 (1)).

[Footnote 5: The first perpendicular marks the limit of the anacrusis.]

2. TYPE B, × ‿̋ | × ‿̋

Two, but not more than two, unaccented syllables may intervene between the stresses. The type of B most frequently occurring is × × ‿̋ | × ‿̋.

(1) ond þâ frêolîc wîf, B. 616, × × ‿̋ | × ‿̋ (2) hê on lust geþeah, B. 619, × × ‿̋ | × ‿̋ (2) þâ se æðeling gîong, B. 2716, × × {´u ×} | × ‿̋ (2) seah on enta geweorc, B. 2718, × × ‿̋ | × × ‿̋ (1) ofer flôda genipu, B. 2809, × × ‿̋ | × × {´u ×} (1) forþam mê wîtan ne þearf, B. 2742, × × × ‿̋ | × × ‿̋ (2) þaes þe hire se willa gelamp, B. 627, × × × × × ‿̋ | × × ‿̋ (1) forþon ne mæg weorþan wîs, W. 64, × × × × ‿̋ | × ‿̋ (1) Næ:fre ic æ:negum [= æ:n'gum] men, B. 656, × × × ‿̋ | × ‿̋

NOTE.--In the last half-line Sievers substitutes the older form #æ:ngum#, and supposes elision of the e in #Næ:fre# (= #Næ:fr-ic#: ××‿̋ | ×‿̋).

3. TYPE C, × ‿̋ | ‿̋ ×

The conditions of this type are usually satisfied by compound and derivative words, and the second stress (not so strong as the first) is frequently on a short syllable. The two arses rarely alliterate. As in B, two unaccented syllables in the first thesis are more common than one.

(1) þæt hêo on æ:nigne, B. 628, × × × ˝ | ˝ × (1) þæt ic ânunga, B. 635, × × ˊ˜ | ˝ × (2) êode gold-hroden, B. 641, × × ˝ | ´u × (1) gemyne mæ:rðo, B. 660, × {´u ×} | ˝ × (1) on þisse meodu-healle, B. 639, × × × {´u ×} | ˝ × (2) æt brimes nosan, B. 2804, × {´u ×} | ´u × (2) æt Wealhþéon [= -þêowan], B. 630, × ˝ | ˝ × (1) geond lagulâde, W. 3, × {´u ×} | ˝ × (1) Swâ cwæð eardstapa, W. 6, × × ˝ | ´u × (2) êalâ byrnwiga, W. 94, × × ˝ | ´u × (2) nô þæ:r fela bringeð, W. 54, × × {´u ×} | ˝ ×

4. TYPE D, { D^1 ˊ˜ | ˊ˜ ˋ˜ × { D^2 ˊ˜ | ˝ × ˋ˜

Both types of D may take one unaccented syllable between the two primary stresses (˝ × | ˊ˜ ˋ˜ ×, ˊ˜ × | ˝ × ˋ˜). The secondary stress in D^1 falls usually on the second syllable of a compound or derivative word, and this syllable (as in C) is frequently short.

(a) D^1 ˊ˜ | ˊ˜ ˋ˜ ×

(1) cwên Hrôðgâres, B. 614, ˊ˜ | ˊ˜ ˋ˜ × (2) dæ:l æ:ghwylcne, B. 622, ˊ˜ | ˊ˜ ˋ˜ × (1) Bêowulf maðelode, B. 632, ˝ × | {´u ×} ˋu × (2) slât unwearnum, B. 742, ˊ˜ | ˊ˜ ˋ˜ × (1) wrâþra wælsleahta, W. 7, ˊ˜ × | ˊ˜ ˋ˜ × (1) wôd wintercearig [= wint'rcearig], W. 24, ˝ | ˝ ˋu × (1) sôhte sele drêorig, W. 25, ˝ × | {´u ×} ˋ˜ × (1) ne sôhte searo-nîðas, B. 2739, × | ˊ˜ × | {´u ×} ˋ˜ ×

NOTE.--There is one instance in the texts (B. 613, (1)) of apparent ˊ˜ × × | ˊ˜ ˋu ×: #word wæ:ron wynsume#. (The triple alliteration has no significance. The sense, besides, precludes our stressing #wæ:ron#.) The difficulty is avoided by bringing the line under the A type: ˝ × × | ˊ˜ {´u ×}.

(b) D^2 ˊ˜ | ˝ × ˋ˜

(2) Forð nêar ætstôp, B. 746, ´˘ | ´˘ x `˘ (2) eorl furður stôp, B. 762, ´˘ | ´˘ x `˘ (2) Denum eallum wearð, B. 768, {´u x} | ´˘ x `˘ (1) grêtte Gêata lêod, B. 626, ´˘ x | ´˘ x `˘ (1) æ:nig yrfe-weard, B. 2732, ´˘ x | ´˘ x `˘ (1) hrêosan hrîm and snâw, W. 48, ´˘ x | ´˘ x `˘ (2) swimmað eft on weg, W. 53, ´˘ x | ´˘ x `˘

Very rarely is the thesis in the second foot expanded.

(2) þegn ungemete till, B. 2722, ´˘ | ´˘ x x x `˘ (1) hrûsan heolster biwrâh, W. 23, ´˘ x | ´˘ x x `˘

5. TYPE E, {E^1 ´˘`˘ x | ´˘ {E^2 ´˘ x `˘ | ´˘

The secondary stress in E^1 falls frequently on a short syllable, as in D^1.

(a) E^1 ´˘`˘ x | ´˘

(1) wyrmlîcum fâh, W. 98, ´˘`˘ x | ´˘ (2) medo-ful ætbær, B. 625, {´u x} `u x | ´˘ (1) sæ:-bât gesæt, B. 634, ´˘`˘ x | ´˘ (1) sige-folca swêg, B. 645, {´u x} `˘ x | ´˘ (2) Norð-Denum stôd, B. 784, ´˘`u x | ´˘ (1) fêond-grâpum fæst, B. 637, ´˘`˘ x | ´˘ (2) wyn eal gedrêas, W. 36, ´˘`˘ x | ´˘ (2) feor oft gemon, W. 90, ´˘`˘ x | ´˘

As in D^2, the thesis in the first foot is very rarely expanded.

(1) wîn-ærnes geweald, B. 655, ´˘`˘ x x | ´˘ (1) Hafa nû ond geheald, B. 659, {´u x} `˘ x x | ´˘ (1) searo-þoncum besmiðod, B. 776, {´u x} `˘ x x | {´u x}

NOTE.--Our ignorance of Old English sentence-stress makes it impossible for us to draw a hard-and-fast line in all cases between D^2 and E^1. For example, in these half-lines (already cited),

wyn eal gedrêas feor oft gemon Forð nêar ætstôp

if we throw a strong stress on the adverbs that precede their verbs, the type is D^2. Lessen the stress on the adverbs and increase it on the verbs, and we have E^1. The position of the adverbs furnishes no clue;

for the order of words in Old English was governed not only by considerations of relative emphasis, but by syntactic and euphonic considerations as well.

(*b*) E^2 ´¯ × `¯ | ´¯

This is the rarest of all types. It does not occur in the texts, there being but one instance of this type (l. 2437 (2)), and that doubtful, in the whole of *Beowulf*.

Abnormal Lines.

The lines that fall under none of the five types enumerated are comparatively few. They may be divided into two classes,
(1) hypermetrical lines, and (2) defective lines.

(1) HYPERMETRICAL LINES.

Each hypermetrical half-line has usually three stresses, thus giving six stresses to the whole line instead of two. These lines occur chiefly in groups, and mark increased range and dignity in the thought. Whether the half-line be first or second, it is usually of the A type without anacrusis. To this type belong the last five lines of the *Wanderer*. Lines 92 and 93 are also unusually long, but not hypermetrical. The first half-line of 65 is hypermetrical, a fusion of A and C, consisting of (´¯ ××× {´u ¯} | ´¯ ×).

(2) DEFECTIVE LINES.

The only defective lines in the texts are B. 748 and 2715 (the second half-line in each). As they stand, these half-lines would have to be scanned thus:

ræ:hte ongêan ´¯ × | × ´¯ bealo-nîð wêoll {´u ×} `¯ | ´¯

Sievers emends as follows:

ræ:hte tôgêanes ´¯ × × | ´¯ × = A bealo-nîðe wêoll {´u ×} ´¯ × | ´¯ = E^1

These defective half-lines are made up of syntactic combinations found on almost every page of Old English prose. That they occur so rarely in poetry is strong presumptive evidence, if further evidence were needed, in favor of the adequacy of Sievers' five-fold classification.

NOTE.--All the lines that could possibly occasion any difficulty to the student have been purposely cited as illustrations under the different types. If these are mastered, the student will find it an easy matter to scan the lines that remain.

SELECTIONS FOR READING.

VI. EXTRACTS FROM BEOWULF.

THE BANQUET IN HEOROT. [Lines 612-662.]

[The Heyne-Socin text has been closely followed. I have attempted no original emendations, but have deviated from the Heyne-Socin edition in a few cases where the Grein-Wülker text seemed to give the better reading.

The argument preceding the first selection is as follows: Hrothgar, king of the Danes, or Scyldings, elated by prosperity, builds a magnificent hall in which to feast his retainers; but a monster, Grendel by name, issues from his fen-haunts, and night after night carries off thane after thane from the banqueting hall. For twelve years these ravages continue. At last Beowulf, nephew of Hygelac, king of the Geats (a people of South Sweden), sails with fourteen chosen companions to Dane-land, and offers his services to the aged Hrothgar. "Leave me alone in the hall to-night," says Beowulf. Hrothgar accepts Beowulf's proffered aid, and before the dread hour of visitation comes, the time is spent in wassail. The banquet scene follows.]

Þæ:r wæs hæleþa hleahtor, hlyn swynsode, word wæ:ron wynsume.
Êode Wealhþêow forð, cwên Hrôðgâres, cynna gemyndig; grêtte
gold-hroden guman on healle, [615] ond þâ frêolîc wîf ful gesealde
æ:rest Êast-Dena êþel-wearde, bæd hine blîðne æt þæ:re bêor-þege,
lêodum lêofne; hê on lust geþeah symbel ond sele-ful, sige-rôf kyning.

[620] Ymb-êode þâ ides Helminga duguðe ond geogoðe dæ:l
æ:ghwylcne, sinc-fato sealde, oð þæt sæ:l âlamp þæt hîo[1] Bêowulfe,
bêag-hroden cwên, môde geþungen, medo[2]-ful ætbær; [625] grêtte
Gêata lêod, Gode þancode wîs-fæst wordum, þæs þe hire se willa
gelamp, þæt hêo on æ:nigne eorl gely:fde fyrena frôfre. Hê þæt ful
geþeah, wæl-rêow wiga, æt Wealhþêon, [630] ond þâ gyddode gûðe
gefy:sed; Bêowulf maðelode, bearn Ecgþêowes: "Ic þæt hogode, þâ ic
on holm gestâh, sæ:-bât gesæt mid mînra secga gedriht, þæt ic
ânunga êowra lêoda [635] willan geworhte, oððe on wæl crunge
fêond-grâpum fæst. Ic gefremman sceal eorlîc ellen, oððe ende-dæg
on þisse meodu[2]-healle mînne gebîdan." Þâm wîfe þâ word wel
lîcodon, [640] gilp-cwide Gêates; êode gold-hroden frêolicu folc-cwên
tô hire frêan sittan. Þâ wæs eft swâ æ:r inne on healle þry:ð-word
sprecen,[3] þêod on sæ:lum, sige-folca swêg, oþ þæt semninga [645]
sunu Healfdenes sêcean wolde æ:fen-ræste; wiste þæ:m âhlæ:can[4]
tô þæ:m hêah-sele hilde geþinged, siððan hîe sunnan lêoht gesêon *ne*
meahton oððe nîpende niht ofer ealle, [650] scadu-helma gesceapu
scrîðan cwôman,[5] wan under wolcnum. Werod eall ârâs; grêtte þâ
giddum guma ôðerne Hrôðgâr Bêowulf, ond him hæ:l âbêad,
wîn-ærnes geweald, ond þæt word âcwæð: [655] "Næ:fre ic
æ:negum[6] men æ:r âly:fde, siððan ic hond ond rond hebban mihte,
ðry:þ-ærn Dena bûton þê nû þâ. Hafa nû ond geheald hûsa sêlest,
gemyne mæ:rþo,[7] mægen-ellen cy:ð, [660] waca wið wrâðum. Ne bið
þê wilna gâd, gif þû þæt ellen-weorc aldre[8] gedîgest."

[1] = hêo. [2] = medu-. [3] = gesprecen. [4] = âglæ:can. [5] = cwômon.
[6] = æ:nigum. [7] = mæ:rþe (acc. sing.). [8] = ealdre (instr. sing.).

[Linenotes:

623: #sinc-fato sealde#. Banning (*Die epischen Formeln im Beowulf*)
shows that the usual translation, *gave costly gifts*, must be given up;
or, at least, that the *costly gifts* are nothing more than *beakers of
mead*. The expression is an epic formula for *passing the cup*.

638-39: #ende-ðæg ... mînne#. This unnatural separation of noun and
possessive is frequent in O.E. poetry, but almost unknown in prose.

641-42: #êode ... sittan#. The poet might have employed #tô sittanne# (§ 108, (1)); but in poetry the infinitive is often used for the gerund. Alfred himself uses the infinitive or the gerund to express purpose after #gân#, #gongan#, #cuman#, and #sendan#.

647-51: #wiste ... cwôman#. A difficult passage, even with Thorpe's inserted #ne#; but there is no need of putting a period after #geþinged#, or of translating #oððe# by *and*: *He (Hrothgar) knew that battle was in store* (#geþinged#) *for the monster in the high hall, after* [= *as soon as*] *they could no longer see the sun's light, or* [= *that is*] *after night came darkening over all, and shadowy figures stalking.* The subject of #cwôman# [= #cwômon#] is #niht# and #gesceapu#.

The student will note that the infinitive (#scrîðan#) is here employed as a present participle after a verb of motion (#cwôman#). This construction with #cuman# is frequent in prose and poetry. The infinitive expresses the kind of motion: #ic côm drîfan# = *I came driving.*]

THE FIGHT BETWEEN BEOWULF AND GRENDEL. [Lines 740-837.]

[The warriors all retire to rest except Beowulf. Grendel stealthily enters the hall. From his eyes gleams "a luster unlovely, likest to fire." The combat begins at once.]

Ne þæt so âglæ:ca yldan þôhte, [740] ac hê gefêng hraðe forman sîðe slæ:pendne rinc, slât unwearnum, bât bân-locan, blôd êdrum dranc, syn-snæ:dum swealh; sôna hæfde unlyfigendes eal gefeormod [745] fêt ond folma. Forð nêar ætstôp, nam þâ mid handa hige-þihtigne rinc on ræste; ræ:hte ongêan fêond mid folme; hê onfêng hraþe inwit-þancum ond wlð earm gesæt. [750] Sôna þæt onfunde fyrena hyrde, þæt hê ne mêtte middan-geardes, eorðan scêatta, on elran men mund-gripe mâran; hê on môde wearð forht, on ferhðe; nô þy: æ:r fram meahte. [755] Hyge wæs him hin-fûs, wolde on heolster flêon, sêcan dêofla gedræg; ne wæs his drohtoð þæ:r, swylce hê on ealder[1]-dagum æ:r gemêtte. Gemunde þâ se gôda mæ:g Higelâces æ:fen-spræ:ce, ûp-lang âstôd [760] ond him fæste wiðfêng; fingras burston; eoten wæs ût-weard; eorl furþur stôp. Mynte se mæ:ra, hwæ:r hê meahte swâ, wîdre gewindan ond on weg þanon flêon on fen-hopu;

wiste his fingra geweald [765] on grames grâpum. Þæt wæs gêocor
sîð, þæt se hearm-scaþa tô Heorute[2] âtêah. Dryht-sele dynede;
Denum eallum wearð ceaster-bûendum, cênra gehwylcum, eorlum
ealu-scerwen. Yrre wæ:ron bêgen [770] rêþe rên-weardas. Reced
hlynsode; þâ wæs wundor micel, þæt se wîn-sele wiðhæfde
heaþo-dêorum, þæt hê on hrûsan ne fêol, fæ:ger fold-bold; ac hê þæs
fæste wæs innan ond ûtan îren-bendum [775] searo-þoncum
besmiðod. Þæ:r fram sylle âbêag medu-benc monig, mîne gefræ:ge,
golde geregnad, þæ:r þâ graman wunnon; þæs ne wêndon æ:r witan
Scyldinga, þæt hit â mid gemete manna æ:nig, [780] betlîc ond
bân-fâg, tôbrecan meahte, listum tôlûcan, nymþe lîges fæðm swulge
on swaþule. Swêg ûp âstâg nîwe geneahhe; Norð-Denum stôd atelîc
egesa, ânra gehwylcum, [785] þâra þe of wealle wôp gehy:rdon,
gryre-lêoð galan Godes ondsacan, sige-lêasne sang, sâr wânigean
helle hæfton.[3] Hêold hine fæste, sê þe manna wæs mægene
strengest [790] on þæ:m dæge þysses lîfes. Nolde eorla hlêo æ:nige
þinga þone cwealm-cuman cwicne forlæ:tan, nê his lîf-dagas lêoda
æ:nigum nytte tealde. Þæ:r genehost bræ:gd [795] eorl Bêowulfes
ealde lâfe, wolde frêa-drihtnes feorh ealgian, mæ:res þêodnes, ðæ:r
hîe meahton swâ. Hîe ðæt ne wiston, þâ hîe gewin drugon,
heard-hicgende hilde-mecgas, [800] ond on healfa gehwone hêawan
þôhton, sâwle sêcan: þone syn-scaðan æ:nig ofer eorðan îrenna cyst,
gûþ-billa nân, grêtan nolde; ac hê sige-wæ:pnum forsworen hæfde,
[805] ecga gehwylcre. Scolde his aldor[4]-gedâl on ðæ:m dæge
þysses lîfes earmlîc wurðan[5] ond se ellor-gâst on fêonda geweald
feor sîðian. Þâ þæt onfunde, sê þe fela æ:ror [810] môdes myrðe
manna cynne fyrene gefremede (hê *wæ:s* fâg wið God), þæt him se
lîc-homa læ:stan nolde, ac hine se môdega[6] mæ:g Hygelâces hæfde
be honda; wæs gehwæþer ôðrum [815] lifigende lâð. Lîc-sâr gebâd
atol æ:glæ:ca[7]; him on eaxle wearð syn-dolh sweotol; seonowe
onsprungon; burston bân-locan. Bêowulfe wearð gûð-hrêð gyfeðe.
Scolde Grendel þonan [820] feorh-sêoc flêon under fen-hleoðu,[8]
sêcean wyn-lêas wîc; wiste þê geornor, þæt his aldres[9] wæs ende
gegongen, dôgera dæg-rîm. Denum eallum wearð æfter þâm
wæl-ræ:se willa gelumpen. [825] Hæfde þâ gefæ:lsod, sê þe æ:r
feorran côm, snotor ond swy:ð-ferhð, sele Hrôðgâres, genered wið
nîðe. Niht-weorce gefeh, ellen-mæ:rþum; hæfde Êast-Denum
Gêat-mecga lêod gilp gelæ:sted; [830] swylce oncy:ððe ealle gebêtte,
inwid-sorge, þe hîe æ:r drugon ond for þrêa-ny:dum þolian scoldon,

torn unly:tel. Þæt wæs tâcen sweotol, syððan hilde-dêor hond âlegde, [835] earm ond eaxle (þæ:r wæs eal geador Grendles grâpe) under gêapne hrôf.

[1] = ealdor-. [2] = Heorote. [3] = hæftan. [4] = ealdor-. [5] = weorðan. [6] = môdiga. [7] = âglæ:ca. [8] = -hliðu. [9] = ealdres.

[Linenotes:

740: #þæt#, the direct object of #yldan#, refers to the contest about to ensue. Beowulf, in the preceding lines, was wondering how it would result.

746: #ætstôp#. The subject of this verb and of #nam# is Grendel; the subject of the three succeeding verbs (#ræ:hte#, #onfêng#, #gesæt#) is Beowulf.

751-52: The O.E. poets are fond of securing emphasis or of stimulating interest by indirect methods of statement, by suggesting more than they affirm. This device often appears in their use of negatives (#ne#, l. 13; p. 140, l. 3; #nô#, p. 140, l. 1 [[lines 752, 757, 755]]), and in the unexpected prominence that they give to some minor detail usually suppressed because understood; as where the narrator, wishing to describe the terror produced by Grendel's midnight visits to Heorot, says (ll. 138-139), "Then was it easy to find one who elsewhere, more commodiously, sought rest for himself." It is hard to believe that the poet saw nothing humorous in this point of view.

755: #nô ... meahte#, *none the sooner could he away*. The omission of a verb of motion after the auxiliaries #magan, môtan, sculan#, and #willan# is very frequent. *Cf.* Beowulf's last utterance, p. 147, l. 17 [[line 2817]].

768: The lines that immediately follow constitute a fine bit of description by indication of effects. The two contestants are withdrawn from our sight; but we hear the sound of the fray crashing through the massive old hall, which trembles as in a blast; we see the terror depicted on the faces of the Danes as they listen to the strange sounds that issue from their former banqueting hall; by these sounds we, too, measure the progress and alternations of the combat. At last we hear only the "terror-lay" of Grendel, "lay of the beaten," and know that Beowulf has made good his promise at the banquet (#gilp gelæ:sted#).

769: #cênra gehwylcum#. The indefinite pronouns (§ 77) may be used as adjectives, agreeing in case with their nouns; but they frequently, as here, take a partitive genitive: #ânra gehwylcum#, *to each one* (= *to each of ones*); #æ:nige# (instrumental) #þinga#, *for any thing* (= *for any of things*); #on healfa gehwone#, *into halves* (= *into each of halves*); #ealra dôgra gehwâm#, *every day* (= *on each of all days*); #ûhtna gehwylce#, *every morning* (= *on each of mornings*).

780: Notice that #hit#, the object of #tôbrecan#, stands for #wîn-sele#, which is masculine. See p. 39, Note 2 [[§ 55, 2]]. #Manna# is genitive after #gemete#, not after #æ:nig#.

787-89: #gryre-lêoð ... hæfton# [= #hæftan#]. Note that verbs of hearing and seeing, as in Mn.E., may be followed by the infinitive. They heard *God's adversary sing* (#galan#) ... *hell's captive bewail* (#wânigean#). Had the present participle been used, the effect would have been, as in Mn.E., to emphasize the agent (the subject of the infinitive) rather than the action (the infinitive itself).

795-96: #þæ:r ... lâfe#. Beowulf's followers now seem to have seized their swords and come to his aid, not knowing that Grendel, having forsworn war-weapons himself, is proof against the best of swords. *Then many an earl of Beowulf's* (= *an earl of B. very often*) *brandished his sword.* That no definite earl is meant is shown by the succeeding #hîe meahton# instead of #hê meahte#. See p. 110, Note. [[Linenote 110.5-6]

799: *They did not know this* (#ðæt#), *while they were fighting*; but the first #Hîe# refers to the warriors who proffered help; the second #hîe#, to the combatants, Beowulf and Grendel. In apposition with #ðæ:t#, stands the whole clause, #þone synscaðan# (object of #grêtan#) #... nolde#. The second, or conjunctional, #ðæt# is here omitted before #þone#. See p. 112, note on ll. 18-19.

837: #grâpe# = genitive singular, feminine, after #eal#.]

BEOWULF FATALLY WOUNDED. [Lines 2712-2752.]

[Hrothgar, in his gratitude for the great victory, lavishes gifts upon Beowulf; but Grendel's mother must be reckoned with. Beowulf finds her at the sea-bottom, and after a desperate struggle slays her. Hrothgar again pours treasures into Beowulf's lap. Beowulf, having now accomplished his mission, returns to Sweden. After a reign of fifty years, he goes forth to meet a fire-spewing dragon that is ravaging his kingdom. In the struggle Beowulf is fatally wounded. Wiglaf, a loyal thane, is with him.]

Þâ sîo[1] wund ongon, þe him se eorð-draca æ:r geworhte, swêlan ond swellan. Hê þæ:t sôna onfand, þæ:t him on brêostum bealo-nîð wêoll [2715] âttor on innan. Þâ se æðeling gîong,[2] þæt hê bî wealle, wîs-hycgende, gesæt on sesse; seah on enta geweorc, hû þâ stân-bogan stapulum fæste êce eorð-reced innan healde. [2720] Hyne þâ mid handa heoro-drêorigne, þêoden mæ:rne, þegn ungemete till, wine-dryhten his wætere gelafede, hilde-sædne, ond his helm onspêon. Bîowulf[3] maðelode; hê ofer benne spræc, [2725] wunde wæl-blêate; wisse hê gearwe, þæt hê dæg-hwîla gedrogen hæfde eorðan wynne; þâ wæs eall sceacen dôgor-gerîmes, dêað ungemete nêah: "Nû ic suna mînum syllan wolde [2730] gûð-gewæ:du, þæ:r mê gifeðe swâ æ:nig yrfe-weard æfter wurde lîce gelenge. Ic ðâs lêode hêold fîftig wintra; næs se folc-cyning ymbe-sittendra œnig þâra, [2735] þe mec gûð-winum grêtan dorste, egesan ðêon. Ic on earde bâd mæ:l-gesceafta, hêold mîn tela, nê sôhte searo-nîðas, nê mê swôr fela âða on unriht. Ic ðæs ealles mæg, [2740] feorh-bennum sêoc, gefêan habban; for-þâm mê wîtan ne ðearf Waldend[4] fîra morðor-bealo[5] mâga, þonne mîn sceaceð lîf of lîce. Nû ðû lungre geong[6] hord scêawian under hârne stân, [2745] Wîglâf lêofa, nû se wyrm ligeð, swefeð sâre wund, since berêafod. Bîo[7] nû on ofoste, þæt ic æ:r-welan, gold-æ:ht ongite, gearo scêawige swegle searo-gimmas, þæt ic ðy: sêft mæge [2750] æfter mâððum-welan mîn âlæ:tan lîf ond lêod-scipe, þone ic longe hêold."

[Linenotes:

2716: #se æðeling# is Beowulf.

2718: #enta geweorc# is a stereotyped phrase for anything that occasions wonder by its size or strangeness.

2720: #healde#. Heyne, following Ettmüller, reads #hêoldon#, thus arbitrarily changing mood, tense, and number of the original. Either mood, indicative or subjunctive, would be legitimate. As to the tense, the narrator is identifying himself in time with the hero, whose wonder was "how the stone-arches ... *sustain* the ever-during earth-hall": the construction is a form of *oratio recta*, a sort of *miratio recta*. The singular #healde#, instead of #healden#, has many parallels in the dependent clauses of *Beowulf*, most of these being relative clauses introduced by #þâra þe# (= *of those that ...* + a singular predicate). In the present instance, the predicate has doubtless been influenced by the proximity of #eorð-reced#, a *quasi*-subject; and we have no more right to alter to #healden# or #hêoldon# than we have to change Shakespeare's *gives* to *give* in

"Words to the heat of deeds too cold breath *gives*." (*Macbeth*, II, i, 61.)

2722: The #þegn ungemete till# is Wiglaf, the bravest of Beowulf's retainers.

2725: #hê ofer benne spræc#. The editors and translators of *Beowulf* invariably render #ofer# in this passage by *about*; but Beowulf says not a word about his wound. The context seems to me to show plainly that #ofer# (cf. Latin *supra*) denotes here opposition = *in spite of*. We read in *Genesis*, l. 594, that Eve took the forbidden fruit #ofer Drihtenes word#. Beowulf fears (l. 2331) that he may have ruled unjustly = #ofer ealde riht#; and he goes forth (l. 2409) #ofer willan# to confront the dragon.

2731-33: #þæ:r mê ... gelenge#, *if so be that* (#þæ:r ... swâ#) *any heir had afterwards been given me* (#mê gifeðe ... æfter wurde#) *belonging to my body.*

2744-45: #geong# [= #gong#] #... scêawian#. See note on #êode ... sittan#, p. 137, ll. 19-20 [[lines 641-42]]. In Mn.E. *Go see, Go fetch,* etc., is the second verb imperative (coördinate with the first), or subjunctive (*that you may see*), or infinitive without *to*?

2751-52: #mîn ... lîf#. See note on #ende-dæg ... mînne#, p. 137, ll. 16-17 [[lines 638-39]].]

[1] = sêo. [2] = gêong. [3] = Bêowulf. [4] = Wealdend. [5] = morðor-bealu. [6] = gong (gang). [7] = Bêo.

BEOWULF'S LAST WORDS. [Lines 2793-2821.]

[Wiglaf brings the jewels, the tokens of Beowulf's triumph. Beowulf, rejoicing to see them, reviews his career, and gives advice and final directions to Wiglaf.]

Bîowulf[1] maðelode, gomel on giohðe (gold scêawode): "Ic þâra frætwa Frêan ealles ðanc, [2795] Wuldur-cyninge, wordum secge ecum Dryhtne, þe ic hêr on starie, þæs þe ic môste mînum lêodum æ:r swylt-dæge swylc gestry:nan. Nû ic on mâðma hord mîne bebohte [2800] frôde feorh-lege, fremmað gê nû lêoda þearfe; ne mæg ic hêr leng wesan. Hâtað heaðo-mæ:re hlæ:w gewyrcean, beorhtne æfter bæ:le æt brimes nosan; sê scel[2] tô gemyndum mînum lêodum [2805] hêah hlîfian on Hrones næsse, þæt hit sæ:-lîðend syððan hâtan[3] Bîowulfes[1] biorh[1] þâ þe brentingas ofer flôda genipu feorran drîfað." Dyde him of healse hring gyldenne [2810] þîoden[1] þrîst-hy:dig; þegne gesealde, geongum gâr-wigan, gold-fâhne holm, bôah ond byrnan, hêt hyne brûcan well. "Þû eart ende-lâf ûsses cynnes, Wæ:gmundinga; ealle wyrd forswêop [2815] mîne mâgas tô metod-sceafte, eorlas on elne; ic him æfter sceal." Þæt wæs þâm gomelan gingeste word brêost-gehygdum, æ:r hê bæ:l cure, hâte heaðo-wylmas; him of hreðre gewât [2820] sâwol sêcean sôð-fæstra dôm.

[1] îo, io = êo, eo. [2] = sceal. [3] = hâten.

[Linenotes:

2795-99: The expression #secgan þanc# takes the same construction as #þancian#; i.e., the dative of the person (#Frêan#) and the genitive (a genitive of cause) of the thing (#þâra frætwa#). Cf. note on #biddan#, p. 45 [[§ 65, 3]]. The antecedent of #þe# is #frætwa#. For the position of #on#, see § 94, (5). The clause introduced by #þæs þe# (*because*) is parallel in construction with #frætwa#, both being causal modifiers of #secge þanc#. The Christian coloring in these lines betrays the influence of priestly transcribers.

2800: *Now that I, in exchange for* (#on#) *a hoard of treasures, have bartered* (#bebohte#) *the laying down* (#-lege# > #licgan#) *of my old life.* The ethical codes of the early Germanic races make frequent mention of blood-payments, or life-barters. There seems to be here a suggestion of the "wergild."

2801: #fremmað gê#. The plural imperative (as also in #Hâtað#) shows that Beowulf is here speaking not so much to Wiglaf in particular as, through Wiglaf, to his retainers in general,--to his *comitatus*.

2806: The desire for conspicuous burial places finds frequent expression in early literatures. The tomb of Achilles was situated "high on a jutting headland over wide Hellespont that it might be seen from off the sea." Elpenor asks Ulysses to bury him in the same way. Æneas places the ashes of Misenus beneath a high mound on a headland of the sea.

2807: #hit = hlæ:w#, which is masculine. See p. 39, Note 2 [[§ 55, 2]].

2810-11: #him ... þîoden#. The reference in both cases is to Beowulf, who is disarming himself (#do-of# > *doff*) for the last time; #þegne# = *to Wiglaf.*

Note, where the personal element is strong, the use of the dative instead of the more colorless possessive; #him of healse#, not #of his healse#.

2817: #ic ... sceal#. See note on #nô ... meahte#, p. 140, l. 1 [[line 755]].

2820: #him of hreðre#. Cf. note on #him ... þîoden#, p. 147, ll. 10-11 [[lines 2810-11]].

2820-21: For construction of #gewât ... sêcean#, see note on #êode ... sittan#, p. 137, ll. 19-20 [[lines 641-42]].]

VII. THE WANDERER.

[Exeter MS. "The epic character of the ancient lyric appears especially in this: that the song is less the utterance of a momentary feeling than the portrayal of a lasting state, perhaps the reflection of an entire life, generally that of one isolated, or bereft by death or exile of protectors and friends." (Ten Brink, *Early Eng. Lit.*, I.) I adopt Brooke's threefold division (*Early Eng. Lit.*, p. 356): "It opens with a Christian prologue, and closes with a Christian epilogue, but the whole body of the poem was written, it seems to me, by a person who thought more of the goddess Wyrd than of God, whose life and way of thinking were uninfluenced by any distinctive Christian doctrine."

The author is unknown.]

PROLOGUE.

Oft him ânhaga âre gebîdeð, Metudes[1] miltse, þêah þe hê môdcearig geond lagulâde longe sceolde hrêran mid hondum hrîmcealde sæ:, wadan wræclæ:stas: wyrd bið ful âræ:d! [5] Swâ cwæð eardstapa earfeþa[2] gemyndig, wrâþra wælsleahta, winemæ:ga hryres:

PLAINT OF THE WANDERER.

"Oft ic sceolde âna ûhtna gehwylce mîne ceare cwîþan; nis nû cwicra nân, þe ic him môdsefan mînne durre [10] sweotule[3] âsecgan. Ic tô sôþe wât þæt biþ in eorle indryhten þêaw, þæt hê his ferðlocan fæste binde, healde his hordcofan, hycge swâ hê wille; ne mæg wêrig môd wyrde wiðstondan [15] nê sê hrêo hyge helpe gefremman: for ðon dômgeorne drêorigne oft in hyra brêostcofan bindað fæste. Swâ ic môdsefan mînne sceolde oft earmcearig êðle bidæ:led, [20] frêomæ:gum feor feterum sæ:lan, siþþan gêara iû goldwine mînne hrûsan heolster biwrâh, and ic hêan þonan wôd wintercearig ofer

waþema gebind, sôhte sele drêorig sinces bryttan, [25] hwæ:r ic feor
oþþe nêah findan meahte þone þe in meoduhealle[4] miltse wisse
oþþe mec frêondlêasne frêfran wolde, wenian mid wynnum. Wât sê þe
cunnað hû slîþen bið sorg tô gefêran [30] þâm þe him ly:t hafað lêofra
geholena: warað hine wræclâst, nâles wunden gold, ferðloca frêorig,
nâlæs foldan blæ:d; gemon hê selesecgas and sincþege, hû hine on
geoguðe his goldwine [35] wenede tô wiste: wyn eal gedrêas! For þon
wât sê þe sceal his winedryhtnes lêofes lârcwidum longe forþolian,
ðonne sorg and slæ:p somod ætgædre earmne ânhagan oft gebindað:
[40] þinceð him on môde þæt hê his mondryhten clyppe and cysse,
and on cnêo lecge honda and hêafod, swâ hê hwîlum æ:r in
gêardagum giefstôles brêac; ðonne onwæcneð eft winelêas guma, [45]
gesihð him biforan fealwe wæ:gas, baþian brimfuglas, bræ:dan feþra,
hrêosan hrîm and snâw hagle gemenged. Þonne bêoð þy: hefigran
heortan benne, sâre æfter swæ:sne; sorg bið genîwad; [50] þonne
mâga gemynd môd geondhweorfeð, grêteð glîwstafum, georne
geondscêawað. Secga geseldan swimmað eft on weg; flêotendra
ferð[5] nô þæ:r fela bringeð cûðra cwidegiedda; cearo[6] bið genîwad
[55] þâm þe sendan sceal swîþe geneahhe ofer waþema gebind
wêrigne sefan. For þon ic geþencan ne mæg geond þâs woruld for
hwan môdsefa mîn ne gesweorce, þonne ic eorla lîf eal geondþence,
[60] hû hî fæ:rlîce flet ofgêafon, môdge maguþegnas. Swâ þês
middangeard ealra dôgra gehwâm drêoseð and fealleþ; for þon ne
mæg weorþan wîs wer, æ:r hê âge wintra dæ:l in woruldrîce. Wita
sceal geþyldig, [65] ne sceal nô tô hâtheort nê tô hrædwyrde, nê tô
wâc wiga nê tô wanhy:dig, nê tô forht nê tô fægen nê tô feohgîfre, nê
næ:fre gielpes tô georn, æ:r hê geare cunne. Beorn sceal gebîdan,
þonne hê bêot spriceð, [70] oþ þæt collenferð cunne gearwe hwider
hreþra gehygd hweorfan wille. Ongietan sceal glêaw hæle hû gæ:stlîc
bið, þonne eall þisse worulde wela wêste stondeð, swâ nû missenlîce
geond þisne middangeard [75] winde biwâune[7] weallas stondaþ,
hrîme bihrorene,[8] hryðge þâ ederas. Wôriað þâ wînsalo,[9] waldend
licgað drêame bidrorene[10]; duguð eal gecrong wlonc bî wealle: sume
wîg fornôm, [80] ferede in forðwege; sumne fugel[11] oþþær ofer
hêanne holm; sumne sê hâra wulf dêaðe gedæ:lde; sumne
drêorighlêor in eorðscræfe eorl gehy:dde: y:þde swâ þisne eardgeard
ælda Scyppend, [85] oþ þæt burgwara breahtma lêase eald enta
geweorc îdlu stôdon. Sê þonne þisne wealsteal wîse geþôhte, and þis
deorce lîf dêope geondþenceð, frôd in ferðe[12] feor oft gemon [90]

wælsleahta worn, and þâs word âcwið: 'Hwæ:r cwôm mearg? hwæ:r cwôm mago[13]? hwæ:r cwôm mâþþumgyfa? hwæ:r cwôm symbla gesetu? hwæ:r sindon seledrêamas? Êalâ beorht bune! êalâ byrnwiga! êalâ þêodnes þrym! hû sêo þrâg gewât, [95] genâp under nihthelm, swâ hêo nô wæ:re! Stondeð nû on lâste lêofre duguþe weal wundrum hêah, wyrmlîcum fâh: eorlas fornômon asca þry:þe, wæ:pen wælgîfru, wyrd sêo mæ:re; [100] and þâs stânhleoþu[14] stormas cnyssað; hrîð hrêosende hrûsan bindeð, wintres wôma, þonne won cymeð, nîþeð nihtscûa, norþan onsendeð hrêo hæglfare hæleþum on andan. [105] Eall is earfoðlîc eorþan rîce, onwendeð wyrda gesceaft weoruld under heofonum: hêr bið feoh læ:ne, hêr bið frêond læ:ne, hêr bið mon læ:ne, hêr bið mæ:g læ:ne; eal þis eorþan gesteal îdel weorþeð!'" [110]

EPILOGUE.

Swâ cwæð snottor on môde, gesæt him sundor æt rune. Til biþ sê þe his trêowe gehealdeð; ne sceal næ:fre his torn tô rycene beorn of his brêostum âcy:þan, nemþe hê æ:r þâ bôte cunne; eorl mid elne gefremman. Wel bið þâm þe him âre sêceð, frôfre tô Fæder on heofonum, þæ:r ûs eal sêo fæstnung stondeð. [115]

[1] = Metodes. [2] = earfoþa. [3] = sweotole. [4] = medu-. [5] = ferhð. [6] = cearu. [7] See bewâwan. [8] See behrêosan. [9] = wînsalu. [10] See bedrêosan. [11] = fugol. [12] = ferhðe. [13] = magu. [14] = -hliðu.

[Linenotcs:

7: The MS. reading is #hryre# (nominative), which is meaningless.

8: For #ûhtna gehwylce#, see note on #cênra gehwylcum#, p. 140 [[*Beowulf* 769]].

10: #þe ... him#. See § 75 (4). Cf. *Merchant of Venice*, II, v, 50-51.

27: For #mine# (MS. #in#), which does not satisfy metrical requirements, I adopt Kluge's plausible substitution of #miltse#; #miltse witan# = *to show* (*know, feel*), *pity*. The #myne wisse# of *Beowulf* (l. 169) is metrically admissible.

37: The object of #wât# is #þinceð him on môde#; but the construction is unusual, inasmuch as both #þæt's# (#þæt# pronominal before #wât# and #þæt# conjunctional before #þinceð#) are omitted. See p. 112, ll. 18-19.

41: #þinceð him on môde# (see note on #him ... þîoden#, p. 147 [[*Beowulf* 2810-11]]). "No more sympathetic picture has been drawn by an Anglo-Saxon poet than where the wanderer in exile falls asleep at his oar and dreams again of his dead lord and the old hall and revelry and joy and gifts,--then wakes to look once more upon the waste of ocean, snow and hail falling all around him, and sea-birds dipping in the spray." (Gummere, *Germanic Origins*, p. 221.)

53-55: #Secga ... cwidegiedda# = *But these comrades of warriors* [= those seen in vision] *again swim away* [= *fade away*]; *the ghost of these fleeting ones brings not there many familiar words*; i.e. he sees in dream and vision the old familiar faces, but no voice is heard: they bring neither greetings to him nor tidings of themselves.

65: #Wita sceal geþyldig#. Either #bêon# (#wesan#) is here to be understood after #sceal#, or #sceal# alone means *ought to be*. Neither construction is to be found in Alfredian prose, though the omission of a verb of motion after #sculan# is common in all periods of Old English. See note on #nô ... meahte#, p. 140 [[*Beowulf* 755]].

75: #swâ nû#. "The Old English lyrical feeling," says Ten Brink, citing the lines that immediately follow #swâ nû#, "is fond of the image of physical destruction"; but I do not think these lines have a merely figurative import. The reference is to a period of real devastation, antedating the Danish incursions. "We might fairly find such a time in that parenthesis of bad government and of national tumult which filled the years between the death of Aldfrith in 705 and the renewed peace of Northumbria under Ceolwulf in the years that followed 729." (Brooke, *Early Eng. Lit.*, p. 355.)

93: #cwôm ... gesetu#. Ettmüller reads #cwômon#; but see p. 107, note on #wæs ... þâ îgland# [[linenote 107.14-15]]. The occurrence of #hwæ:r cwôm# three times in the preceding line tends also to hold #cwôm# in the singular when its plural subject follows. Note the influence of a somewhat similar structural parallelism in *seas hides* of these lines (*Winter's Tale*, IV, iv, 500-502):

"Not for ... all the *sun sees* or The close *earth wombs* or the profound *seas hides* In unknown fathoms, will I break my oath."

111: #gesæt ... rûne#, *sat apart to himself in silent meditation.*

114: #eorl ... gefremman#. Supply #sceal# after #eorl#.]

I. GLOSSARY.

OLD ENGLISH--MODERN ENGLISH.

[The order of words is strictly alphabetical, except that ð follows t. The combination æ follows ad.

Gender is indicated by the abbreviations, m. (= masculine), f. (= feminine), n. (= neuter). The usual abbreviations are employed for the cases, nom., gen., dat., acc., and instr. Other abbreviations are sing. (= singular), pl. (= plural), ind. (= indicative mood), sub. (= subjunctive mood), pres. (= present tense), pret. (= preterit tense), prep. (= preposition), adj. (= adjective), adv. (= adverb), part. (= participle), conj. (= conjunction), pron. (= pronoun), intrans. (= intransitive), trans. (= transitive).

Figures not preceded by § refer to page and line of the texts.]

[[Transcriber's Note: References to verse selections (pages 136-153) are followed by the actual line number in [[double brackets]].]

#A.#

â, *ever, always, aye.* abbudisse, f., *abbess* [Lat. abbatissa]. âbêodan (§ 109), *bid, offer;* him hæ:l âbêad 138, 9 [[*Beowulf* 654]] = *bade him hail, wished him health.* âbrecan (§ 120, Note 2), *break down, destroy.* âbûgan (§ 109, Note 1), *give way, start* [bow away]. ac, conj., *but.* âcweðan (§ 115), *say, speak.* âcy:ðan (§ 126), *reveal, proclaim* [cûð]. âd, m., *funeral pile.* adesa, m., *adze, hatchet.* æ: (æ:w), f., *law.* æ:dre

(êdre), f., *stream, canal, vein*; blôd êdrum dranc 139, 4 [[*Beowulf* 743]]
= *drank blood in streams* (instr.). æ:fæstnis, f., *piety.* æ:fen-ræst, f.,
evening rest. æ:fen-spræ:c, f., *evening speech.* æ:f[e,]st (æ:wf[e,]st),
law-abiding, pious. æ:f[e,]stnis, see æ:fæstnis. æ:fre, *ever, always.*
æ:fter, prep. (§ 94, (1)), *after*; æ:fter ðæ:m, *after that, thereafter*; æfter
ðæ:m ðe, conj., *after.* æfter, adv., *after, afterwards.* æ:ghwâ (§ 77,
Note), *each, every.* æ:ghwilc (§ 77, Note), *each, any.* æ:glæ:ca, see
âglæ:ca. æ:gðer (æ:ghwæðer, âðer) (§ 77, Note), *each, either*; æ:gðer
... ôðer ... ôðer, *either ... or ... or*; æ:gðer ge ... ge (§ 95, (2)), *both ...
and*; æ:gðer ge ... ge ... ge, *both ... and ... and.* æ:ht, f., *property,
possession* [âgan]. æ:lc (§ 77), *each.* ælde (ielde) (§ 47), m. pl., *men*;
gen. pl., ælda. ælmihtig, *almighty.* æ:metta, m., *leisure* [*empti*-ness].
æ:nig (§ 77), *any*; æ:nige ðinga 141, 22 [[*Beowulf* 792]] = *for anything.*
(See 140, 15 [[*Beowulf* 769]], Note.) æ:r, adv., *before, formerly,
sooner*; nô þy: æ:r 140, 1 [[*Beowulf* 755]] = *none the sooner*; æ:ror,
comparative, *before, formerly*; æ:rest, superlative, *first.* æ:r, conj. (§
105, 2), *ere, before* = æ:r ðæ:m ðe. æ:r, prep, with dat., *before* (time);
æ:r ðæ:m ðe, conj. (§ 105, 2), *before.* ærcebisceop, m., *archbishop*
[Lat. archiepiscopus]. æ:rendgewrit, n., *message, letter.* æ:rendwreca
(-raca), m., *messenger.* æ:rest, adj. (§ 96, (4)), *first.* ærnan (§ 127),
ride, gallop [iernan]. æ:rra, adj. (§ 96, (4)), *former.* æ:rwela, m., *ancient
wealth.* æsc, m., *ash, spear*; gen. pl., asca. Æscesdûn, f., *Ashdown* (in
Berkshire). æstel, m., *book-mark* [Lat. hastula]. æt (§ 94, (1)), *at, in*;
with leornian, *to learn*, geðicgan, *to receive*, and other verbs of similar
import, æt = *from*: 115, 18; 137, 8 [[*Beowulf* 630]], etc. ætberan (§
114), *bear to, hand.* ætgæd(e)re, adv., *together.* ætsteppan (§ 116),
step up, advance; pret. sing., ætstôp. æðele, *noble, excellent.* æðeling,
m., *a noble, prince.* Æðelwulfing, m., *son of Ethelwulf.* Æðered, m.,
Ethelred. âfeallan (§ 117), *fall.* âfierran (§ 127), *remove* [feor]. âgan (§
136), *to own, possess.* âgen, adj.-part., *own*; dat. sing., âgnum [âgan].
âgiefan (§ 115), *give back.* âglæ:ca (æ:glæ:ca), m., *monster,
champion.* âhton, see âgan. âlæ:tan (§ 117), *let go, leave.* aldor, see
ealdor. âl[e,]cgan (§ 125, Note), *lay down* [licgan]; past part., âlêd.
Âlîesend, m., *Redeemer* [âlîesan = *release, ransom*]. âlimpan (§ 110),
befall, occur. âly:fan (§ 126), *entrust, permit.* ambor, m., *measure*; gen.
pl., ambra (§ 27, (4)). ambyre, *favorable.* ân (§ 89), *one*; âna, *alone,
only*; ânra gehwylcum 141, 15 [[*Beowulf* 785]] = *to each one.* (See 140,
15, Note. [[*Beowulf* 769]]) anda, m., *zeal, injury, indignation*; hæleðum
on andan 153, 6 [[*Wanderer* 105]] = *harmful to men.* andêfn, f.,

proportion, amount. andgiet (-git), n., *sense, meaning.* andgitfullîce, *intelligibly*; -gitfullîcost, *superlative.* andswaru, f., *answer.* andwyrdan (§ 127), *to answer*; pret., andwyrde. Angel, n., *Anglen* (in Denmark); dat. sing., Angle (§ 27 (4)). Angelcynn, n., *English kin, English people, England.* ânhaga (-hoga), m., *a solitary, wanderer* [ân + hogian, *to meditate*]. ânlîpig, *single, individual.* ânunga (§ 93, (2)), *once for all* [ân]. apostol, m., *apostle* [Gr. +apostolos+]. âr, f., *honor, property, favor*; âre gebîdeð 148, 3 [[*Wanderer* 1]] = *waits for divine favor* (gen.). âræ:d, adj., *inexorable.* âræ:dan (§ 126), *read.* âr[e,]cc(e)an (§ 128), *translate, expound.* ârfæstnis, f., *virtue.* ârîsan (§ 102), *arise.* asca, see aesc. âs[e,]cgan (§ 132), *say, relate.* âs[e,]ttan (§ 127), *set, place.* âsingan (§ 110), *sing.* âsp[e,]ndan (§ 127), *spend, expend.* âstîgan (§ 102), *ascend, arise.* âst[o,]ndan (§ 116), *stand up.* âtêah, see âtêon. atelîc, *horrible, dire.* âtêon (§ 118), *draw, draw away, take* (as a journey). atol, *horrible, dire.* âttor, n., *poison.* âtuge, see âtêon. âð, m., *oath.* âðer, see æ:gðer. âw[e,]ccan (§ 128), *awake, arouse*; pret. sing., âweahte, âw[e,]hte. aweg, *away.* âw[e,]ndan (§ 127), *turn, translate.* âwrîtan (§ 102), *write, compose.* âwyrcan (§ 128), *work, do, perform.*

#B.#

Bâchs[e,]cg, m., *Bagsac.* bæcbord, n., *larboard, left side of a ship.* bæ:l, n., *funeral fire, funeral pile.* bân, n., *bone.* bân-fâg, *adorned with bones* or *antlers.* bân-loca, m., *flesh* [bone-locker]. Basengas, m. pl., *Basing* (in Hantshire). be (bî) (§ 94, (1)), *by, about, concerning, near, along, according to*; be norðan þæ:m wêstenne (§ 94, (1)), *north of the waste (desert)*; be fullan, *fully, perfectly.* bêag, see bûgan. bêag-hroden, *ring-adorned.* bêah (bêag), m., *ring, bracelet, collar* [bûgan]. bealo-nîð, m., *dire hatred, poison, venom.* bearn, n., *child, son* [bairn]. bebêodan (§ 109), *command, bid, entrust* (with dat.). bebîo-, see bebêo-. bebohte, see bebycgan. bebycgan (§ 128), *sell.* bêc, see bôc. becuman (§ 114), *come, arrive, befall.* bedæ:lan (§ 126), *separate, deprive.* bedrêosan (§ 109), *deprive*; past part. pl., bedrorene (bidrorene) [dross, dreary]. befæ:stan (§ 127), *fasten, implant.* befêolan (§ 110), *apply one's self*; ðâra ðe ðâ spêda hæbben ðæ:t hîe ðæ:m befêolan mægen 119, 20 = *of those who have the means by which they may apply themselves to it.* beforan, prep. with dat., *before.* bêgen (declined like twêgen, § 89), *both.* begeondan (begiondan), prep. with dat., *beyond.* begietan (§ 115), *get, obtain, find.* beginnan (§ 110), *begin.* beheonan (behionan), prep. with dat., *on this side of.* behreôsan (§ 109), *fall upon, cover*; past part. pl., behrorene (bihrorene). belimpan (§ 110), *pertain, belong.* beniman (§ 114), *take, derive.* b[e,]nn, f., *wound* [bana = *murderer*]. bêon (bîon) (§ 134), *be, consist.* beorh (beorg, biorh), m., *mound* [barrow]. beorht, *bright, glorious.* Beormas, m. pl., *Permians.* beorn, m., *man, hero, chief.* bêor-þ[e,]gu, f., *beer-drinking* [þicgan = *receive*]. bêot, n., *boast.* beran (§ 114), *bear.* berêafian (§ 130), *bereave*; since berêafod 145, 22 [[*Beowulf* 2747]] = *bereft of treasure.* beren, adj., *of a bear, bear.* berstan (§ 110), *burst, crack.* besmiðian (§ 130), *make hard* (as at the forge of a smith). b[e,]t, see wel (§ 97, (2)). bêtan (§ 126), *make good, requite*; past part. pl., gebêtte. b[e,]tera (b[e,]tra), see gôd (§ 96, (3)). betlîc, *excellent.* b[e,]tsta, see gôd (§ 96, (3)). betuh (betux) (§ 94, (1)), *between.* betwêonan (§ 94, (1)), *between.* bety:nan (§ 126), *close, end* [tûn = *enclosure*]. bewâwan (§ 117), *blow upon*; past part. pl., bewâune (biwâune, bewâwene). bewrêon (§ 118, 1), *enwrap*; pret. 3d sing., bewrâh (biwrâh). bî, see be. bi-, see be-. bîdan (§ 102), *bide, await, expect, endure* (with gen.). biddan (§ 115, Note 2), *bid, pray, request* (§ 65, Note 3); bæd hine blîône 136, 7 [[*Beowulf* 618]] = *bade him be blithe.* bindan (§ 110), *bind.* bîo, see bêo (imperative sing.). bisceop (biscep), m., *bishop* [Lat. episcopus]. bisceop-stôl, m., *episcopal seat, bishopric.* bisigu, f., *business, occupation*; dat. pl., bisgum. bîtan (§ 102), *bite, cut.* biwrâh, see bewrêon. blæ:d, m., *glory, prosperity* [blâwan = *blow, inflate*]. Blêcinga-êg, f., *Blekingen.* bliss, f., *bliss* [blîðe]. blîðe, *blithe, happy.* blôd, n., *blood.* bôc (§ 68, (1), Note 1), f., *book.* bôcere, m., *scribe* [bôc]. b[o,]na (bana), m., *murderer* [bane]. bôt, f., *boot, remedy, help, compensation.* brâd (§ 96, (1)), *broad.* bræ:dan (§ 126), *extend, spread* [brâd]. bræ:dra, see brâd. brægd, see bregdan. brêac, see brûcan. breahtm, m., *noise, revelry*; burgwara breahtma lêase 152, 10 [[*Wanderer* 86]] = *bereft of the revelries of citizens.* bregdan (§ 110), *brandish, draw* [braid]; pret. ind. 3d sing., brægd. brenting, m., *high ship.* brêost, n., *breast* (the pl. has the same meaning as the sing.). brêost-cofa, m., *breast-chamber, heart, mind.* brêost-gehygd, n., *breast-thought, thought of the heart, emotion.* brim, n., *sea, ocean.* brimfugol, m., *sea-fowl.* bringan (§ 128), *bring.* brôhte, brôhton, see bringan. brôðor (brôður) (§ 68, (2)), m., *brother.* brûcan (§ 109, Note 1), *use, enjoy* (§ 62, Note 1; but Alfred frequently employs the acc. with brûcan). brycg, f., *bridge.* bry:cð, see brûcan. brytta, m., *distributor, dispenser* [brêotan = *break in pieces*]. bûan (§ 126, Note 2),

dwell, cultivate [bower]. bûde, see bûan. bufan, prep. with dat. and
acc., *above.* bûgan (§ 109, Note 1), *bow, bend, turn.* bune, f., *cup.*
burg (burh) (§ 68, (1), Note), f., *city, borough*; dat. sing., byrig.
Burgenda, m. gen. pl., *of the Burgundians*; Burgenda land, *Bornholm.*
burgware (§ 47), m. pl., *burghers, citizens.* burh, see burg. bûtan
(bûton), prep. (§ 94, (1)), *without, except, except for, but.* bûtan
(bûton), conj., *except that, unless.* bûtû, *both* (= *both--two.* The word is
compounded of the combined neuters of bêgen and twêgen, but is m.
and f. as well as n.). by:n (§ 126, Note 2), *cultivated.* byrde, adj., *of
high rank, aristocratic.* byrig, see burg. byrne, f., *byrnie, corselet, coat
of mail.* byrnwiga, m., *byrnie-warrior, mailed soldier.* byrð, see beran.

#C.#

canôn, m., *sacred canon, Bible* [Lat. canon, Gr. +kanôn+]. cearu
(cearo), f., *care.* ceaster-bûend, m., *castle-dweller.* cêne, *keen, bold,
brave.* cêosan (§ 109), *choose, accept, encounter.* cild, n., *child.* cirice,
f., *church*; nom. pl., ciricean. cirr (cierr), m., *turn, time, occasion* [char,
chore, ajar = on char, on the turn]. cirran (§ 127), *turn.* clæ:ne, *clean,
pure.* clæ:ne, adv., *entirely* ["clean out of the way," Shaks.]. clûdig,
rocky [having boulders or masses like *clouds*]. clyppan (§ 127),
embrace, accept [clip = clasp for letters, papers, etc.]. cnapa, m., *boy*
[knave]. cnêo (cnêow), n., *knee*; acc. pl., cnêo. cniht, m., *knight,
warrior.* cnyssan (§ 125), *beat.* collenferð (-ferhð), *proud-minded,
fierce.* costnung, f., *temptation.* Crêcas (Crêacas), m. pl., *Greeks.*
cringan (§ 110), *cringe, fall.* Crîst, m., *Christ.* Crîsten, *Christian*; nom.
pl. m., Crîstene, Crîstne. cuma, m., *new-comer, stranger.* cuman (§
114), *come.* (See p. 138, Note on ll. 2-6.) cunnan (§ 137), *know, can,
understand.* cunnian (§ 130), *make trial of, experience* [cunnan]. cure,
see cêosan. cûð, *well-known, familiar* [past part. of cunnan: cf.
uncouth]. cüðe, cüðen, cüðon, see cunnan. cwæ:den, cwæ:don, see
cweðan. cwalu, f., *death, murder* [cwelan]. cwealm-cuma, m.,
murderous comer. cwelan (§ 114), *die* [to quail]. cwên, f., *queen.*
Cwênas, m. pl., *a Finnish tribe.* cweðan (§ 115), *say, speak* [quoth,
bequeath]. cwic, *living, alive* [quicksilver; the quick and the dead].
cwidegiedd, n., *word, utterance* [cweðan and gieddian, both meaning
to speak]. cwîðan (§ 126), *bewail* (trans.). cwôm, see cuman. cyle
(ciele), m., *cold* [chill]; cyle gewyrcan 110, 7 = *produce cold, freeze.*
cyme, m., *coming* [cuman]. cyn(n), n., *kin, race.* cyn(n), adj. (used only

in pl.), *fitting things, etiquette, proprieties, courtesies*; cynna gemyndig 136, 3 [[*Beowulf* 614]] = *mindful of courtesies*. cynerîce, n., *kingdom*. cyning, m., *king*. cyssan (§ 125), *kiss*. cyst, f., *the choice, the pick, the best* [cêosan]. cy:ðan (§ 126), *make known, display*, [cûð]; 2d sing. imperative, cy:ð.

#D.#

dæ:d, f., *deed*. dæg, m., *day*. dæg-hwîl, f., *day-while, day*; hê dæg-hwîla gedrogen hæfde eorðan wynne 145, 2 [[*Beowulf* 2727]] = *he had spent his days of earth's joy*. dæg-rîm, n., number of days [day-rime]; dôgera daeg-rîm 143, 7 [[*Beowulf* 824]] = *the number of his days*. dæl, n., *dale*. dæ:l, m., *part, deal, division*. dêad, *dead*. dêað, m., *death*. dêman (§ 126), *deem, judge*. D[e,]namearc, see D[e,]nemearc. D[e,]ne (§ 47), m. pl., *Danes*. D[e,]nemearc (D[e,]nemearce), f., *Denmark*; dat. sing., D[e,]nemearce (strong), D[e,]nemearcan (weak). D[e,]nisc, *Danish*; ðâ D[e,]niscan, *the Danes*. dêofol, m., n., *devil*; gen. sing., dêofles (§ 27, (4)). dêope, *deeply, profoundly* [dêop]. dêor, n., *wild animal* [deer]. deorc, *dark, gloomy*. dôgor, n., *day*; gen. pl., dôgora, dôgera, dôgra. dôgor-gerîm, n., *number of days, lifetime*. dôm, m., *doom, judgment, glory*. dômgeorn, adj., *eager for glory* [*doom-yearning*]. dôn (§ 135), *do, cause, place, promote, remove*. dorste, dorston, see durran. drêam, m., *joy, mirth* [dream]. drêogan (§ 109), *endure, enjoy, spend* [Scotch dree]. drêorig, *dreary, sad*. drêorighlêor, adj., *with sad face* [hlêor = *cheek, face, leer*]. drêosan (§ 109), *fall, perish* [dross]. drîfan (§ 102), *drive*. drihten, see dryhten. drincan (§ 110), *drink*. drohtoð (-að), m., *mode of living, occupation* [drêogan]. drugon, see drêogan. dryhten (drihten), m., *lord, Lord*; dat. sing., dryhtne. dryht-s[e,]le, m., *lordly hall*. duguð, f., *warrior-band, host, retainers* [doughtiness]. In duguð and geogoð, the higher (older) and lower (younger) ranks are represented, the distinction corresponding roughly to the mediæval distinction between knights and squires. durran (§ 137), *dare*. duru, f., *door*. dyde, see dôn. dynnan (§ 125), resound [din]. dy:re (dîere, dêore, dîore), *dear, costly*.

#E.#

êa, f., *river*; gen. sing., êas; dat. and acc. sing., êa. êac, *also, likewise* [a nickname = an eek-name. See § 65, Note 2]; êac swilce (swelce)

112, 3 = *also*. êaca, m., *addition* [êac]; tô êacan = *in addition to* (§ 94, (4)). êage, n., *eye*. eahta, *eight*. êalâ, *oh! alas!* ealað, see ealu. eald (§ 96, (2)), *old*. ealdor (aldor), n., *life*; gif ðû ðæt [e,]llenweorc aldre gedîgest 138, 17 [[*Beowulf* 662]] = *if thou survivest that feat with thy life* (instr.). ealdor-dæg (aldor-, ealder-), m., *day of life*. ealdor-gedâl (aldor-), n., *death* [life-deal]. ealdorm[o,]n, m., *alderman, chief, magistrate*. ealgian, (§ 130), *protect, defend*. eall (eal), *all*; ealne weg, *all the way* (§ 98, (1)); ealneg (< ealne weg), *always*; ealles (§ 98, (3)), adv., *altogether, entirely*. Eall (eal) is frequently used with partitive gen. = *all of*: 143, 19 [[*Beowulf* 836]]; 145, 3 [[*Beowulf* 2728]]. ealu (ealo) (§ 68), n., *ale*; gen. sing., ealað. ealu-scerwen, f., *mortal panic* [ale-spilling]. eard, m., *country, home* [eorðe]. eardgeard, m. *earth* [earth-yard]. eardian (§ 130), *dwell* [eard]. eardstapa, m., *wanderer* [earth-stepper]. êare, n., *ear*. earfoð (earfeð), n. *hardship, toil*; gen. pl., earfeða. earfoðlîc, adj., *full of hardship, arduous*. earm, m., *arm*. earm, adj., *poor, wretched*. earmcearig, *wretched, miserable*. earmlîc, *wretched, miserable*. earnung, f., *merit* [earning]. êast, *east*. êastan (§ 93, (5)), *from the east*. Êast-D[e,]ne (§ 47), *East-Danes*. êasteweard, *eastward*. êastrihte (êastryhte) (§ 93, (6)), *eastward*. Êastron, pl., *Easter*. êaðe, *easily*. êaðmôdlîce, *humbly*. eaxl, f., *shoulder* [axle]. Ebrêisc, adj., *Hebrew*. êce, *eternal, everlasting*. [e,]cg, f., *sword* [edge]. edor, m., *enclosure, dwelling*; nom. pl., ederas. êdrum, see æ:dre. efne, adv., *just, only* [evenly]. eft, adv., *again, afterwards* [aft]. [e,]gesa, m., *fear, terror* [awe]. [e,]llen, n., *strength, courage*; mid [e,]lne = *boldly*; on [e,]lne 147, 17 [[*Beowulf* 2817]] = *mightily, suddenly*, or *in their (earls') strength (prime)*. [e,]llen-mæ:ðu, f. *fame for strength, feat of strength*. [e,]llen-weorc, n., *feat of strength*. [e,]llenwôdnis, f., *zeal, fervor*. [e,]llor-gâst, m., *inhuman monster* [alien ghost]. [e,]ln, f., *ell* [el-bow]. [e,]lne, *see* [e,]llen. [e,]lra, adj. comparative, *another* [*[e,]le cognate with Lat. alius]; on [e,]lran m[e,]n 139, 14 [[*Beowulf* 753]] = *in another man*. emnlong (-lang), *equally long*; on emnlange = *along* (§ 94, (4)). [e,]nde, m., *end*. [e,]ndebyrdnes, f., *order*. [e,]nde-dæg, m., *end-day, day of death*. [e,]nde-lâf, f., *last remnant* [end-leaving]. [e,]ngel, m., *angel* [Lat. angelus]. [E,]nglafeld (§ 51), m., *Englefield* (in Berkshire). [E,]ngle (§ 47), m. pl., *Angles*. [E,]nglisc, adj., *English*; on [E,]nglisc 117, 18 and 19 = *in English, into English*. [E,]ngliscgereord, n., *English language*. [e,]nt, m., *giant*. êode, see gân. eodorcan (§ 130), *ruminate*. eorl, m., *earl, warrior, chieftain*. eorlîc, *earl-like, noble*. eorð-draca, m., *dragon* [earth-drake]. eorðe, f., *earth*. eorð-r[e,]ced, n., *earth-hall.* eorðscræf, n., *earth-cave, grave.* eoten, m., *giant, monster.* êow, see ôû. Êowland, n., *Öland* (an island in the Baltic Sea). [e,]rian (§ 125), *plow* [to ear]. Estland, n., *land of the Estas* (on the eastern coast of the Baltic Sea). Estm[e,]re, m., *Frische Haff.* Estum, dat. pl., *the Estas.* etan (§ 115), *eat* [ort]. [e,]ttan (§ 127), *graze* [etan]. êðel, m., *territory, native land* [allodial]. êðel-weard, m., *guardian of his country.*

#F.#

fæc, n., *interval, space.* fæder (§ 68, (2)), m., *father.* fægen, *fain, glad, exultant.* fæger (fæ:ger), *fair, beautiful.* fæ:lsian (§ 130), *cleanse.* fæ:rlîce, *suddenly* [fæ:r = *fear*]. fæst, *fast, held fast.* fæste, adv., *fast, firmly.* fæstnung, f., *security, safety.* fæt, n., *vessel* [wine-fat, vat]. fæ:tels, m., *vessel*; acc. pl., fæ:tels. fæðm, m., *embrace, bosom* [fathom = the space *embraced* by the extended arms]. fâg (fâh), *hostile*; hê wæs fâg wið God 142, 18 [[*Beowulf* 812]] = *he was hostile to God.* fâh (fâg), *variegated, ornamented.* Falster, *Falster* (island in the Baltic Sea). fandian (§ 130), *try, investigate* [findan]. faran (§ 116), *go* [fare]. feallan (§ 117), *fall, flow.* fealu, *fallow, pale, dark*; nom. pl. m., fealwe. fêawe (fêa, fêawa), pl., *few.* fela (indeclinable), *much, many* (with gen.). feld (§ 51), m., *field.* fell (fel), n., *fell, skin, hide.* fêng, see fôn. f[e,]n-hlið, n., *fen-slope.* f[e,]n-hop, n., *fen-retreat.* feoh, n., *cattle, property* [fee]; gen. and dat. sing., fêos, fêo. feohgîfre, *greedy of property, avaricious.* feohtan (§ 110), *fight.* fêol, see feallan. fêond (§ 68, (3)), m., *enemy, fiend.* fêond-grâp, f., *fiend-grip.* feor (§ 96, (4)), adj., *far, far from* (with dat.). feor, adv., *far, far back* (time). feorh, m., n., *life.* feorh-b[e,]nn, f., *life-wound, mortal wound.* feorh-l[e,]gu, f., *laying down of life.* (See p. 146, Note on l. 13. [[*Beowulf* 2800]]) feorh-sêoc, *life-sick, mortally wounded.* feorm (fiorm), f., *use, benefit* (*food, provisions*) [farm]. feormian (§ 130), *eat, devour.* feorran, *from afar.* fêowertig, *forty*; gen., fêowertiges (§ 91, Note 1). ferhð (ferð), m., *heart, mind, spirit.* f[e,]rian (§ 125), *carry, transport* [to ferry]; f[e,]rede in forðwege 152, 5 [[*Wanderer* 81]] = *carried away.* fers, n., *verse* [Lat. versus]. fersc, *fresh.* ferðloca (ferhð-), m., *heart, mind, spirit* [heart-locker]. fêt, see fôt. fetor, f., *fetter* [fôt]; instr. pl., feterum. feðer, f., *feather*; acc. pl., feðra. fierd, f., *English army* [faran]. fîf, *five.* fîftîene, *fifteen.* fîftig, *fifty*; gen. sing., fîftiges (§ 91, Note 1); dat. pl., fîftegum (§ 91, Note 3). findan (§ 110), *find.* finger, m., *finger.* Finnas, m. pl., *Fins.* fiorm, see feorm. fîras, m. pl., *men* [feorh]; gen. pl., fîra; dat. pl., fîrum.

firrest (fierrest), see feor (§ 96, (4)). first, m., *time, period.* fiscað (fiscnað), m., *fishing.* fiscere, m., *fisherman.* fiscnað, see fiscað. flêon (§ 118, II.), *flee.* flêotan (§ 109), *float.* fl[e,]t, n., *floor of the hall.* flôd, m., *flood, wave.* folc, n., *folk, people.* folc-cwên, f., *folk-queen.* folc-cyning, m., *folk-king.* folcgefeoht, n., *folk-fight, battle, general engagement.* fold-bold, n., *earth-building, hall.* folde, f., *earth, land, country* [feld]. folm, f., *hand* [fêlan = *feel*]. fôn (§ 118), *seize, capture, take* [fang]; tô rîce fôn = *come to (ascend) the throne.* for (§ 94, (1)), *for, on account of*; for ðæ:m (ðe), for ðon (ðe), *because*; for ðon, for ðy:, for ðæ:m (for-ðâm), *therefore.* fôr, see faran. forbærnan (§ 127), *burn thoroughly* [for is intensive, like Lat. per]. forgiefan (-gifan) (§ 115), *give, grant.* forh[e,]rgian (§ 130), *harry, lay waste.* forhogdnis, f., *contempt.* forht, *fearful, afraid.* forhwæga, *about, at least.* forlæ:tan (§ 117), *abandon, leave.* forlêt, forlêton, see forlæ:tan. forma, *first*; forman sîðe, *the first time* (instr.). forniman (§ 114), *take off, destroy.* forsp[e,]ndan (§ 127), *spend, squander.* forst[o,]ndan (-standan) (§ 116), *understand.* forswâpan (§ 117), *sweep away*; pret. 3d sing. indic., forswêop. forsw[e,]rian (§ 116), *forswear* (with dat.); past part., forsworen. forð, *forth, forward.* forðolian (§ 130), *miss, go without* (with dat.) [not to *thole* or experience]. forðweg, m., *way forth*; in forðwege, *away.* fôt (§ 68, (1)), m. *foot.* Fræ:na, m., *Frene.* frætwe, f. pl., *fretted armor, jewels* [fret]. fram, see fr[o,]m. frêa, m., *lord, Lord.* frêa-drihten, m., *lord, master.* frêfran (§ 130), *console, cheer* [frôfor]. fr[e,]mde, *strange, foreign*; ðâ fr[e,]mdan, *the strangers.* fr[e,]mman (§ 125), *accomplish, perform, support* [to frame]. fr[e,]msumnes (-nis), f., *kindness, benefit.* frêo (frîo), *free*; gen. pl., frêora (frîora). frêodôm, m., *freedom.* frêolîc, *noble* [free-like]. frêomæ:g, m., *free kinsman.* frêond (§ 68, (3)), m., *friend.* frêondlêas, *friendless.* frêondlîce, *in a friendly manner.* frêorig, *cold, chill* [frêoran]. frîora, see frêo. frið, m., n., *peace, security* [bel-*fry*]. frôd, *old, sage, prudent.* frôfor, f., *comfort, consolation, alleviation*; fyrena frôfre 137, 7 [[*Beowulf* 629]] = *as an alleviation of outrages* (dat.). fr[o,]m (fram) (§ 94, (1)), *from, by.* fr[o,]m, adv., *away, forth.* fruma, m., *origin, beginning* [fr[o,]m]. frumsceaft, f., *creation.* fugela, see fugol. fugelere, m., *fowler.* fugol (fugel), m., *fowl, bird*; gen. pl., fugela. ful, n., *cup, beaker.* fûl, *foul.* fûlian (§ 130), *grow foul, decompose.* full (ful), adj., *full* (with gen.); be fullan, *fully, perfectly.* full (ful) adv., *fully, very.* fultum, m., *help.* furðor (furður), adv., *further.* furðum, adv., *even.* fylð, see feallan. fyren (firen), f., *crime, violence, outrage.* fyrhtu, f., *fright, terror*; dat. sing., fyrhtu. fyrst, adj., superlative, *first, chief.* fy:san (§ 126), *make ready, prepare* [fûs = *ready*]; gûðe gefy:sed 137, 9 [[*Beowulf* 631]] = *ready for battle.*

#G.#

gâd, n., *lack.* gæ:st, see gâst. gafol, n., *tax, tribute.* galan (§ 116), *sing* [nightingale]. gâlnes, f., *lust, impurity.* gân (§ 134), *go.* gâr, m., *spear* [gore, gar-fish]. gâr-wiga, m., *spear-warrior.* gâst (gæ:st), m., *spirit, ghost.* gâstlîc (gæ:stlîc), *ghastly, terrible.* ge, *and*; see æ:gðer. gê, *ye*; see ðû. geador, *together.* geæ:metigian (§ 130), *disengage from* (with acc. of person and gen. of thing) [empty]. geærnan (§ 127), *gain by running* [iernan]. gêap, *spacious.* gêar, n., *year*; gen. pl., gêara, is used adverbially = *of yore, formerly.* gêardæg, m., *day of yore.* geare (gearo, gearwe), *readily, well, clearly* [yarely]. Gêat, m., *a Geat, the Geat* (i.e. Beowulf). Gêatas, m. pl., *the Geats* (a people of South Sweden). Gêat-mecgas, m. pl., *Geat men* (= the fourteen who accompanied Beowulf to Heorot). gebêorscipe, m., *banquet, entertainment.* gebêtan (§ 126), *make amends for* [bôt]. gebîdan (§ 102), *wait, bide one's time* (intrans.); *endure, experience* (trans., with acc.). gebind, n., *commingling.* gebindan (§ 110), *bind.* gebrêowan (§ 109), *brew.* gebrowen, see gebrêowan. gebûd, gebûn, see bûan (§ 126, Note 2). gebyrd, n., *rank, social distinction.* gecêosan (§ 109), *choose, decide.* gecnâwan (§ 117), *know, understand.* gecoren, see gecêosan. gecringan (§ 110), *fall, die* [cringe]. gedæ:lan (§ 126), *deal out, give*; dêaðe gedæ:lde 152, 7 [[*Wanderer* 83]] = *apportioned to death* (dat.), or, *tore (?) in death* (instr.). gedafenian (§ 130), *become, befit, suit* (impersonal, usually with dat., but with acc. 112, 10). gedîgan (§ 126), *endure, survive.* gedôn (§ 135), *do, cause, effect.* gedræg, n., *company.* gedrêosan (§ 109), *fall, fail.* gedriht (gedryht), n., *band, troop.* gedrogen, see drêogan. gedrync, n., *drinking.* ge[e,]ndian (§ 130), *end, finish.* gefaran (§ 116), *go, die.* gefêa, m., *joy.* gefeaht, see gefeohtan. gefeh, see gefêon. gefêng, see gefôn. gefeoht, n., *fight, battle.* gefeohtan (§ 110), *fight.* gefêon (§ 118, v.), *rejoice at* (with dat.); pret. 3d sing., gefeah, gefeh. gefêra, m., *companion, comrade* [co-farer]. geflîeman (§ 126), *put to flight* [flêon]. gefohten, see gefeohtan. gefôn (§ 118, vii.), *seize.* gefôr, see gefaran. gefræ:ge, n., *hearsay, report*; mîne gefræ:ge (instr.) 141, 7 [[*Beowulf* 777]] = *as I have heard say, according to my information.* gefr[e,]mman (§ 125), *perform, accomplish, effect.* gefultumian (§ 130), *help* [fultum]. gefylce, n., *troop, division* [folc]; dat. pl., gefylcum, gefylcium. gefyllan (§ 127), *fill* (with gen.); past part. pl., f., gefylda. gegl[e,]ngan (§ 127), *adorn.* gehâtland, n., *promised land* [gehâtan = *to promise*]. gehealdan (§ 117), *hold, maintain.* gehîeran (gehy:ran) (§ 126), *hear.* gehîersumnes, f., *obedience.* gehola, m., *protector* [helan]. gehwâ (§ 77, Note), *each*; on healfa gehwone 142, 7 [[*Beowulf* 801]] (see Note 140, 15 [[*Beowulf* 769]]. Observe that the pron. may, as here, be masc. and the gen. fem.). gehwæðer (§ 77, Note), *each, either, both.* gehwylc (gehwilc) (§ 77, Note), *each* (with gen. pl. See Note 140, 15 [[*Beowulf* 769]]). gehwyrfan (§ 127), *convert, change.* gehy:dan (§ 126), *hide, conceal, consign.* gehygd, f., n., *thought, purpose.* gehy:ran, see gehîeran. gehy:rnes, f., *hearing*; eal ðâ hê in gehy:rnesse geleornian meahte 115, 14 = *all things that he could learn by hearing.* gelæ:dan (§ 126), *lead.* gelæ:red, part.-adj., *learned*; superlative, gelæ:redest. gelafian (§ 130), *lave.* gel[e,]nge, *along of, belonging to* (with dat.). geleornian (-liornian) (§ 130), *learn.* gelîce, *likewise*; *in like manner to* (with dat.). gelîefan (gely:fan) (§ 126), *believe*; ðæt hêo on æ:nigne eorl gely:fde 137, 6 [[*Beowulf* 628]] = *that she believed in any earl.* gelimpan (§ 110), *happen, be fulfilled.* gelimplîc, *proper, fitting.* gely:fan, see gelîefan. gely:fed, *weak, infirm* [left (hand)]. gêmde, see gîeman. gemet, n., *meter, measure, ability.* gemêtan (§ 126), *meet.* gem[o,]n, see gemunan. gemunan (§ 136), *remember*; indic. pres. 1st and 3d sing., gem[o,]n; pret. sing., gemunde. gemynd, n., *memory, memorial*; tô gemyndum 147, 5 [[*Beowulf* 2805]] = *as a memorial.* gemyndgian (-mynian) (§ 130), *remember*; mid hine gemyndgade 115, 15 = *he treasured in his memory*; gemyne mæ:rðo 138, 15 [[*Beowulf* 660]] = *be mindful of glory* (imperative 2d sing.). gemyndig, *mindful of* (with gen.). genâp, see genîpan. geneahhe, *enough, often*; genehost, superlative, *very often.* genip, n., *mist, darkness.* genîpan (§ 102), *grow dark.* genîwian (§ 130), *renew.* genôh, *enough.* genumen, see niman. geoc, n., *yoke.* gêocor, *dire, sad.* geogoð, f., *youth, young people, young warriors.* (See duguð.) geond (giond) (§ 94, (2)), *throughout* [yond]. geondhweorfan (§ 110), *pass over, traverse, recall*; ðonne mâga gemynd môd geondhweorfeð 150, 15 [[*Wanderer* 51]] = *then his mind recalls the memory of kinsmen.* geondscêawian (§ 130), survey, review; georne geondscêawað 150, 16 [[*Wanderer* 52]] = *eagerly surveys them.* geondð[e,]nc(e)an (§ 128), *think over, consider.* geong (§ 96, (2)), *young*; giengest, (gingest), superlative, *youngest, latest, last.* geong = g[o,]ng, see g[o,]ngan (imperative 2d sing.). gêong (gîong), see g[o,]ngan (pret. 3d sing.). georn (giorn), *eager, desirous, zealous, sure* [yearn]. georne, *eagerly, certainly*; wiste ðê geornor 143, 5 [[*Beowulf* 822]] = *knew the more certainly*. geornfulnes, f., *eagerness, zeal*. geornlîce, *eagerly, attentively*. geornor, see georne. ger[e,]cednes, f., *narration* [r[e,]ccan]. gerisenlîc, *suitable, becoming*. gery:man (§ 126), *extend*, (trans.) [rûm]. gesæ:liglîc, *happy, blessed* [silly]. gesamnode, see ges[o,]mnian. gesceaft, f., *creature, creation, destiny* [scieppan]. gesceap, n., *shape, creation, destiny* [scieppan]. gescieldan (§ 127), *shield, defend*. gesealde, see ges[e,]llan. geseglian (§ 130), *sail*. geselda, m., *comrade*. ges[e,]llan (§ 128), *give*. gesêon (gesîon) (§ 118), *see*, observe; pres. indic. 3d sing., gesihð. geset, n., *habitation, seat*. ges[e,]ttan (§ 127), *set, place, establish*. gesewen, see sêon, gesêon (past part.). gesewenlîc, *seen, visible* [seen-like]. gesiglan (§ 127), *sail*. gesihð, see gesêon. gesittan (§ 115, Note 2), *sit* (trans., as *to sit a horse, to sit a boat*, etc.); *sit, sit down* (intrans.). geslægen, see slêan (§ 118). ges[o,]mnian (§ 130), *assemble, collect*. ges[o,]mnung, f., *collection, assembly*. gestâh, see gestîgan. gestaðelian (§ 130), *establish, restore* [standan]. gesteal, n., *establishment, foundation* [stall]. gestîgan (§ 102), *ascend, go* [stile, stirrup, sty (= a *rising* on the eye)]. gestrangian (§ 130), *strengthen*. gestrêon, n., *property*. gestry:nan (§ 126), *obtain, acquire* [gestrêon]. gesweorcan (§ 110), *grow dark, become sad*; For ðon ic geð[e,]ncan ne mæg geond ðâs woruld for hwan môdsefa mîn ne gesweorce 151, 3-4 [[lines 58-59]] = *Therefore in this world I may not understand wherefore my mind does not grow "black as night."* (Brooke.) geswîcan (§ 102), *cease, cease from* (with gen.). getæl, n., *something told, narrative*. getruma, m., *troop, division*. geðanc, m., n., *thought*. geðeah, see geðicgan. geð[e,]nc(e)an (§ 128), *think, remember, understand, consider*. geðêodan (§ 126), *join*. geðêode (-ðîode), n., *language, tribe*. geðêodnis, f., *association*; but in 112, 2 this word is used to render the Lat. *appetitus = desire*. geðicg(e)an (§ 115, Note 2), *take, receive*; pret. indic. 3d sing., geðeah. geðungen, part.-adj., *distinguished, excellent* [ðêon, *to thrive*]. geðyldig, *patient* [ðolian]. geweald (gewald), n., *control, possession, power* [wield]. geweorc, n., *work, labor*. geweorðian (§ 130), *honor* [to attribute *worth* to]. gewîcian (§ 130), *dwell*. gewin(n), n., *strife, struggle*. gewindan (§ 110), *flee* [wend]. gewissian (§ 130), *guide, direct*. gewîtan (§ 102), *go, depart*. geworht, see gewyrcan. gewrit, n., *writing, Scripture*. gewunian (§ 130), *be accustomed, be wont*. gewyrc(e)an (§ 128), *work, create*, *make, produce.* gid(d), n., *word, speech.* giefan (§ 115), *give.* giefstôl, m., *gift-stool, throne.* giefu (gifu), f., *gift.* gielp (gilp), m., n., *boast* [yelp]. gîeman (gêman) (§ 126), *endeavor, strive.* gîet (gît, gy:t), *yet, still.* gif (gyf), *if* [not related to *give*]. gifeðe (gyfeðe), *given, granted.* gilp, see gielp. gilp-cwide, m., *boasting speech* [*yelp*-speech]. gingest, see geong (adj.). giohðo (gehðu), f., *care, sorrow, grief.* giû (iû), *formerly, of old.* glæd (glæ:d), *glad.* glêaw, *wise, prudent.* glîwstæf, m., *glee, joy*; instr. pl. (used adverbially), glîwstafum 150, 16 [[*Wanderer* 52]] = *joyfully.* God, m., *God.* gôd (§ 96, (3)), *good*; mid his gôdum 115, 12 = *with his possessions (goods).* godcund, *divine* [God]. godcundlîce, *divinely.* gold, n., *gold.* gold-æ:ht, f., *gold treasure.* gold-fâh, *gold-adorned.* gold-hroden, part.-adj., *gold-adorned.* goldwine, m., *prince, giver of gold, lord* [gold-friend]. gomel (gomol), *old, old man.* g[o,]ngan (gangan) (§ 117), *go* [gang]; imperative 2d sing., geong; pret. sing., gêong, gîong, gêng; past part., geg[o,]ngen, gegangen. The most commonly used pret. is êode, which belongs to gân (§ 134). Gotland, n., *Jutland* (in *Ohthere's Second Voyage*), *Gothland* (in *Wulfstan's Voyage*). gram, *grim, angry, fierce, the angry one.* grâp, f., *grasp, clutch, claw.* grêtan (§ 126), *greet, attack, touch.* grôwan (§ 117, (2)), *grow.* gryre-lêoð, n., *terrible song* [grisly lay]. guma, m., *man, hero* [groom; see § 65, Note 1]. gûð, f., *war, battle.* gûð-bill, n., *sword* [war-bill]. gûð-gewæ:de, n., *armor* [war-weeds]. gûð-hrêð, f., *war-fame.* gûð-wine, m., *sword* [war-friend]. gyddian (§ 130), *speak formally,* chant [giddy; the original meaning of *giddy* was *mirthful,* as when one sings]. gyf, see gif. gyfeðe, see gifeðe. gyldan (gieldan) (§ 110), *pay*; indic. 3d sing., gylt. gyldon, *golden* [gold].

#H.#

habban (§ 133), *have.* hâd, m., *order, rank, office, degree* [-hood, -head]. hæfta, m., *captive.* hægel (hagol), m., *hail*; instr. sing., hagle. hæglfaru, f., *hail-storm* [hail-faring]. hæle, see hæleð. hæ:l, f., *hail, health, good luck.* hæleð (hæle), m., *hero, warrior.* hæ:t, see hâtan. hæ:ðen, *heathen.* Hæ:ðum (æt Hæ:ðum), *Haddeby* (= *Schleswig*). hâl, *hale, whole.* hâlettan (§ 127), *greet, salute* [to hail]. Halfd[e,]ne, *Halfdane* (proper name). hâlga, m., *saint.* Hâlgoland, *Halgoland* (in ancient Norway). hâlig, *holy.* hâlignes, f., *holiness.* hâm, m., *home*; dat. sing., hâme, hâm (p. 104, Note); used adverbially in hâm êode 112, 18 = *went home.* hand, see h[o,]nd. hâr, *hoary, gray.* hât, *hot.* hâtan (§

117, Note 2), *call, name, command*; pret. sing., heht, hêt. hâtheort, *hot-hearted*. hâtte, see hâtan. hê, hêo, hit (§ 53), *he, she, it*. hêafod, n., *head*. hêah (§ 96, (2)), *high*; acc. sing, m., hêanne. hêah-s[e,]le, m., *high hall*. hêahðungen, *highly prosperous, aristocratic* [hêah + past part. of ðêon (§ 118)]. healdan (§ 117), *hold, govern, possess*; 144, 9 [[*Beowulf* 2720]] = *hold up, sustain*. healf, adj., *half*. healf, f., *half, side, shore*. heall, f., *hall*. heals, m., *neck*. hêan, *abject, miserable*. hêanne, see hêah. heard, *hard*. heard-hicgende, *brave-minded* [hard-thinking]. hearm-scaða, m., *harmful foe* [harm-scather]. hearpe, f., *harp*. heaðo-dêor, *battle-brave*. heaðo-mæ:re, *famous in battle*. heaðo-wylm, m., *flame-surge, surging of fire* [battle-welling]. hêawan (§ 117), *hew, cut*. h[e,]bban, hôf, hôfon, gehafen (§ 117), *heave, lift, raise*. h[e,]fig, *heavy, oppressive*. heht, see hâtan. helan (§ 114), *conceal*. h[e,]ll, f., *hell*. helm, m., *helmet*. Helmingas, m. pl., *Helmings* (Wealtheow, Hrothgar's queen, is a Helming). help, f., *help*. helpan (§ 110), *help* (with dat.). heofon, m., *heaven*. heofonlîc, *heavenly*. heofonrîce, n., *kingdom of heaven*. hêold, see healdan. heolstor (-ster), n., *darkness, concealment, cover* [holster]. heora (hiera), see hê. heord, f., care, guardianship [hoard]. heoro-drêorig, *bloody* [sword-dreary]. Heorot, *Heorot, Hart* (the famous hall which Hrothgar built). heorte, f., *heart*. hêr, *here, hither*; in the *Chronicle* the meaning frequently is *at this date, in this year*: 99, 1. h[e,]re, m., *Danish army*. h[e,]renis, f., *praise*. h[e,]rgian (§ 130), *raid, harry, ravage* [h[e,]re]. h[e,]rgung, f., *harrying, plundering*. h[e,]rian (h[e,]rigean) (§ 125), *praise*. hêrsumedon, see hîersumian. hêt, see hâtan. hider (hieder), *hither*. hiera, see hê. hîeran (hy:ran) (§ 126), *hear, belong*. hierde, m., *shepherd, instigator* [keeper of a *herd*]. hierdebôc, f., *pastoral treatise* [shepherd-book, a translation of Lat. *Cura Pastoralis*]. hîerra, see hêah. hîersumian (hy:r-, hêr-) (§ 130), *obey* (with dat.). hige (hyge), m., *mind, heart*. hige-ðihtig, *bold-hearted*. hild, f., *battle*. hilde-dêor, *battle-brave*. hilde-mecg, m., *warrior*. hilde-sæd, *battle-sated*. hin-fûs, *eager to be gone* [hence-ready]. hira, see hê. hlæ:w (hlâw), m., *mound, burial mound* [Lud*low* and other place-names, *low* meaning *hill*]. hlâford, m., *lord, master* [loaf-ward?]. hleahtor, m., *laughter*. hlêo, m., *refuge, protector* [lee]. hlîfian (§ 130), *rise, tower*. hlyn, m., *din, noise*. hlynsian (§ 130), *resound*. hof, n., *court, abode*. hogode, see hycgan. holm, m., *sea, ocean*. h[o,]nd (hand), f., *hand*; on gehwæðre h[o,]nd, *on both sides*. hord, m., n., *hoard, treasure*. hordcofa, m., *breast, heart* [hoard-chamber] hors, n., *horse*. horshwæl, m., *walrus*. hrædwyrde, *hasty of speech* [hræd = *quick*]. hrægel, n., *garment*; dat. sing., hrægle. hrân, m., *reindeer*. hraðe, *quickly, soon* [*rath*-er]. hrêo (hrêoh), *rough, cruel, sad*. hrêosan (§ 109), *fall*. hrêran (§ 126), *stir*. hreðer, m., n., *breast, purpose*; dat. sing., hreðre. hrîm, m., *rime, hoarfrost*. hrîmceald, *rime-cold*. hring, m., *ring, ring-mail*. hrîð, f. (?), *snow-storm*. hrôf, m., *roof*. Hrones næss, literally *Whale's Ness, whale's promontory*; see næss. hrûse, f., *earth* [hrêosan: deposit]. hryre, m., *fall, death* [hrêosan]. hry:ðer, n., *cattle* [rinder-pest]. hryðig, *ruined* (?), *storm-beaten*; nom. pl. m., hryðge. hû, *how*. Humbre, f., *river Humber*. hund, *hundred*. hunig, n., *honey*. hunta, m., *hunter*. huntoð (-tað), m., *hunting*. hûru, adv., *about*. hûs, n., *house*. hwâ, hwæt (§ 74), *who? what?* swâ hwæt swâ (§ 77, Note), *whatsoever*; indefinite, *any one, anything*; for hwan (instr.), *wherefore*. hwæl, m., *whale*. hwælhunta, m., *whale-hunter*. hwælhuntað, m., *whale-fishing*. hwæ:r, *where?* hwæ:r ... swâ, *wheresoever*; wel hwæ:r, *nearly everywhere*. hwæthwugu, *something*. hwæðer, *whether, which of two?* hwæðre, *however, nevertheless*. hwêne, see hwôn. hweorfan (§ 110), *turn, go*. hwider, *whither*. hwîl, f., *while, time*; ealle ðâ hwîle ðe, *all the while that*; hwîlum (instr. pl.), *sometimes*. hwilc (hwylc, hwelc) (§ 74, Note 1), *which? what?* hwôn, n., *a trifle*; hwêne (instr. sing.), *somewhat, a little*. hw[o,]nan, *when*. hy:, see hîe. hycgan (§ 132), *think, resolve*; pret. 3d sing., hogode. hy:d, f., *hide, skin*. hyge, see hige. hyra (hiera), see hê. hy:ran, see hîeran. hyrde, see hierde. hys (his), see hê. hyt (hit), see hê.

#I.#

ic (§ 72), *I*. îdel, *idle, useless, desolate*. ides, f., *woman, lady*. ieldra, adj., see eald. ieldra, m., *an elder, parent, ancestor*. iernan (yrnan) (§ 112), *run*. îgl[o,]nd (îgland), n., *island*. ilca (ylca), *the same* [of that ilk]. Ilting, *the Elbing*. in, *in, into* (with dat. and acc.); in on, *in on, to, toward*. inbryrdnis (-nes), f., *inspiration, ardor*. indryhten, *very noble*. ing[o,]ng, m., *entrance*. innan, adv., *within, inside*; on innan, *within*. innanbordes, adv.-gen., *within borders, at home*. inne, adv., *within, inside*. intinga, m., *cause, sake*. inweardlîce, *inwardly, fervently*. inwid-sorg (inwit-sorh), f., *sorrow caused by an enemy*. inwit-ðanc, m., *hostile intent*. Îraland, n., *Ireland* (but in *Ohthere's Second Voyage, Iceland* is probably meant). îren, n., *iron, sword*; gen. pl., îrenna, îrena. îren-b[e,]nd, m., f., *iron-band*. îu, see gîu.

#K.#

kynerîce, see cynerîce. kyning, see cyning. kyrtel, m., *kirtle, coat.*

#L.#

Læ:den, *Latin.* Læ:dengeðêode (-ðîode), n., *Latin language.*
Læ:denware (§ 47), m. pl., *Latin people, Romans.* læ:fan (§ 126),
leave. læ:ge, see licgan. Læ:land, n., *Laaland* (in Denmark). læ:n, n.,
loan; tô læ:ne 121, 2 = *as a loan.* læ:ne, adj., *as a loan, transitory,
perishable.* læ:ran (§ 126), *teach, advise, exhort* [lâr]. læ:ssa, læ:sta,
see ly:tel. læ:stan (§ 127), *last, hold out* (intrans.); *perform, achieve*
(trans.). læ:tan (§ 117), *let, leave.* lâf, f., *something left, remnant,
heirloom* (often a *sword*); tô lâfe, *as a remnant, remaining.* lagulâd, f.,
sea [lake-way, lâd = *leading, direction, way*]. land, see l[o,]nd. lang,
see l[o,]ng. Langaland, n., *Langeland* (in Denmark). lâr, f., *lore,
teaching.* lârcwide, m., *precept, instruction,* [cwide < cweðan]. lârêow,
m., *teacher* [lâr + ðêow]. lâst, m., *track, footprint* [shoemaker's last]; on
lâst(e), *in the track of, behind* (with dat.). lâð, *loathsome, hateful.* lêas,
loose, free from, bereft of (with gen.). lêasung, f., *leasing, deception,
falsehood.* l[e,]cgan (§ 125, Note), *lay.* lêfdon, see lîefan. leger, n.,
lying in, illness [licgan]. l[e,]ng, see l[o,]nge. l[e,]ngra, see l[o,]ng. lêod,
m., *prince, chief.* lêod, f., *people, nation* (the plural has the same
meaning). lêod-scipe, m., *nation* [people-ship]. lêof, *dear* [lief]. leoht,
adj., *light.* lêoht, n., *light, brightness.* leornere, m., *learner, disciple.*
leornian (§ 130), *learn.* leornung (liornung), f., *learning.* lêoð, n., *song*
[lay?]. lêoðcræft, m., *poetic skill* [lay-craft]. lêoðs[o,]ng, n., *song, poem.*
lêt, see læ:tan. libban (§ 133), *live;* pres. part., lifigende, *living, alive.*
lîc, n., *body, corpse* [lich-gate, Lichfield]. licgan (§ 115, Note 2), *lie,
extend, flow, lie dead;* 3d sing. indic. pres., ligeð, lîð. lîchama
(-h[o,]ma), m., *body* [body-covering]. lîcian (§ 130), *please* (with dat.)
[like]. lîc-sâr, n., *body-sore, wound in the body.* lîefan (lêfan) (§ 126),
permit, allow (with dat.) [grant *leave* to]. lîf, n., *life.* lîf-dagas, m. pl.,
life-days. lifigende, see libban. lîg, m., *flame, fire.* ligeð, see licgan. lim,
n., *limb.* list, f., *cunning;* dat. pl., listum, is used adverbially = *cunningly.*
lîð, see licgan. lof, m., *praise, glory.* l[o,]nd (land), n., *land, country.*
l[o,]ng (lang) (§ 96, (2)), *long.* l[o,]nge (lange) (§ 97, (2)), *long;* l[o,]nge
on dæg, *late in the day.* lufan, see lufu. lufian (lufigean) (§ 131), *love.*
luflîce, *lovingly.* lufu, f., *love;* dat. sing. (weak), lufan. lungre, *quickly.*

lust, m., *joy* [lust]; on lust, *joyfully.* ly:t, indeclinable, *little, few* (with partitive gen.). ly:tel (lîtel) (§ 96, (2)), *little, small.*

#M.#

mâ, see micle (§ 97, (2)). mæg, see magan. mæ:g, m., *kinsman*; nom. pl., mâgas (§ 27, (2)). mægen n., *strength, power* [might and *main*]. mægen-[e,]llen, n., *main strength, mighty courage.* mæ:gð, f., *tribe.* mægðhâd, m., *maidenhood, virginity.* mæ:l-gesceaft, f., *appointed time* [mæ:l = *meal, time*]. mæ:ran (§ 126), *make famous, honor.* mæ:re, *famous, glorious, notorious.* mæ:rðo (mæ:rðo, mæ:rð), f., *glory, fame.* mæsseprêost, m., *mass-priest.* mæ:st, see micel. magan (§ 137), *be able, may.* mâgas, see mæ:g. magu (mago), m., *son, man.* maguðegn, m., *vassal, retainer.* man(n), see m[o,]n(n). mancus, m., *mancus, half-crown*; gen. pl., mancessa. mândæ:d, f., *evil deed.* manig, see m[o,]nig. manigfeald, see m[o,]nigfeald. mâra, see micel. maðelian (§ 130), *harangue, speak.* mâðum (mâððum), m., *gift, treasure, jewel*; gen. pl., mâðma. mâððumgyfa, m., *treasure-giver, lord.* mâððum-wela, m., *wealth of treasure.* mê, see ic. meaht, f., *might, power.* meahte, see magan. mearc, f., *boundary, limit* [mark, march]. mearg (mearh), m., *horse*; nom. pl., mêaras. mearð, m., *marten.* mec, see ic. medmicel, *moderately large, short, brief.* medu (medo), m., *mead.* medu-b[e,]nc, f., *mead-bench.* medu-ful, n., *mead-cup.* medu-heall, f., *mead-hall.* m[e,]n, see m[o,]n(n). m[e,]ngan (§ 127), *mingle, mix.* m[e,]nigu (m[e,]nigeo), f., *multitude* [many]. m[e,]nniscnes, f., *humanity, incarnation* [man]. meolc, f., *milk.* Mêore, Möre (in Sweden). m[e,]re, m., *lake, mere, sea* [mermaid]. Meretûn, m., *Merton* (in Surrey). mêtan (§ 126), *meet, find.* Metod (Meotod, Metud), m., *Creator, God.* metod-sceaft, f., *appointed doom, eternity.* micel (§ 96, (3)), *great, mighty, strong, large* [mickle]; mâra, *more, stronger, larger.* micle (micele), *greatly, much.* mlclum, (§ 93, (4)), *greatly.* mid, *with, amid, among* (with dat. and acc.). middangeard, m., *earth, world* [middle-yard]. middeweard, *midward, toward the middle.* Mierce, m. pl., *Mercians.* mihte, see *magan.* mîl, f., *mile* [Lat. mille]. mildheortnes, f., *mild-heartedness, mercy.* milts, f., *mildness, mercy.* mîn (§ 76), *my, mine.* mislîc, *various.* missenlîc, *various.* môd, n., *mood, mind, courage.* môdcearig, *sorrowful of mind.* môdega, môdga, see môdig. môdgeðanc, m., *purpose of mind.* môdig, *moody, brave, proud.* môdor, f., *mother.* môdsefa, m., *mind, heart.* m[o,]n(n) (man, mann) (§ 68; §

70, Note), m., *man, one, person, they*. môna, m., *moon*. mônað (§ 68, (1), Note), m., *month* [môna]; dat. sing., mônðe. m[o,]n(n)cynn, n., *mankind*. m[o,]ndryhten, m., *liege lord*. m[o,]nian (manian) (§ 130), *admonish*. m[o,]nig (manig, m[o,]neg, mænig), *many*. m[o,]nigfeald (manig-), *manifold, various*. mônðe, see mônað. môr, m., *moor*. morgen, m., *morning*; dat. sing., morgen(n)e. morðor-bealu (-bealo), n., *murder* [murder-bale]; see ðurfan. môste, see môtan. môtan (§ 137), *may, be permitted, must*. mund-gripe, m., *hand-grip*. munuc, m., *monk* [Lat. monachus]. munuchâd, m., *monkhood, monastic rank*. mûð, m., *mouth*. myntan (§ 127), *be minded, intend*; pret. indic. 3d sing., mynte. mynster, n., *monastery* [Lat. monasterium]; dat. sing., mynstre. my:re, f., *mare* [mearh]. myrð, f., *joy, mirth*; môdes myrðe 142, 17 [[*Beowulf* 811]] = *with joy of heart*.

#N.#

nâ (nô), *not* [ne â = *n-ever*]; nâ ne, *not, not at all*. nabban (p. 32, Note), *not to have*. næ:dre, f., *serpent, adder*. næfde, see nabban. næ:fre, *never*. næ:nig (§ 77), *no one, no, none*. næ:re, næ:ren, næ:ron, see § 40, Note 2. næs = ne wæs, see § 40, Note 2. næss, m., *ness, headland*. nâht, see nôht. nâlæs (nâles), *not at all* [nâ ealles]. nam, see niman. nama, see n[o,]ma. nâmon, see niman. nân, *not one, no, none* [ne ân]. nânwuht, n., *nothing* [no whit]. ne, *not*. nê, *nor*; nê ... nê, *neither ... nor*. nêah (§ 96, (4)), *near*. nêah, adv., *nigh, near, nearly, almost*; comparative, nêar, *nearer*. neaht, see niht. nêalêcan (-læ:can) (§ 126), *draw near to, approach* (with dat.). nêar, see nêah, adv. nêat, n., *neat, cattle*. n[e,]mnan (§ 127), *name*. nemðe, (nymðe), *except, unless*. n[e,]rian (§ 125), *save, preserve*. nêten, see nîeten. nîedbeðearf, *needful, necessary*. nîehst, see nêah (§ 96, (4)). nîeten (nêten), n., *neat, beast, cattle*. nigontîene, *nineteen*. niht (neaht) (§ 68, (1), Note), *night*. nihthelm, m., *night-helm, shade of night*. nihtscûa, m., *shadow of night*. niht-weorc, n., *night-work*. niman (§ 114), *take, gain* [nimble, numb]. nîpan (§ 102), *grow dark, darken*. nis, see § 40, Note 2. nîð, m., *malice, violence*. nîwe, *new, novel, startling*. nô, see nâ. nôht (nâht, nâ-wiht), n., *not a whit, naught, nothing*; *not, not at all*. nôhwæðer (nâhwæðer), *neither*; nôhwæðer nê ... ne ... nê ... ne 118, 8 = *neither ... nor*. nolde, noldon = ne wolde, ne woldon, see willan. n[o,]ma (nama), m., *name*. norð (§ 97, (1)), *north, in the north, northwards*. norðan (§ 93, (5)), *from the north*; be norðan, see § 94,

(4). Norð-D[e,]ne, m. pl., *North-Danes.* norðeweard, *northward.*
Norðhymbre, m. pl., *Northumbrians.* Norðmanna, see Norðm[o,]n.
Norðm[e,]n, see Norðm[o,]n. norðmest, see norð. Norðm[o,]n (-man) (§
68, (1)), *Norwegian.* norðor, see norð. norðryhte, *northward.*
norðweard, *northward.* Norðweg, *Norway.* nose, f., *cape, naze* [ness,
nose]. notu, f., *office, employment.* nû, *now; now that, seeing that;* nû
ðâ 138, 13 [[*Beowulf* 658]] = *now then.* ny:hst (nîehst), see nêah.
nymðe, see nemðe. nysse, see nytan. nyste, see nytan. nyt(t), *useful,
profitable.* nytan (nitan < ne witan, § 136), *not to know;* 3d sing. pret.,
nysse, nyste.

#O.#

of (§ 94, (1)), *of, from, concerning.* ofer (§ 94, (2)), *over, across, after,
in spite of* (see 144, 14 [[*Beowulf* 2725]]); ofer eorðan 142, 9 [[*Beowulf*
803]] = *on earth.* ofer, adv., *over, across.* oferfêran (§ 126), *go over,
traverse.* oferfrêosan (§ 109), *freeze over.* oferfroren, see oferfrêosan.
ofgiefan (§ 115), *give up, relinquish.* ofost, f., *haste.* ofslægen, see
ofslêan. ofslêan (§ 118), *slay off, slay.* ofslôge, see ofslêan. oft, *oft,
often;* superlative, oftost. on (§ 94, (3)), *in, into, on, against, to, among,
during;* on fîf oððe syx 109, 6 = *into five or six parts;* on weg 140, 10
[[*Beowulf* 764]] = *away;* on innan 144, 5 [[*Beowulf* 2716]] = *within;* on
unriht 145, 15 [[*Beowulf* 2740]] = *falsely.* onbærnan (§ 126), *kindle,
inspire.* oncy:ðð, f., *distress, suffering.* [o,]nd (and), *and.* [o,]ndsaca,
m., *adversary.* [o,]ndswarian (§ 130), *answer.* [o,]ndweard, adj.,
present. onfêng, see onfôn. onfeohtan (§ 110), *fight.* onfindan (§ 110),
find out, discover; pret. indic. 3d sing., onfunde. onfôn (§ 118), *receive,
seize violently.* onfunde, see onfindan. ongêan, prep., *against, towards*
(with dat. and acc.). ongêan, adv., *just across, opposite.* [O,]ngelcynn
(Angel-), n., *Angle kin, English people, England.* [O,]ngelðêod (Angel-),
f., *the English people or nation.* ongemang (-m[o,]ng), *among* (with
dat.). ongietan (-gitan) (§ 115), *perceive, see, understand.* onginnan (§
110), *begin, attempt.* onlûtan (§ 109), *bow, incline* (intrans.) [lout = a
stooper]. onrîdan (§ 102), *ride against, make a raid on.* ons[e,]ndan (§
127), *send.* onslæ:pan (onslêpan) (§ 126), *fall asleep, sleep.*
onsp[o,]nnan (§ 117), *loosen* [unspan]; pret. 3d sing. indic., onspêon.
onspringan (§ 110), *spring apart, unspring.* onstâl, m., *institution,
supply.* onst[e,]llan (§ 128), *establish;* pret. 3d sing. indic., onstealde.
onwæcnan (§ 127), *awake* (intrans.). onweald (-wald), m., *power,*

authority [wield]. onw[e,]ndan (§ 127), *change, overturn* [to wind]. ôr,
n., *beginning.* oð (§ 94, (2)), *until, as far as* (of time and place); oð ðæt,
oð ðe, *until.* oðberan (§ 114), *bear away.* ôðer, *other, second*; ôðer ...
ôðer, *the one ... the other.* oðfæstan (§ 127), *set to* (a task). oðfeallan
(§ 117) *fall off, decline.* oððe, *or*; oððe ... oððe, *either ... or.*

#P.#

plega, m., *play, festivity.* port, m., *port* [Lat. portus].

#R.#

râd, f., *raid.* ræ:can (§ 126), *reach*; pret. 3d sing., ræ:hte. ræst, see
r[e,]st. Rêadingas, m. pl., *Reading* (in Berkshire). r[e,]ccan (§ 128),
narrate, tell; pret. pl. indic., r[e,]hton, reahton. r[e,]ccelêas, *reckless,
careless.* r[e,]ced, n., *house, hall.* regnian (rênian) (§ 130), *adorn,
prepare*; past part., geregnad. regollîc (-lec), *according to rule, regular.*
rên-weard, m., *mighty warden, guard, champion.* r[e,]st (ræst), f., *rest,
resting-place, bed.* rêðe, *fierce, furious.* rîce, *rich, powerful,
aristocratic.* rîce, n., *realm, kingdom* [bishopric]. rîcsian (§ 130), *rule.*
rîdan (§ 102), *ride.* rîman (§ 126), *count* [rime]. rinc, m., *man, warrior.*
rôd, f., *rood, cross*; rôde tâcen, *sign of the cross.* Rômware, m. pl.,
Romans. r[o,]nd (rand), m., *shield.* rûn, f., *rune, secret meditation* [to
round = to whisper]. rycene (ricene), *quickly, rashly.* ryhtnorðanwind,
m., *straight north-wind.*

#S.#

sæ:, f., *sea.* sæ:-bât, m., *sea-boat.* sæ:d, n., *seed.* sæ:de, see
s[e,]cgan. sæ:l, m., f., *time, happiness* [sil-ly]; on sæ:lum 137, 22
[[*Beowulf* 644]] = *joyous, merry.* sæ:lan (§ 126), *bind.* sæ:-lîðend (§ 68,
(3)), m., *seafarer* (nom. and acc. pl. same as nom. and acc. sing.).
sam ... sam, *whether ... or.* same, *similarly*; swâ same, *just the same,
in like manner.* samod, see s[o,]mod. sanct, m., f., *saint* [Lat. sanctus];
gen. sing., sanctæ, f., sancti, m. sang, see s[o,]ng. sâr, f., n., *sore,
pain, wound.* sâr, adj., *sore, grievous.* sâre, *sorely.* sâwan (§ 117,)
sow. sâwol, f., *soul*; oblique cases, sing., sâwle (§ 39, Note). scacan
(sceacan) (§ 116), *shake, go, depart*; past part., scacen, sceacen.
scadu-helm, m., *cover of night, shadow-covering* [shadow-helm];

scadu-helma gesceapu, see Note on 138, 2-6 [[lines 647-51]]. sceal, see sculan. scêap, n., *sheep.* scêat, m., *corner, region, quarter* [sheet]; eorðan scêatta 139, 14 [[*Beowulf* 753]] = *in the regions of earth* (gen. used as locative). scêawi(g)an (§ 130), *view, see* [shew]. scêawung, f., *seeing.* sceolde, see sculan. scêop (scôp), see scieppan. scêowyrhta, m., *shoe-maker.* sc[e,]ððan (§ 116), *injure, scathe* (with dat.). scieppan (§ 116), *create.* Scieppend, m., *Creator.* scînan (§ 102), *shine.* scip (scyp), n., *ship.* scipen, n., *stall.* sciprâp, m., *ship-rope, cable.* scîr, f., *shire, district.* Sciringeshêal, m., *Sciringesheal* (in Norway). scolde, see sculan. sc[o,]mu, f., *shame, dishonor.* Scônêg, f., *Skaane* (southern district of the Scandinavian peninsula). scopgereord, n., *poetic language.* scrîðan (§ 102), *stride, stalk.* sculan (§ 136; § 137, Note 2), *shall, have to, ought.* Scyldingas, m. pl., *Scyldings, Danes.* scyp, see scip. Scyppend, see Scieppend. sê, sêo, ðæt (§ 28; § 28, Note 3), *the; that; he, she, it; who, which, that;* ðæs, *from then, afterwards, therefore;* ðæs ðe (p. 110, l. 2), *with what;* ðy: ... ðæt (p. 110, ll. 7-8), *for this reason ... because;* tô ðæ:m ... swâ, *to such an extent ... as;* ðy (ðê), *the* (adverbial, with comparatives); ðy: ... ðy:, *the ... the.* seah, see sêon. sealde, see s[e,]llan. searo-gimm, m., *artistic gem, jewel.* searo-nîð, m., *cunning hatred, plot.* searo-ð[o,]nc, m., *cunning thought, device.* Seaxe, m. pl., *Saxons, Saxony.* sêc(e)an (§ 128), *to seek, visit, meet.* s[e,]cg, m., *man, warrior.* s[e,]cgan (§ 132), *say, tell.* sefa, m., *mind, spirit.* sêfte, *more easily* (comparative of sôfte). segel, m., n., *sail;* dat. sing. = segle. seglian (§ 130), *sail.* s[e,]le, m., *hall.* s[e,]ledrêam, m., *hall joy, festivity.* s[e,]le-ful, n., *hall cup.* s[e,]les[e,]cg, m., *hall warrior, rctaincr.* sêlcst, bcst (no positive). self (sylf), *self, himself* (declined as strong or weak adjective). s[e,]llan (syllan) (§ 128), *give* [sell, han(d)sel]. s[e,]mninga, *forthwith, straightway.* s[e,]ndan (§ 127), *send.* sêo, see sê. sêoc, *sick.* seofon (syfan), *seven.* seolh, m., *seal;* gen. sing. = sêoles (§ 27, (3)). sêon (§ 118), *see, look.* seonu, f., *sinew;* nom. pl., seonowe. sess, m., *seat.* slbb, f., *friendship, peace* [gos*sip*]. sidu (siodu), m., *custom, morality, good conduct.* sîe, see bêon. siex, *six;* syxa (siexa) sum, see sum. siextig, *sixty.* sige, m., *victory.* sige-folc, n., *victorious people.* sige-lêas, *victory-less, of defeat.* sige-rôf, victory-famed, *victorious.* sige-wæ:pen, n., *victory-weapon.* siglan (§ 127), *sail.* Sillende, *Zealand.* sinc, n., *treasure, prize.* sinc-fæ:t, n., see 137, 1 [[*Beowulf* 623]] [treasure-vat]. sinc-ð[e,]gu, f., *receiving of treasure* [ðicgan]. sind, sint, sindon, see bêon. singan (§ 110), *sing.* sittan (§ 115, Note 2), *sit, take position.* sîð, m., *journey, time*; forman sîðe 139, 2 [[*Beowulf* 741]] = *the first time* (instr. sing.). sîðian (§ 130), *journey*. siððan, *after that, afterwards, after*. slæ:p, m., *sleep*. slæ:pan (§ 117), *sleep*. slêan (§ 118), *slay* [slow-worm]. slîtan (§ 102), *slit, tear to pieces*. slîðen, *savage, perilous*. smæl, *narrow*. smalost, see smæl. snâw, m., *snow*. snot(t)or, *wise, prudent*. sôhte, see sêcan. s[o,]mod (samod), *together*. sôna, *soon*. s[o,]ng, m., n., *song, poem*. s[o,]ngcræft, m., *art of song and poetry*. sorg (sorh), f., *sorrow*. sôð, *true*. sôð, n., *truth*; tô sôðe, *for a truth, truly, verily*. sôð-fæst, *truthful, just*. sôðlîce, *truly*. spêd, f., *possessions, success, riches* [speed]. spêdig, *rich, prosperous*. spell, n., *story, tale* [gospel]. spêow, see spôwan. spere, n., *spear*. spor, n., *track, footprint*. spôwan (§ 117), *succeed* (impersonal with dat.). spræ:c, f., *speech, language*. sprecan (§ 115), *speak*. spyrian (spyrigean) (§ 130), *follow* (intrans.) [spor]. stæf, *staff, rod*; pl. = *literature, learning*. stælhrân, m., *decoy-reindeer*. stælwierðe, *serviceable* (see p. 56, Note 2). stæ:r, n., *story, narrative* [Lat. historia]. stæð, n., *shore*. stân, m., *stone, rock*. stân-boga, m., *stone-arch* [stone-bow]. standan, see st[o,]ndan. stânhlið (-hleoð), n., *stone-cliff*. stapol, m., *column* [staple]. starian (§ 125), *stare, gaze*. st[e,]de, m., *place*. stelan (§ 114), *steal*. st[e,]nt, see st[o,]ndan. stêorbord, n., *starboard, right side of a ship*. st[e,]ppan (§ 116), *step, advance*; pret. indic. 3d sing., stôp. stilnes, f., *stillness, quiet*. st[o,]ndan (§ 116), *stand*. stôp, see st[e,]ppan. storm, m., *storm*. stôw, f., *place* [stow, and in names of places]. strang, see str[o,]ng. str[e,]ngest, see str[o,]ng. str[o,]ng (§ 96, (2)), *strong*. styccemæ:lum, *here and there*. sum (§ 91, Note 2), *some, certain, a certain one*; hê syxa sum 104, 25 = *he with five others*. sumera, see sumor. sumor, m., *summer*; dat. sing. = sumera. sumorlida, m., *summer-army*. sundor, *apart*. sunne, f., *sun*. sunu, m., *son*. sûð, *south, southwards*. sûðan (§ 93, (5)), *from the south*; be sûðan, *south of* (§ 94, (4)). sûðeweard, *southward*. sûðryhte, *southward*. swâ (swæ:), *so, as, how, as if*; swâ swâ, *just as, as far as*; swâ ... swâ, *the ... the, as ... as*; swâ hwæt swâ, *whatsoever* (§ 77, Note). swæ:s, *beloved, own*. swæð, n., *track, footprint* [swath]. swaðul, m.? n.?, *smoke*. swealh, see swelgan. swefan (§ 115), *sleep, sleep the sleep of death*. swefn, n., *sleep, dream*. swêg, m., *sound, noise*. swegle, *bright, clear*. swêlan (§ 126), *burn* [sweal]. swelgan (§ 110), *swallow*; pret. indic. 3d sing., swealh; subj., swulge. swellan (§ 110), *swell*. Swêoland, n., *Sweden*. Swêom, m., dat. pl., *the Swedes*. sweotol, *clear*. sweotole, *clearly*. sw[e,]rian (§ 116), *swear*. swête, *sweet*. swêtnes (-nis), f., *sweetness*. swift (swyft), *swift.* swilc (swylc) (§ 77), *such.* swilce, *in such manner, as, likewise;* *as if, as though* (with subj.). swimman (§ 110), *swim.* swîn (swy:n), n., *swine, hog.* swînsung, f., *melody, harmony.* swîðe (swy:ðe), *very, exceedingly, greatly.* swîðost, *chiefly, almost.* swôr, see sw[e,]rian. swulge, see swelgan. swuster (§ 68, (2)), f., *sister.* swylce (swelce), see swilce. swy:n, see swîn. swynsian (§ 130), *resound.* swy:ðe, see swîðe. swy:ð-ferhð, *strong-souled.* sylf, see self. syll, f., *sill, floor.* syllan, see s[e,]llan. symbel, n., *feast, banquet.* symle, *always.* synd, see bêon. syn-dolh, n., *ceaseless wound, incurable wound.* syndriglîce, *specially.* synn, f., *sin.* syn-scaða, m., *ceaseless scather, perpetual foe.* syn-snæ:d, f., *huge bit* [ceaseless bit]. syððan, see siððan. syx, see siex. syxtig, see siextig.

#T.#

tâcen, n., *sign, token;* dat. sing., tâcne (§ 33, Note). tæ:can (§ 128), *teach.* tam, *tame.* tela, *properly, well* [til]. t[e,]llan (§ 128), *count, deem* [tell]; pret. 3d sing., tealde. T[e,]mes, f., *the Thames.* têon, *arrange, create;* pret. sing., têode. Terfinna, m., gen. pl., *the Terfins.* têð, see tôð. tîd, f., *tide, time, hour.* tîen (ty:n), *ten.* til(l), *good.* tîma, m., *time.* tintreglîc, *full of torment.* tô (§ 94, (1)), *to, for, according to, as;* tô hrôfe 114, 2 = *for (as) a roof* [cf. Biblical *to wife,* modern *to boot*]. tô, adv., *too.* tôbrecan (p. 81, Note 2), *break to pieces, knock about.* tôdæ:lan (§ 126), *divide.* tôemnes (tô emnes) (§ 94, (4)), *along, alongside.* tôforan (§ 94, (1)), *before.* tôgeðêodan (§ 126), *join.* tôhopa, m., *hope.* tôlicgan (§ 115, Note 2), *separate, lie between;* 3d sing, indic. = tôlîð. tôlîð, see tôlicgan. tolûcan (§ 109, Note 1), *destroy* [the prefix tô reverses the meaning of lûcan, *to lock*]. torn, m., *anger, insult.* tôð (§ 68, (1)), m., *tooth.* tôweard (§ 94, (1)), *toward.* tôweard, adj., *approaching, future.* trêow, f., *pledge, troth.* trêownes, f., *trust.* Trûsô, *Drausen* (a city on the Drausensea). tûn, m., *town, village.* tunge, f., *tongue.* tûngerêfa, m., *bailiff* [town-reeve; so sheriff = shire-reeve]. tungol, n., *star.* twâ, see twêgen. twêgen, (§ 89), *two, twain.* twêntig, *twenty.* ty:n, see tîen.

#Ð.#

ðâ, *then, when;* ðâ ... ðâ, *when ... then;* ðâ ðâ, *then when* = *when.* ðâ, see sê. ðæ:r, *there, where;* ðæ:r ðæ:r, *there where* = *where;* ðæ:r ... swâ 142, 4 [[Beowulf 798]] = *wheresoever;* 145, 6 [[Beowulf 2731]] = *if*

so be that. ðæs, *afterwards, therefore, thus, because*; see sê. ðæt
(ðætte = ðæt ðe), *that, so that.* ðafian (§ 130), *consent to.* ðanc, see
ð[o,]nc. ðancian (ð[o,]ncian) (§ 130), *thank.* ðanon, see ð[o,]nan. ðâs,
see ðês. ðê, see sê (instr. sing.) and ðû. ðe (§ 75), *who, whom, which,*
that. ðêah, *though, although*; ðêah ðe, *though, although.* ðearf, see
ðurfan. ðearf, f., *need, benefit.* ðêaw, m., *habit, custom* [thews]. ðegn
(ðegen), m., *servant, thane, warrior.* ð[e,]nc(e)an (§ 128), *think, intend.*
ðening (-ung), f., *service*; the pl. may mean *book of service* (117, 17).
ðêod, f., *people, nation.* ðêoden, m., *prince, lord.* ðêodscipe, m.,
discipline. ðêon (ðy:wan) (§ 126), *oppress* [ðêow]. ðêow, m., *servant.*
ðêowa, m., *servant.* ðêowotdôm (ðîowot-), m., *service.* ðês (§ 73), *this.*
ðider, *thither.* ðiderweard, *thitherward.* ðîn (§ 76), *thine.* ðing, n., *thing*;
æ:nige ðinga, see 140, 15 [[*Beowulf* 769]], Note. ðingan (§ 127),
arrange, appoint. ðis, see ðês. ðissum, see ðês. ðôhte, ðôhton, see
ð[e,]ncean. ðolian (§ 130), *endure* [thole]. ð[o,]nan, *thence.* ð[o,]nc, m.,
thanks. ðone, see sê. ðonne, *than, then, when*; ðonne ... ðonne, *when*
... then. ðrâg, f., *time.* ðrêa-ny:d, f., *compulsion, oppression, misery*
[throe-need]. ðrêora, see ðrîe. ðridda, *third.* ðrie (ðry:) (§ 89), *three.*
ðrîm, see ðrîe. ðrîst-hy:dig, *bold-minded.* ðrîtig, *thirty.* ðrôwung, f.,
suffering. ðry:, see ðrîe. ðrym(m), m., *renown, glory, strength.* ðry:ð, f.,
power, multitude (pl. used in sense of sing.); asca ðry:ðe 152, 23
[[*Wanderer* 99]] = *the might of spears.* ðry:ð-ærn, n., *mighty house,*
noble hall. ðry:ð-word, n., *mighty word, excellent discourse.* ðû (§ 72),
thou. ðûhte, see ðyncan. ðurfan (§ 136), *need*; pres. indic. 3d sing.,
ðearf; pret. 3d sing., ðorfte; for-ðâm mê wîtan ne ðearf Waldend fîra
morðor-bealo mâga 145, 17 [[*Beowulf* 2742]] = *therefore the Ruler of*
men need not charge me with the murder of kinsmen. ðurh (§ 94, (2)),
through. ðus, *thus.* ðûsend, *thousand.* ðy:, see sê. ðyder, see ðider.
ðyncan (§ 128), *seem, appear* (impersonal); mê ðyncð, *methinks, it*
seems to me; him ðûhte, *it seemed to him.*

#U.#

ûhta, m., *dawn*; gen. pl., ûhtna. unbeboht, *unsold* [bebycgan = *to sell*].
uncûð, *unknown, uncertain* [uncouth]. under, *under* (with dat. and
acc.). underst[o,]ndan (§ 116), *understand.* underðêodan (-ðîedan) (§
126), *subject to*; past part. underðêoded = *subjected to, obedient to*
(with dat.). unforbærned, *unburned.* unfrið, m., *hostility.* ungefôge,
excessively. ungemete, *immeasurably, very.* ungesewenlîc, *invisible*

[past part. of sêon + lîc]. unlyfigend, *dead, dead man* [unliving].
unly:tel, *no little, great.* unriht, n., *wrong*; on unriht, see on.
unrihtwîsnes, f., *unrighteousness.* unspêdig, *poor.* unwearnum,
unawares. ûp (ûpp), *up.* ûpâstîgnes, f., *ascension* [stîgan]. ûp-lang,
upright. ûre (§ 76), *our.* usses = gen. sing. neut. of ûser, see ic. ût, *out,
outside.* ûtan, *from without, outside.* ûtanbordes, *abroad.* ûtg[o,]ng, m.,
exodus. uton, *let us* (with infin.) [literally *let us go* with infin. of purpose
(see 137, 19-20, Note [[lines 641-42]]); uton = wuton, corrupted form of
1st pl. subj. of wîtan, *to go*]. ût-weard, *outward bound, moving
outwards.*

#W.#

wâc, *weak, insignificant.* wacian (§ 130), *watch, be on guard*;
imperative sing., waca. wadan (§ 116), *go, tread* [wade]. wæ:g, m.,
wave. Wæ:gmundigas, m. *Wægmundings* (family to which Beowulf
and Wiglaf belonged). wæl, n., *slaughter, the slain.* wæl-blêat, *deadly*
[slaughter-pitiful]. wælgîfre, *greedy for slaughter.* wæl-ræ:s, m., *mortal
combat* [slaughter-race]. wæl-rêow, *fierce in strife.* wælsliht (-sleaht),
m., *slaughter.* wælstôw, f., *battle-field* [slaughter-place]; wælstôwe
gewald, *possession of the battle-field.* wæ:pen, n., *weapon.* wæ:re,
see bêon. wæs, see bêon. wæter, n., *water.* waldend, see *wealdend.*
wan (w[o,]n), *wan, dark.* wanhy:dig, *heedless, rash.* wânigean (wânian)
(§ 130), *bewail, lament* (trans.) [whine]. warian (§ 130), *attend,
accompany.* wât, see witan. waðum, m., *wave*; gen. pl., waðema.
weal(l), m., *wall, rampart.* wealdend (§ 68, (3)), *wielder, ruler, lord.*
wealh, m., *foreigner, Welshman.* wealhstôd, m., *interpreter, translator.*
weallan (§ 117), *well up, boil, be agitated*; pret. 3d. sing. indic., wêoll.
wealsteal(l), m., *wall-place, foundation.* weard, m., *ward, keeper.*
wearð, see weorðan. weaxan (§ 117), *wax, grow.* weg, m., *way*; hys
weges, see § 93, (3); on weg, see on. wel(l), *well, readily.* wela, m.,
weal, prosperity, riches. welm, see wielm. wênan (§ 126), *ween, think,
expect.* w[e,]ndan (§ 127), *change, translate* [wend, windan]. w[e,]nian
(§ 130), *entertain*; w[e,]nian mid wynnum 149, 20 [[*Wanderer* 29]] =
entertain joyfully; w[e,]nede tô wiste 149, 27 [[*Wanderer* 36]] = *feasted*
(trans.). Weonodland (Weonoðland), n., *Wendland.* weorc, n., *work,
deed.* weorold (weoruld), see woruld. weorpan (§ 110), *throw.* weorðan
(§ 110), *be, become.* wer, m., *man* [werwulf]. wêrig, *weary, dejected.*
werod, n., *army, band.* wesan, see bêon. Wesseaxe, m. pl., *West*

Saxons; gen. pl. = Wesseaxna. west, *west, westward*. westanwind, m., *west wind*. wêste, *waste*. wêsten, n., *waste, desert*. Westsæ:, f., *West Sea* (west of Norway). Westseaxe, m. pl., *West Saxons, Wessex*. wîc, n., *dwelling* [bailiwick]. wîcian (§ 130), *stop, lodge, sojourn* [wîc]. wîdre, adv., *farther, more widely* (comparative of wîde). wîdsæ:, f., *open sea*. wielm (welm), m., *welling, surging flood* [weallan]. wîf, n., *wife, woman*. wîg, m., n., *war, battle*. wiga, m., *warrior*. wild, *wild*. wildor, n., *wild beast, reindeer*; dat. pl. = wildrum (§ 33, Note). willa, m., *will, pleasure*; gen. pl., wilna (138, 16 [[*Beowulf* 661]]). willan (§ 134; § 137, Note 3), *will, intend, desire*. wilnung, f., *wish, desire*; for ðæ:re wilnunga 119, 4 = *purposely*. Wiltûn, m., *Wilton* (in Wiltshire). wîn, n., *wine*. wîn-ærn, n., *wine-hall*. Wînburne, f., *Wimborne* (in Dorsetshire). wind, m., *wind*. wine, m., *friend*. Winedas, m. pl., *the Wends, the Wend country*. wine-dryhten, m., *friendly lord*. winelêas, *friendless*. winemæ:g, m., *friendly kinsman*. wîngeard, m., *vineyard*. winnan (§ 110), *strive, fight* [win]. wînsæl, n., *wine-hall*. wîn-s[e,]le, m., *wine-hall*. winter, m., *winter*; dat. sing. = wintra. wintercearig, *winter-sad, winter-worn*. wîs, *wise*. wîsdôm, m., *wisdom*. wîse, *wisely*. wîse, f., *manner, matter, affair* [in this wise]. wîs-fæst, *wise* [wise-fast; cf. shame-faced = shamefast]. wîs-hycgende, *wise-thinking*. Wîsle, f., *the Vistula*. Wîslemûða, m., *the mouth of the Vistula*. wisse, see witan. wist, f., *food, feast*. wita, m., *wise man, councillor*. witan (§ 136), *know, show, experience*. wîtan (§ 102), *reproach, blame* (with acc. of thing, dat. of person). wîte, n., *punishment*. Wîtland, n., *Witland* (in Prussia). wið (§ 94, (3)), *against, toward, with*; wið êastan and wið ûpp on emnlange ðæ:m by:num lande, *toward the east, and upwards along the cultivated land*; wið earm gesæt 139, 11 [[*Beowulf* 750]] = *supported himself on his arm*; gen[e,]red wið nîðe (dat.) 143, 11 [[*Beowulf* 828]] = *had preserved it from (against) violence*. wiðerwinna, m., *adversary*. wiðfôn (§ 118), *grapple with* (with dat.). wiðhabban (§ 133), *withstand, resist* (with dat.). wiðst[o,]ndan (§ 116), *withstand, resist* (with dat.). wl[o,]nc, *proud*. wôd, see wadan. wolcen, n., *cloud* [welkin]; dat. pl., wolcnum. wolde, see willan. wôma, m., *noise, alarm, terror*. w[o,]n, see wan. wôp, n., *weeping*. word, n., *word*. wôrian (§ 130), *totter, crumble*. worn, m., *large number, multitude*. woruld, f., *world*; tô worulde bûtan æ:ghwilcum [e,]nde 102, 18 = *world without end*. woruldcund, *worldly, secular*. woruldhâd, m., *secular life* [world-hood]. woruldrîce, n., *world-kingdom, world*. woruldðing, n., *worldly affair*. wræclâst, m., *track or path of an exile*. wrâð, *wroth, angry*; *foe, enemy*. wrîtan (§ 102), *write.* wucu, f., *week.* wudu, m., *wood, forest.* wuldor, n., *glory.* Wuldorfæder (§ 68, (2)), m., *Father of glory*; gen. sing., Wuldorfæder. Wuldur-cyning, m., *King of glory.* wulf, m., *wolf.* wund, f., *wound.* wund, *wounded.* wunden, *twisted, woven, convolute* (past part. of windan). wundor, n., *wonder, marvel.* wundrian (§ 130), *wonder at* (with gen.). wurdon, see weorðan. wurðan, see weorðan. wylf, f., *she wolf.* wyllað, see willan. wyn-lêas, *joyless.* wynn, f., *joy, delight.* wynsum, *winsome, delightful.* wyrc(e)an (§ 128), *work, make, compose.* wyrd, f., *weird, fate, destiny.* wyrhta, m., *worker, creator* [-wright]. wyrm, m., *worm, dragon, serpent.* wyrmlîca, m., *serpentine ornamentation.* wyrð (weorð), *worthy*; see 114, 7-9, Note.

#Y.#

ylca, see ilca. yldan (§ 127), *delay, postpone* [eald]. yldu, f., *age* [eld]. ymbe (ymb) (§ 94, (2)), *about, around, concerning* [*um*while]; ðæs ymb iii niht 99, 2 = *about three nights afterwards.* ymb-êode, see ymb-gân. ymbe-sittend, *one who sits (dwells) round about another, neighbor.* ymb-gân (§ 134), *go about, go around, circle* (with acc.). yrfe-weard, m., *heir.* yrnan, see iernan. yrre, *ireful, angry.* yteren, *of an otter* [*otor*]. y:ðan (§ 126), *lay waste* (as by a deluge) [y:ð = *wave*].

II. GLOSSARY.

MODERN ENGLISH--OLD ENGLISH.

#A.#

a, *ân* (§ 77). abide, *bîdan* (§ 102), *âbîdan.* about, *be* (§ 94, (1)), *ymbe* (§ 94, (2)); to write about, *wrîtan be*; to speak about (= of), *sprecan ymbe*; about two days afterwards, *ðæs ymbe twêgen dagas.* adder, *næ:dre* (§ 64). afterwards, *ðæs* (§ 93, (3)). against, *wið* (§ 94, (3)), *on* (§ 94, (3)). Alfred, *Ælfred* (§ 26). all, *eall* (§ 80). also, *êac.* although, *ðêah* (§ 105, 2). always, *â*; *ealne weg* (§ 98, (1)). am, *eom* (§ 40). an, see a. and, *[o,]nd* (*and*). angel, *[e,]ngel* (§ 26). animal, *dêor* (§ 32). are, *sind, sint, sindon* (§ 40). army, *werod* (§ 32); Danish army, *h[e,]re* (§ 26); English army, *fierd* (§ 38). art, *eart* (§ 40). Ashdown, *Æscesdûn* (§ 38). ask, *biddan* (§ 65, Note 3; § 115, Note 2). away, *aweg.*

#B.#

battle-field, *wælstôw* (§ 38). be, *bêon* (§ 40); not to be, see § 40, Note 2. bear, *beran* (§ 114). because, *for ðæ:m (ðe), for ðon (ðe).* become, *weorðan* (§ 110). before (temporal conjunction), *æ:r, æ:r ðæ:m ðe* (§ 105, 2). begin, *onginnan* (§ 107, (1); § 110). belong to, *belimpan tô* + dative (§ 110). best, see good. better, see good. bind, *bindan* (§ 110). bird, *fugol* (§ 26). bite, *bîtan* (§ 102). body, *lîc* (§ 32). bone, *bân* (§ 32). book, *bôc* (§ 68). both ... and, *æ:gðer ge ... ge.* boundary, *mearc* (§ 38). boy, *cnapa* (§ 64). break, *brêotan* (§ 109), *brecan, âbrecan* (§ 114). brother, *brôðor* (§ 68, (2)). but, *ac.* by, *fr[o,]m (fram)* (§ 94, (1); § 141, Note 1).

#C.#

Cædmon, *Cædm[o,]n* (§ 68, (1)). call, *hâtan* (§ 117, (1)). cease, cease from, *geswîcan* (§ 102). child, *bearn* (§ 32). choose, *cêosan* (§ 109). Christ, *Crîst* (§ 26). church, *cirice* (§ 64). come, *cuman* (§ 114). comfort, *frôfor* (§ 38). companion, *gefêra* (§ 64). consolation, *frôfor* (§ 38). create, *gescieppan* (§ 116).

#D.#

Danes, *D[e,]ne* (§ 47). day, *dæg* (§ 26). dead, *dêad* (§ 80). dear (= beloved), *lêof* (§ 80). deed, *dæ:d* (§ 38). die, *cwelan* (§ 114). division (of troops), *gefylce* (§ 32), *getruma* (§ 64). do, *dôn* (§ 134). door, *dor* (§ 32), *duru* (§ 52). drink, *drincan* (§ 110). during, *on* (§ 94, (3)). See also § 98. dwell in, *bûan on* (§ 126, Note 2).

#E.#

earl, *eorl* (§ 26). endure, *drêogan* (§ 109). England, *[E,]nglal[o,]nd* (§ 32). enjoy, *brûcan* (§ 62, Note 1; § 109, Note 1). every, *æ:lc* (§ 77). eye, *êage* (§ 64).

#F.#

father, *fæder* (§ 68, (2)). field, *feld* (§ 51). fight, *feohtan, gefeohtan* (§ 110). find, *findan* (§ 110). finger, *finger* (§ 26). fire, *fy:r* (§ 32).

fisherman, *fiscere* (§ 26). foreigner, *wealh* (§ 26). freedom, *frêodôm* (§ 26). friend, *wine* (§ 45), *frêond* (§ 68, (3)). friendship, *frêondscipe* (§ 45). full, *full* (with genitive) (§ 80).

#G.#

gain the victory, *sige habban, sige niman.* gift, *giefu* (§ 38). give, *giefan* (with dative of indirect object) (§ 115). glad, *glæd* (§ 81). glove, *glôf* (§ 38). go, *gân* (§ 134), *faran* (§ 116). God, *God* (§ 26). good, *gôd* (§ 80).

#H.#

Halgoland, *Hâlgoland* (§ 32). hall, *heall* (§ 38). hand, *h[o,]nd* (§ 52). hard, *heard* (§ 80). have, *habban* (§ 34); not to have, *nabban* (p. 32, Note). he, *hê* (§ 53). head, *hêafod* (§ 32). hear, *hîeran* (§ 126). heaven, *heofon* (§ 26). help, *helpan* (with dative) (§ 110). herdsman, *hierde* (§ 26). here, *hêr.* hither, *hider.* hold, *healdan* (§ 117, (2)). holy, *hâlig* (§ 82). horse, *mearh* (§ 26), *hors* (§ 32). house, *hûs* (§ 32).

#I.#

I, *ic* (§ 72). in, *on* (§ 94, (3)). indeed, *sôðlîce.* injure, *sc[e,]ððan* (with dative) (§ 116). it, *hit* (§ 53).

#K.#

king, *cyning* (§ 26). kingdom, *rîce* (§ 32), *cynerîce* (§ 32).

#L.#

land, *l[o,]nd* (§ 32). language, *spræ:c* (§ 38), *geðéode* (§ 32). large, *micel* (§ 82). leisure, *æ:metta* (§ 64). let us, *uton* (with infinitive). limb, *lim* (§ 32). little, *lytel* (§ 82). live in, *bûan on* (§ 126, Note 2). lord, *hlâford* (§ 26). love, *lufian* (§ 131). love (noun), *lufu* (§ 38).

#M.#

make, *wyrcan* (§ 128). man, *s[e,]cg* (§ 26), *m[o,]n* (§ 68, (1)). many, *m[o,]nig* (§ 82). mare, *my:re* (§ 64). mead, *medu* (§ 51). Mercians,

Mierce (§ 47). milk, *meolc* (§ 38). month, *mônað* (§ 68, (1), Note 1).
mouth, *mûð* (§ 26). much, *micel* (§ 96, (3)), *micle* (§ 97, (2)). murderer,
b[o,]na (§ 64). my, *mîn* (§ 76).

#N.#

natives, *l[o,]ndlêode* (§ 47). nephew, *nefa* (§ 64). new, *nîwe* (§ 82).
Northumbrians, *Norðymbre* (§ 47). not, *ne*.

#O.#

of, see about. on, *on* (§ 94, (3)), *ofer* (§ 94, (2)). one, *ân* (§ 89); the one
... the other, *ôðer ... ôðer*. other, *ôðer* (§ 77). our, *ûre* (§ 76). ox, *oxa* (§
64).

#P.#

place, *stôw* (§ 38). plundering, *h[e,]rgung* (§ 38). poor, *earm* (§ 80),
unspêdig (§ 82). prosperous, *spêdig* (§ 82).

#Q.#

queen, *cwên* (§ 49).

#R.#

reindeer, *hrân* (§ 26). remain, *bîdan* (§ 102), *âbîdan*. retain possession
of the battle-field, *âgan wælstôwe gewald*. rich, *rîce* (§ 82), *spêdig* (§
82). ride, *rîdan* (§ 102).

#S.#

say, *cweðan* (§ 115), *s[e,]cgan* (§ 133). scribe, *bôcere* (§ 26). seal,
seolh (§ 26). see, *sêon* (§ 118), *gesêon*. serpent, *næ:dre* (§ 64).
servant, *ðêowa* (§ 64), *ðegn* (§ 26). shall, *sculan* (§ 136; § 137,
Note 2). she, *hêo* (§ 53). shepherd, *hierde* (§ 26). ship, *scip* (§ 32).
shire, *scîr* (§ 38). shoemaker, *scêowyrhta* (§ 64). side, on both sides,
on gehwæðre h[o,]nd. six, *siex* (§ 90). slaughter, *wæl* (§ 32), *wælsliht*
(§ 45). small, *ly:tel* (§ 82). son, *sunu* (§ 51). soul, *sâwol* (§ 38). speak,

sprecan (§ 115). spear, *gâr* (§ 26), *spere* (§ 32). stand, *st[o,]ndan* (§ 116). stone, *stân* (§ 26). stranger, *wealh* (§ 26), *cuma* (§ 64). suffer, *drêogan* (§ 109). sun, *sunne* (§ 64). swift, *swift* (§ 80).

#T.#

take, *niman* (§ 110). than, *ðonne* (§ 96, (6)). thane, *ðegn* (§ 26). that (conjunction), *ðæt*. that (demonstrative), *sê, sêo, ðæt* (§ 28). that (relative), *ðe* (§ 75). the, *se, sêo, ðæt* (§ 28). then, *ðâ, ðonne*. these, see this. they, *hîe* (§ 53). thing, *ðing* (§ 32). thirty, *ðrîtig*. this, *ðês, ðêos, ðis* (§ 73). those, see that (demonstrative). thou, *ðû* (§ 72). though, *ðêah* (§ 105, 2). three, *ðrîe* (§ 89). throne, ascend the throne, *tô rîce fôn*. throw, *weorpan* (§ 110). to, *tô* (§ 94, (1)). tongue, *tunge* (§ 64). track, *spor* (§ 32). true, *sôð* (§ 80). truly, *sôðlîce*. two, *twêgen* (§ 89).

#V.#

very, *swîðe*. vessel, *fæt* (§ 32). victory, *sige* (§ 45).

#W.#

wall, *weall* (§ 26). warrior, *s[e,]cg* (§ 26), *eorl* (§ 26). way, *weg* (§ 26). weapon, *wæ:pen* (§ 32). well, *wel* (§ 97, (2)). Welshman, *Wealh* (§ 26). went, see go. westward, *west, westrihte*. whale, *hwæl* (§ 26). what? *hwæt* (§ 74). when, *ðâ, ðonne*. where? *hwæ:r*. which, *ðc* (§ 75). who? *hwâ* (§ 74). who (relative), *ðe* (§ 75). whosoever, *swâ hwâ swâ* (§ 77, Note). will, *willan* (§ 134; § 137, Note 3). Wilton, *Wiltûn* (§ 26). win, see gain. wine, *wîn* (§ 32). wisdom, *wîsdôm* (§ 26). wise, *wîs* (§ 80). with, *mid* (§ 94, (1)); to fight with (= against), *gefeohtan wið* (§ 94, (3)). withstand, *wiðst[o,]ndan* (with dative) (§ 116). wolf, *wulf* (§ 26), *wylf* (§ 38). woman, *wîf* (§ 32). word, *word* (§ 32). worm, *wyrm* (§ 45).

#Y.#

ye, *gê* (§ 72). year, *gêar* (§ 32). yoke, *geoc* (§ 32). you, *ðû* (singular), *gê* (plural) (§ 72). your, *ðîn* (singular), *êower* (plural) (§ 76).

* * * * * * * * * * * * *

Errata

The spelling "Fins" (translating "ðâ Finnas") is used consistently. Errors were trivial, generally missing punctuation. Shakespeare citations have been silently regularized to "I, ii, 3" form. The Old English text was not checked for misprints.

Numbered Sections:

9 Note to t.: #settan#, *to set* [to t.] 39 NOTE.--Syncopation occurs as in masculine and neuter a-stems. [*final . missing*] 41 sêo hâlignes[1], *holiness.* [*comma missing*] 95 for ðæ:m, } [*comma missing*] 104 corresponding with its function in Mn.E. [*final . missing*] 130 eard-ian, eard-ode ... [*first comma missing*] 131 NOTE 1. [NOTE. 1.] 132 hæf-de, lif-de, secg-an, [*all commas missing*]

Readings:

Poetry: Structure: Meter: Type B: The type of B most frequently occurring is × × ´¯ | × ´¯. [*final . missing*]

Beowulf: The Banquet in Heorot (page 138). [8] = ealdre (instr. sing.). [*final . missing*]

Glossary:

âbûgan (§ 109, Note 1) [Note, 1] dêofol, m., n., *devil*; [m. n.,] intinga, m., *cause, sake.* [intinga.] lagulâd, f., *sea* [lake-way, lâd = *leading, direction, way*]. [*closing bracket printed as parenthesis*] norðan (§ 93, (5)), *from the north*; [*second closing parenthesis missing*] sæ:l, m., f., *time, happiness* [sil-ly]; [m. f.,] sêfte, *more easily* (comparative of sôfte). [*closing parenthesis missing*] Swêom, m., dat. pl., *the Swedes.* [*final . missing*] tolûcan (§ 109, Note 1), *destroy* ... [*section mark § missing*] wið (§ 94, (3)), ... [*section mark § missing*]

End of the Project Gutenberg EBook of Anglo-Saxon Grammar and Exercise Book, by C. Alphonso Smith

http://gutenberg.net/license).

Section 1. General Terms of Use and Redistributing Project Gutenberg-tm electronic works

1.A. By reading or using any part of this Project Gutenberg-tm electronic work, you indicate that you have read, understand, agree to and accept all the terms of this license and intellectual property (trademark/copyright) agreement. If you do not agree to abide by all the terms of this agreement, you must cease using and return or destroy all copies of Project Gutenberg-tm electronic works in your possession. If you paid a fee for obtaining a copy of or access to a Project Gutenberg-tm electronic work and you do not agree to be bound by the terms of this agreement, you may obtain a refund from the person or entity to whom you paid the fee as set forth in paragraph 1.E.8.

1.B. "Project Gutenberg" is a registered trademark. It may only be used on or associated in any way with an electronic work by people who agree to be bound by the terms of this agreement. There are a few things that you can do with most Project Gutenberg-tm electronic works even without complying with the full terms of this agreement. See paragraph 1.C below. There are a lot of things you can do with Project Gutenberg-tm electronic works if you follow the terms of this agreement and help preserve free future access to Project Gutenberg-tm electronic works. See paragraph 1.E below.

1.C. The Project Gutenberg Literary Archive Foundation ("the Foundation" or PGLAF), owns a compilation copyright in the collection of Project Gutenberg-tm electronic works. Nearly all the individual works in the collection are in the public domain in the United States. If an individual work is in the public domain in the United States and you are located in the United States, we do not claim a right to prevent you from copying, distributing, performing, displaying or creating derivative works based on the work as long as all references to Project Gutenberg are removed. Of course, we hope that you will support the Project Gutenberg-tm mission of promoting free access to electronic works by freely sharing Project Gutenberg-tm works in compliance with the terms of this agreement for keeping the Project Gutenberg-tm name associated with the work. You can easily comply with the terms of this agreement by keeping this work in the same format with its attached full Project Gutenberg-tm License when you share it without charge with others.

1.D. The copyright laws of the place where you are located also govern what you can do with this work. Copyright laws in most countries are in a constant state of change. If you are outside the United States, check the laws of your country in addition to the terms of this agreement before downloading, copying, displaying, performing, distributing or creating derivative works based on this work or any other Project Gutenberg-tm work. The Foundation makes no representations concerning the copyright status of any work in any country outside the United States.

1.E. Unless you have removed all references to Project Gutenberg:

1.E.1. The following sentence, with active links to, or other immediate access to, the full Project Gutenberg-tm License must appear prominently whenever any copy of a Project Gutenberg-tm work (any work on which the phrase "Project Gutenberg" appears, or with which the phrase "Project Gutenberg" is associated) is accessed, displayed, performed, viewed, copied or distributed:

This eBook is for the use of anyone anywhere at no cost and with almost no restrictions whatsoever. You may copy it, give it away or re-use it under the terms of the Project Gutenberg License included with this eBook or online at www.gutenberg.net

1.E.2. If an individual Project Gutenberg-tm electronic work is derived from the public domain (does not contain a notice indicating that it is posted with permission of the copyright holder), the work can be copied and distributed to anyone in the United States without paying any fees or charges. If you are redistributing or providing access to a work with the phrase "Project Gutenberg" associated with or appearing on the work, you must comply either with the requirements of paragraphs 1.E.1 through 1.E.7 or obtain permission for the use of the work and the Project Gutenberg-tm trademark as set forth in paragraphs 1.E.8 or 1.E.9.

1.E.3. If an individual Project Gutenberg-tm electronic work is posted with the permission of the copyright holder, your use and distribution must comply with both paragraphs 1.E.1 through 1.E.7 and any additional terms imposed by the copyright holder. Additional terms will be linked to the Project Gutenberg-tm License for all works posted with the permission of the copyright holder found at the beginning of this work.

1.E.4. Do not unlink or detach or remove the full Project Gutenberg-tm License terms from this work, or any files containing a part of this work or any other work associated with Project Gutenberg-tm.

1.E.5. Do not copy, display, perform, distribute or redistribute this electronic work, or any part of this electronic work, without prominently displaying the sentence set forth in paragraph 1.E.1 with active links or immediate access to the full terms of the Project Gutenberg-tm License.

1.E.6. You may convert to and distribute this work in any binary, compressed, marked up, nonproprietary or proprietary form, including any word processing or hypertext form. However, if you provide access to or distribute copies of a Project Gutenberg-tm work in a format other than "Plain Vanilla ASCII" or other format used in the official version posted on the official Project Gutenberg-tm web site (www.gutenberg.net), you must, at no additional cost, fee or expense to the user, provide a copy, a means of exporting a copy, or a means of obtaining a copy upon request, of the work in its original "Plain Vanilla ASCII" or other form. Any alternate format must include the full Project Gutenberg-tm License as specified in paragraph 1.E.1.

1.E.7. Do not charge a fee for access to, viewing, displaying, performing, copying or distributing any Project Gutenberg-tm works unless you comply with paragraph 1.E.8 or 1.E.9.

1.E.8. You may charge a reasonable fee for copies of or providing access to or distributing Project Gutenberg-tm electronic works provided that

- You pay a royalty fee of 20% of the gross profits you derive from the use of Project Gutenberg-tm works calculated using the method you already use to calculate your applicable taxes. The fee is owed to the owner of the Project Gutenberg-tm trademark, but he has agreed to donate royalties under this paragraph to the Project Gutenberg Literary Archive Foundation. Royalty payments must be paid within 60 days following each date on which you prepare (or are legally required to prepare) your periodic tax returns. Royalty payments should be clearly marked as such and sent to the Project Gutenberg Literary Archive Foundation at the address specified in Section 4, "Information about donations to the Project Gutenberg Literary Archive Foundation."

- You provide a full refund of any money paid by a user who notifies you in writing (or by e-mail) within 30 days of receipt that s/he does not agree to the terms of the full Project Gutenberg-tm License. You must require such a user to return or destroy all copies of the works possessed in a physical medium and discontinue all use of and all access to other copies of Project Gutenberg-tm works.

- You provide, in accordance with paragraph 1.F.3, a full refund of any money paid for a work or a replacement copy, if a defect in the electronic work is discovered and reported to you within 90 days of receipt of the work.

- You comply with all other terms of this agreement for free distribution of Project Gutenberg-tm works.

1.E.9. If you wish to charge a fee or distribute a Project Gutenberg-tm electronic work or group of works on different terms than are set forth in this agreement, you must obtain permission in writing from both the Project Gutenberg Literary Archive Foundation and Michael Hart, the owner of the Project Gutenberg-tm trademark. Contact the Foundation as set forth in Section 3 below.

1.F.

1.F.1. Project Gutenberg volunteers and employees expend considerable effort to identify, do copyright research on, transcribe and proofread public domain works in creating the Project Gutenberg-tm collection. Despite these efforts, Project Gutenberg-tm electronic works, and the medium on which they may be stored, may contain "Defects," such as, but not limited to, incomplete, inaccurate or corrupt data, transcription errors, a copyright or other intellectual property infringement, a defective or damaged disk or other medium, a computer virus, or computer codes that damage or cannot be read by your equipment.

1.F.2. LIMITED WARRANTY, DISCLAIMER OF DAMAGES - Except for the "Right of Replacement or Refund" described in paragraph 1.F.3, the Project Gutenberg Literary Archive Foundation, the owner of the Project Gutenberg-tm trademark, and any other party distributing a Project Gutenberg-tm electronic work under this agreement, disclaim all liability to you for damages, costs and expenses, including legal fees. YOU AGREE THAT YOU HAVE NO REMEDIES FOR NEGLIGENCE, STRICT LIABILITY, BREACH OF WARRANTY OR BREACH OF CONTRACT EXCEPT THOSE PROVIDED IN PARAGRAPH F3. YOU AGREE THAT THE FOUNDATION, THE TRADEMARK OWNER, AND ANY DISTRIBUTOR UNDER THIS AGREEMENT WILL NOT BE LIABLE TO YOU FOR ACTUAL, DIRECT, INDIRECT, CONSEQUENTIAL, PUNITIVE OR INCIDENTAL DAMAGES EVEN IF YOU GIVE NOTICE OF THE POSSIBILITY OF SUCH DAMAGE.

1.F.3. LIMITED RIGHT OF REPLACEMENT OR REFUND - If you discover a defect in this electronic work within 90 days of receiving it, you can receive a refund of the money (if any) you paid for it by sending a written explanation to the person you received the work from. If you received the work on a physical medium, you must return the medium with your written explanation. The person or entity that provided you with the defective work may elect to provide a replacement copy in lieu of a refund. If you received the work electronically, the person or entity providing it to you may choose to give you a second opportunity to receive the work electronically in lieu of a refund. If the second copy is also defective, you may demand a refund in writing without further opportunities to fix the problem.

1.F.4. Except for the limited right of replacement or refund set forth in paragraph 1.F.3, this work is provided to you 'AS-IS' WITH NO OTHER

WARRANTIES OF ANY KIND, EXPRESS OR IMPLIED, INCLUDING BUT NOT LIMITED TO WARRANTIES OF MERCHANTIBILITY OR FITNESS FOR ANY PURPOSE.

1.F.5. Some states do not allow disclaimers of certain implied warranties or the exclusion or limitation of certain types of damages. If any disclaimer or limitation set forth in this agreement violates the law of the state applicable to this agreement, the agreement shall be interpreted to make the maximum disclaimer or limitation permitted by the applicable state law. The invalidity or unenforceability of any provision of this agreement shall not void the remaining provisions.

1.F.6. **INDEMNITY**

- You agree to indemnify and hold the Foundation, the trademark owner, any agent or employee of the Foundation, anyone providing copies of Project Gutenberg-tm electronic works in accordance with this agreement, and any volunteers associated with the production, promotion and distribution of Project Gutenberg-tm electronic works, harmless from all liability, costs and expenses, including legal fees, that arise directly or indirectly from any of the following which you do or cause to occur: (a) distribution of this or any Project Gutenberg-tm work, (b) alteration, modification, or additions or deletions to any Project Gutenberg-tm work, and (c) any Defect you cause.

Section 2. Information about the Mission of Project Gutenberg tm

Project Gutenberg-tm is synonymous with the free distribution of electronic works in formats readable by the widest variety of computers including obsolete, old, middle-aged and new computers. It exists because of the efforts of hundreds of volunteers and donations from people in all walks of life.

Volunteers and financial support to provide volunteers with the assistance they need are critical to reaching Project Gutenberg-tm's goals and ensuring that the Project Gutenberg-tm collection will remain freely available for generations to come. In 2001, the Project Gutenberg Literary Archive Foundation was created to provide a secure and permanent future for Project Gutenberg-tm and future generations. To learn more about the Project Gutenberg Literary Archive Foundation and how your efforts and donations can help, see Sections 3 and 4 and the Foundation web page at http://www.pglaf.org.

Section 3. Information about the Project Gutenberg Literary Archive Foundation

The Project Gutenberg Literary Archive Foundation is a non profit 501(c)(3) educational corporation organized under the laws of the state of Mississippi and granted tax exempt status by the Internal Revenue Service. The Foundation's EIN or federal tax identification number is 64-6221541. Its 501(c)(3) letter is posted at http://pglaf.org/fundraising. Contributions to the Project Gutenberg Literary Archive Foundation are tax deductible to the full extent permitted by U.S. federal laws and your state's laws.

The Foundation's principal office is located at 4557 Melan Dr. S. Fairbanks, AK, 99712., but its volunteers and employees are scattered throughout numerous locations. Its business office is located at 809 North 1500 West, Salt Lake City, UT 84116, (801) 596-1887, email business@pglaf.org. Email contact links and up to date contact information can be found at the Foundation's web site and official page at http://pglaf.org

For additional contact information: Dr. Gregory B. Newby Chief Executive and Director gbnewby@pglaf.org

Section 4. Information about Donations to the Project Gutenberg Literary Archive Foundation

Project Gutenberg-tm depends upon and cannot survive without wide spread public support and donations to carry out its mission of increasing the number of public domain and licensed works that can be freely distributed in machine readable form accessible by the widest array of equipment including outdated equipment. Many small donations ($1 to $5,000) are particularly important to maintaining tax exempt status with the IRS.

The Foundation is committed to complying with the laws regulating charities and charitable donations in all 50 states of the United States. Compliance requirements are not uniform and it takes a considerable effort, much paperwork and many fees to meet and keep up with these requirements. We do not solicit donations in locations where we have not received written confirmation of compliance. To SEND DONATIONS or determine the status of compliance for any particular state visit http://pglaf.org

While we cannot and do not solicit contributions from states where we have not met the solicitation requirements, we know of no prohibition against accepting unsolicited donations from donors in such states who approach us with offers to donate.

International donations are gratefully accepted, but we cannot make any statements concerning tax treatment of donations received from outside the United States. U.S. laws alone swamp our small staff.

Please check the Project Gutenberg Web pages for current donation methods and addresses. Donations are accepted in a number of other ways including including checks, online payments and credit card donations. To donate, please visit: http://pglaf.org/donate

Section 5. General Information About Project Gutenberg-tm electronic works.

Professor Michael S. Hart is the originator of the Project Gutenberg-tm concept of a library of electronic works that could be freely shared with anyone. For thirty years, he produced and distributed Project Gutenberg-tm eBooks with only a loose network of volunteer support.

Project Gutenberg-tm eBooks are often created from several printed editions, all of which are confirmed as Public Domain in the U.S. unless a copyright notice is included. Thus, we do not necessarily keep eBooks in compliance with any particular paper edition.

Most people start at our Web site which has the main PG search facility:

http://www.gutenberg.net

This Web site includes information about Project Gutenberg-tm, including how to make donations to the Project Gutenberg Literary Archive Foundation, how to help produce our new eBooks, and how to subscribe to our email newsletter to hear about new eBooks.

Anglo-Saxon Grammar and Exercise Book, by

A free ebook from http://manybooks.net/

9588632R00112

Printed in Germany
by Amazon Distribution
GmbH, Leipzig